LOST BOYS

James Bloodworth's work has appeared in *The Times, New York Review of Books, Guardian, Prospect* and elsewhere. He is also the author of *The Myth of Meritocracy* and *Hired: Six Months in Low-Wage Britain*.

LOST BOYS

A Personal Journey Through the Manosphere

JAMES BLOODWORTH

Atlantic Books
London

Some names and identifying details have been changed in order to protect the privacy of those profiled in the book.

First published in trade paperback in Great Britain in 2025 by
Atlantic Books, an imprint of Atlantic Books Ltd.

Copyright © James Bloodworth, 2025

The moral right of James Bloodworth to be identified as the author of this work has been asserted by him in accordance with the Copyright, Designs and Patents Act of 1988.

All rights reserved. No part of this publication may be reproduced, stored in a retrieval system, or transmitted in any form or by any means, electronic, mechanical, photocopying, recording, or otherwise, without the prior permission of both the copyright owner and the above publisher of this book.

No part of this book may be used in any manner in the learning, training or development of generative artificial intelligence technologies (including but not limited to machine learning models and large language models (LLMs)), whether by data scraping, data mining or use in any way to create or form a part of data sets or in any other way.

Every effort has been made to trace or contact all copyright holders. The publishers will be pleased to make good any omissions or rectify any mistakes brought to their attention at the earliest opportunity.

10 9 8 7 6 5 4 3 2 1

A CIP catalogue record for this book is available from the British Library.

Trade Paperback ISBN: 978 1 78649 979 0
E-book ISBN: 978 1 78649 980 6

Printed and bound by CPI (UK) Ltd, Croydon CR0 4YY

Atlantic Books
An imprint of Atlantic Books Ltd
Ormond House
26–27 Boswell Street
London
WC1N 3JZ

www.atlantic-books.co.uk

Product safety EU representative: Authorised Rep Compliance Ltd., Ground Floor, 71 Lower Baggot Street, Dublin, D02 P593, Ireland. www.arccompliance.com

For Grandma (1929–2022)

The Manosphere [man–uh–sfeer]: a loosely affiliated network of masculinist websites, blogs and online forums.[1]

'Only by being terrible do they avoid being comic.'
C.S. Lewis, *The Four Loves*

CONTENTS

Part One: The Blue Pill

1. Body Count — 3
2. Return of the Brute — 37
3. Angry Men on the Internet — 61
4. The 10 Commandments of Game — 73

Part Two: The Red Pill

5. Origins of the Red Pill — 83
6. Make Men Great Again — 99
7. 'War is Coming': The Story of Lyndon McLeod — 115
8. Waiting for Caesar — 135
9. Interlude — 157

Part Three: The Black Pill

10. Men of Action — 163
11. Alpha Fucks, Beta Bucks — 191
12. Surplus Men — 213
13. Top G — 245

Epilogue — 267
Acknowledgements — 285
Endnotes — 287

PART 1

The Blue Pill

'As social life becomes more and more warlike and barbaric, personal relations, which ostensibly provide relief from these conditions, take on the character of combat.'

Christopher Lasch, *The Culture of Narcissism*, 1979

1

BODY COUNT

Leicester Square, London, March 2006

'What's your body count?'

'Two,' replies a diminutive man who has recently introduced himself as Dan. He has a gaunt and ghoulish look and his bony shoulders sag down and inwards as if he wants to shield his solar plexus from the outside world. His voice is barely audible above the hum and clatter of the coffee shop.

'Louder,' says the instructor with an imperious gesture of the hand. There are four of us sitting round the coffee-stained table. The two men either side of me are wide-eyed and alert. My own hands feel hot and clammy. There is a sense of trepidation among our little group as the instructor takes turns barking the question at each of us. When he reaches me his eyes narrow; he is looking for signs of low status, categorising me based on the thousands of clients who have come before. And then the question:

'What's your body count?'

'One,' I reply before surreptitiously scanning the faces of the other men for signs of laughter – a self-conscious tick I've internalised over the years.

This is the first time I've been asked for my 'body count'. I briefly wonder if I have inadvertently walked into a serial killers' meet-up. And yet this is the agreed rendezvous point: Starbucks, Leicester Square, 7 p.m.

The men sitting next to me don't look like serial killers, if there is a 'look'. Adam is in his mid-twenties and has high cheekbones, an expensive-looking tan and a carefully coiffured chestnut bouffant that bounces when he talks. He has on a light-blue, button-up shirt and his cloying aftershave mixes incongruously with the smell of cappuccino. He has a job in finance, which is precisely where you'd place him if you were to take a guess.

Sitting next to Adam is Bruce, a stocky white South African with brown curls cropped neatly into a short back and sides. Bruce is also in his mid-twenties and is smartly dressed in a sleeveless puffer jacket and stone-coloured chinos. Though a little on the short side, Bruce is conventionally good-looking. He works in sales and peppers stories of his dating exploits with industry patter. A woman's phone number is 'put through the funnel' before he 'handles her objections'. If things go well he 'closes the deal'. He says he hopes this weekend will be a 'game changer' for his dating life.

Adam and Bruce boast of double figure 'body counts'. Dan and I look on deferentially as they reel off a succession of seedy anecdotes. Both men have always been good with 'girls'.[1] But as far as they see it you can always get better.

According to the seduction community's template of the world, a woman's most important trait is her physical beauty, which can be rated on a scale from one to ten. When 'Tux' asks Adam and Bruce what their dating goals are, both say they want to meet 'the genuine nines and tens'.

I decide early on that I'm going to stick closely to a third student, whose social deficiencies make me feel less self-conscious about my own. Dan is twenty-two years old and ghostly pale. He struggles to hold eye contact and has jittery body movements. He is a man of few words, though this is a by-product of social paralysis rather than enigmatic mystery. When he does speak there is a nasal voice that resembles the sound of a leaky gas pipe. He possesses an energy that sucks the air out of the room.

Dan and I feel an immediate kinship. Tux on the other hand has identified Dan as the runt of the litter – i.e. as the lowliest member of our little group. 'What makes you think some little hottie in the club is gonna want to choose *you*?' he asks Dan pointedly. Dan gives a hangdog look, writhes in his chair and looks at the floor in ponderous silence. Adam and Bruce's downfall comes when they open their mouths. Mine and Dan's comes when we don't. Instead we look on in awkward silence, our nervous laughter ringing out pathetically as the other men banter.

Each of us has spent nearly £2,000 to be here. This is how much it costs in 2006 to learn how to be a pickup artist. We'll be spending the weekend with Tux, one of the best in the business. Tux is short for tuxedo, which is purely metaphorical: he has on a black dress shirt that sits snugly under a charcoal grey blazer, and black jeans. The moniker is a pseudonym intended to communicate an aura of debonair sophistication. Tux's skills with women are legendary in the community. His fans say he combines the smoothness of James Bond with the wit of Oscar Wilde. And he does exude a certain narcissistic blasé, rumoured to be the afterglow of hundreds of successful conquests: the seducer's aura.

For the next three days and nights, Tux will be our guru and guide. We will do as he says, however ridiculous or terrifying this initially sounds. The instructors are reprogramming us with a new belief system and it is incumbent on us to suspend any lingering scepticism for the duration of the weekend. It's apparently for our own good.

Tux is a conspiracy theorist. He believes in the existence of a secret society that 52 per cent of the population are part of. Of that 52 per cent, 50 per cent are women and 2 per cent are men. Of that 2 per cent, 1 per cent are gay and the other 1 per cent are sexually attractive 'alpha males'. This is the real world according to Tux's employer Real Social Dynamics, a company that makes its money teaching the hapless 48 per cent how to mimic the traits of the sexual elite of 'alphas' and 'naturals'. Boot camps like this one are supposed to begin the process of rewiring our neural pathways through repetition until the performance becomes natural. Tux is a member of the 1 per cent and he's going to elevate us to his level.

BODY COUNT

The pickup forums[2] encouraged men to steer clear of the mainstream media – to avoid, say, the radio lest it brainwash you with its steady diet of gooey love songs. It was important not to let your newly discovered faith be shaken. According to Tux, everything we have been told about male–female dynamics up to now – by family and friends, by films and soap operas, by popular music – has been a lie. We've been brainwashed by a society that wants us only to conform and consume. The soppy advice to buy women flowers and being a nice guy? Propaganda to keep us soft and passive. Tux brings a fist crashing down on the table as his speech reaches its rhetorical climax. Other Starbucks patrons look over quizzically as they file past clutching their mochaccinos and flat whites. Tux's speech has stirred something in us. Ready to break away from their world, we stare back at their blank and complacent faces with feelings of supercilious contempt.

*

It's 8 o'clock and we've been sitting in Starbucks for nearly an hour. Through gaps in the condensation on the windows we see partygoers stagger across damp cobbles. They mingle effortlessly as if guided by a social instinct that is unfamiliar to at least two of us on this side of the glass. I look on with a tightening feeling in my stomach. Several times on the walk over to Starbucks I nearly went back to my hotel off Trafalgar Square. My head swam with rationalisations as to why it would be no great shame to retreat, order room service and accept my fate. And yet bravely I have soldiered on. An hour later and the warmth of the coffee shop has become congenial. It's the prospect of mingling with the crowds that scares me.

Suddenly Tux receives a message on his Nokia 3310 and pivots hurriedly towards us. He clasps his hands together, wraps his arms around us and ushers us towards the exit. 'We're here to get girls, guys. It's time to step up,' he bawls in an Australian drawl. He gets a chant going with Adam and Bruce as he ushers us out of the coffee shop. 'RIGHT HERE, RIGHT NOW... RIGHT HERE, RIGHT NOW... RIGHT HERE, RIGHT NOW.'

Dan and I join in, reluctantly at first but with more gusto until we're bellowing the words into the night air. A group of Chinese tourists cautiously files past. They glare at us and we try to look menacing. 'RIGHT HERE, RIGHT NOW,' we chant as they hurry through the doors to join their tour party. I laugh with the other students and feel vaguely powerful as I do.

It's bitterly cold out on Leicester Square, a clear and crisp night lit up by a moon that's flaring in the sky like a white-hot coin. We've been told to do warm-up approaches while we wait for the other instructors to arrive. At first we look around gravely, each of us waiting for someone else to take the initiative. I look at Dan whose countenance is wearing the most desolate expression I have ever seen.

All of a sudden, Bruce has darted off in the direction of three women in their early twenties; this is what the pickup artists call a 'three set'. The women are wearing stiletto heels, miniskirts and tight-fitting jackets pulled over even smaller crop tops. Bruce moves towards them, loops round and comes back again to position himself so he's approaching the group diagonally from the front. He stops momentarily and bounces from foot to foot, exhaling deeply as he gets ready to go in. The vapour on his breath is visible as he starts the preamble for his opener. 'Ex... cuse me...', 'Ex... cuse me,' Bruce says while tapping one of the women gingerly on the shoulder as if touching something scalding hot. Straight away, a mass of blonde hair swivels round and two eyes scan Bruce up and down. The woman's upper lip begins to curl and retract, exposing a set of luminous white teeth. The blonde turns back towards her two friends and eye-codes them before the group starts to slowly edge away from Bruce. The entire scene unfolds in a matter of seconds. Even after the brush-off, Bruce continues to unload a fusillade of scripted one-liners at the women. He seems oblivious to the fact that it isn't working, like a fly stupidly bashing itself against a windowpane. When the group is nearly out of sight, Bruce turns around and trundles back towards us pursing his lips. 'Did you open them?' asks Adam. 'Negative,' says Bruce. 'I didn't talk loud enough.' Bruce is shaking his head. 'Fuck, I messed up man. *Fuck!*'

We awkwardly slap Bruce on the back and tell him 'great job'. We tell him that rejection doesn't matter – that it's just a game like Tux said in Starbucks. And yet I feel profoundly disconcerted by the scene I've just witnessed. The camaraderie of the coffee shop has been replaced by a grim and solemn atmosphere. Bruce wears a horrifying grimace on a stricken face that appears to have collapsed in on itself. He reaches for a cigarette with a hand that's visibly shaking. First blood of the night has been drawn. I try to put the episode to the back of my mind.

Bruce has performed what the pickup artists call a 'cold approach' (this contrasts with a warm approach, which is when a woman has given some indication that she wants to be approached). The cold approach requires a single-minded willingness to potentially embarrass yourself in the hope that if you repeat the process enough times, proficiency will be attained. It's called the 'game' because viewing the process like a video game is supposed to make it easier and take the sting out of rejection.

Pressure is now on the rest of us to start approaching. Since leaving Starbucks I've been floundering. I pretend not to see women passing right beside me. I notice imaginary boyfriends or AMOGs (alpha male other guys) who I tell myself will unleash violence on me if I talk to their girl. I dismiss almost every woman I see as not my type – as too old, too young, too fat ('she's just a five, bro'); as wearing too much make-up; as probably not able to understand English anyway – as if someone in my position can afford to be choosy.

I resolve to do my first approach before Tux comes back and catches sight of me standing around shivering. That's when I spot a potential 'target': a woman in a white dress with a black and gold sash draped over her shoulder. She's trailed by a small group of slightly inebriated women, all wearing different outfits but each with the same black and gold sash flopping diagonally across the body. I hesitate for a moment and then I hear Tux's admonition ringing in my head – 'RIGHT HERE, RIGHT NOW'.

I've rehearsed this moment dozens of times in the mirror at home. Yet despite knowing what to do on a theoretical level, my feet remain planted to the spot. My brain is pulling me in two different directions. On the one hand I want to break through the anxiety and stop feeling like such a coward. At the same time I want to run away. Amid this indecision, I begin to question whether the circumstances that brought me to Leicester Square this Friday night are as bad as I've been making them out to be. Maybe fate will take care of my dating life if I give it its proper due? That's when it hits me like a bucket of ice-cold water: I've paid nearly £2,000 to be here. In Starbucks, Tux had talked about how our ancestors had killed giant mammals with their bare hands and fought in bloody wars. Why then was I petrified of women? The answer wasn't easily forthcoming – though my body seemed determined to remind me of its verity: despite the sub-zero temperatures I can feel droplets of perspiration running down the back of my neck. After a minute or so of mental torment, I decide that the women in the hen party are not good enough for me. They're too prettified and bimbo-ish; we wouldn't have anything in common. I feel superior to them in some ill-defined way – yet still I want them. I bounce from one foot to the other, my skin clammy and grey. A sense of resignation washes over me. I catch the eye of an Alsatian dog standing on the cobblestones next to its owner; it glances over mournfully at me and we briefly lock eyes; then it too turns its head away in disgust.

*

In 2006, pickup artistry is a multi-million-dollar industry. Whether you want to add more notches to your bedpost or find a girlfriend and fall in love, the industry's gurus claim to have the secret formula that can induce any woman to fall under your spell. All it takes is a willingness to hand over your money, memorise some canned material and head out to the bars and clubs to practise on unsuspecting women.

I blame the American writer Neil Strauss. Pickup artists went mainstream the previous year largely thanks to Strauss's book, *The Game: Undercover in the Secret Society of Pickup Artists*. An overnight bestseller, *The Game* would go on to sell two and a half million copies. Strauss, a journalist for *Rolling Stone* and the *New York Times*, had immersed himself in Los Angeles's seduction community. The resulting book has piqued the interest of libidinous men the world over. Thanks to *The Game*, seduction boot camps are in high demand in cities across the world.[3] Ask a pickup student how they first discovered the subculture and the reply inevitably comes: 'I read *The Game*.' Not only have the students on this boot camp read it but they have studied it, scrutinised it and imbibed every piece of dubious wisdom contained within its pages. Published in a sleek black imitation leather cover with gold typeface, their copies are defiled with thumbprints and scribbled notes. The contents of the book are treated with a reverence usually accorded to the words of kings or prophets. *The Game* is a holy book and this boot camp, I suppose, is our pilgrimage.

Though ostensibly an investigation into an unusual subculture, the book doubled up as a scintillating male fantasy told through the concupiscent antics of Strauss's alter ego, Style. Strauss hadn't simply investigated the community – he'd 'gone native', becoming a venerated pickup artist in the process. The book produced by the experience was a rags-to-riches story transposed on to the world of sex. It was also a *vade mecum* for the aspiring pickup artist: an instruction manual through which the reader could learn the revelatory techniques that Strauss had uncovered during his two-year stint in the community. The chapters of *The Game* were even arranged in the chronological order in which a seduction was supposed to go down, from Step 1: 'Select a Target', to Step 5: 'Isolate the Target', to the most horrifying of all, Step 10: 'Blast Last-Minute Resistance'.

The Game had added a carnal twist to the traditional hero's arc. Strauss had gone on an adventure, learned a lesson, won a victory, and then returned to his old life with his newfound knowledge. Throughout the book, Strauss leans heavily on his purported ordinariness prior to discovering the pickup scene. He describes himself in the opening chapters as a short, balding and malnourished-looking man with beady eyes and a nose too big for his face. Yet by rehearsing the scripts and techniques imparted to him by Mystery – a charismatic pickup artist from Toronto who claimed to have distilled seduction into a step-by-step formula – Strauss is able to overcome these physical shortcomings and date a spectacular array of beautiful women. Eventually the student manages to surpass the master and Strauss's new friends vote him the world's number one pickup artist.

For a book that would inspire thousands of would-be Casanovas, *The Game's* opening sequence is less than hopeful. The story begins with Strauss checking Mystery into a Hollywood psychiatric facility. His mentor is suicidal following a break-up with his latest girlfriend. Meanwhile, Project Hollywood, the mansion that Strauss and the other pickup artists had hoped to turn into something akin to the notorious Playboy mansion, has degenerated into 'a madhouse'. Doors are smashed off hinges and used condoms float around in a filthy pool. Moreover, the men who live there have come to hate each other.

The scene is presented by Strauss as a dark portent of things to come. Having immersed himself in the pickup community for two years, Strauss reaches the belated realisation that building your life around the pursuit of one-night stands is hollow and soul-destroying. The pickup artists may have been able to make a drunken woman giggle at a nightclub, but when the scripted material ran out, their contrived personas imploded. Women rarely stuck around once they realised they were dealing with losers. Strauss's final love interest in the book drives the point home by giving him an ultimatum: retire his pickup alter ego or lose her. 'I want you to just be Neil: balding, nerdy, glasses and all,' she tells the writer.

Had Strauss not spent the intervening four hundred pages mesmerising male readers with a puerile account of sexual conquest, these hints at a deeper self-awareness might have felt genuine. Yet as with the quotes from celebrated feminists that Strauss decided to place at the beginning of each chapter, such well-timed nods to remorse and contrition felt like an attempt by the author to have it both ways: to retain his journalistic credibility and – should the book be poorly received – leave enough space to wriggle out of any unfortunate associations.

Whether or not *The Game* really had started life as a journalistic endeavour – Strauss insisted that it had – its author had decided to go all-in on the techniques he had purportedly set out to expose. Once the commercial success of *The Game* was assured, Strauss quickly released his own three-volume guide to picking up women. The book consisted of autobiographical stories, scripted routines and a thirty-day instructional programme. Strauss had claimed in the closing chapters of *The Game* that 'to win the game was to leave it'. Yet he would spend the next few years flying around the world teaching the very material he claimed to have outgrown. As for the rest of us, we wanted to know what it was that Style – Strauss's irresistible alter ego – possessed that we didn't.

*

Tux saunters out of Starbucks carrying a flat white. As he does so he makes a sidelong glance at two brunettes walking by.

When he returns his attention to us, the remnants of a strange leer are plastered across his face. 'How you getting on, boys?' he asks. We mumble various noises in the affirmative.

Tux informs us that the club of choice tonight will be Tiger Tiger, a venue in Piccadilly spanning two floors. It's a popular nightclub with tourists and Tux assures us it'll be target-rich. Most pickup artists I've spoken to don't enjoy nightclubs. Underneath the smooth patter they are nerds who would rather be at home playing Xbox or watching the Discovery Channel. But nightclubs are where many of the most beautiful women hang out. They are also a discomfiting environment in which to talk to people, which means they are good places to practise the game. In a club, you are competing with alcohol, loud music and bright lights. You are competing with people who are cooler than you, more attractive than you. If you can nail the art of the approach in a nightclub you can do it anywhere. You're also less likely to ruin your reputation there. Chatting somebody up in the club isn't frowned upon like it is elsewhere.[4] Moreover, the nightclub has no memory. However badly it goes, there's a good chance you'll be quickly forgotten. The nightclub is therefore the perfect place for us to make utter fools of ourselves.

As we approach the venue, Tux makes us split into pairs. Dan and I hang back as the others march ahead. The big clubs aren't keen on groups of men rolling up because of the heady mix of alcohol and testosterone.

The queue for Tiger Tiger is enormous. It's so long in fact that I have ample time to run through every possible failure scenario in my head. Worse, when we do finally reach the front, the arm of a bouncer – a granite monolith of a man – shoots out mechanically, halting my forward momentum. Affronted by the crumpled T-shirt I have on underneath my blazer, he makes a grunting sound and fixes me with a grim and serious stare. Fortunately, Tux intervenes, informing the gum-chewing beefcake that my name is on the guest list.

It's mayhem once we get inside. Women with heavily painted faces and tiny dresses yell and raise their glasses high in the air as the DJ plays a track by Shakira. Men in collared shirts teeter past sloshing jars of lager. Lights pulsate and the music makes the floor vibrate. I cower a little. The gears in my brain start grinding away. I don't belong here. Everyone is smiling and laughing at some joke I'm not privy to. It's only a matter of time until I'm exposed as an interloper. I feel acutely aware of my limbs: the jerky movements of my legs and my arms hanging awkwardly by my sides. The club is like a panopticon, ready to enact its unforgiving judgement on my ungainly bearing.

Seeking sanctuary, I find the bathroom and dive into a toilet cubicle. I then proceed to linger around the sinks for a bit before elbowing my way back through the crowds to the bar. I stop off to buy a beer which I quickly drain. I then catch sight of the one person I am trying to forestall my introduction to: my instructor. I see him by the dance floor, head bobbing and foot tapping to the music. He also sees me. 'Hey, man,' he says enthusiastically through a toothy grin. He sticks out a hand and introduces himself as Ox. He seems friendly.

He's from Cuba originally and has flown in from Barcelona where he lives in exile from the dictatorship that rules over his homeland. He's thirty-seven, has chin-length brown hair and is wearing a tight-fitting white T-shirt with *'De Puta Madre'* across the front in striking yellow typeface. His accent is strong but endearing. Ox is highly respected in the community for his skill on the dance floor and what he calls 'getting physical'. He tells me to 'treat every girl as if she is a child or your little sister'. Before I have time to ask any questions about this instruction, Ox puts his hands on my shoulders and spins me vertiginously in the direction of two brunettes standing by the bar. They look deep in conversation but Ox says this is just my brain looking for excuses not to go over. 'Look down, look what you have... your organ is a spear,' Ox shouts into my ear. 'Be the prize,' he rasps, before gently shoving me towards the bar. His breath smells strongly of aniseed. I make eye contact with Dan as I set off in the direction of the two women. We look at each other with a stricken lucidity.

*

I mainly encountered two types of men in the community. I will call them The Manipulator and The Dabbler. The Manipulator tended to view all social interactions as a means to an end. He was more or less indifferent to most ethical considerations that might arise during an interaction. Women were viewed as inanimate objects who responded in predictable ways to scripted stimuli. The Manipulator probably represented about a quarter of the men I encountered in the pickup scene, though possibly less (a disproportionately high number of instructors fitted this mould). Taking to heart the advice of certain self-help gurus, The Manipulator clinically audited those around him, expelling from his life anybody (friend, relative or partner) thought to be holding him back. Those who crossed paths with The Manipulator were unfailingly assessed on the basis of how much 'value' they were bringing to the table.

The Dabbler occupied a more ambiguous place, morally speaking, than The Manipulator. He might become a Manipulator with time (over a period of months or years perhaps) but he didn't usually start off that way. Most men in the community were dilettantes. They found the pickup material and briefly experimented with it before forgetting about the community once they had found a woman who liked them. The one thing pickup did have going for it was its insistence that men had to put themselves out there. A lot. They had to go out to 'target-rich' environments four nights a week and approach x number of women. Over and over again. Statistically speaking, this alone hugely improved the chances of meeting someone. And then, later on, when they were quietly getting on with their lives, The Dabblers probably realised that it was *them* – and not the pickup lines – that had got the girl. And then they forgot all about it again.

As for me, I was a Dabbler, but then most of The Manipulators probably said that. All I knew was that flirting was a foreign language to me. In 2006 I was almost certainly sexist by today's standards. But then, to depict the pickup community as *uniquely* sexist might be to let wider society off the hook. The 1990s and 2000s were the era of publications such as *Loaded, Maxim, FHM, Nuts* and *Zoo*. Women were typically presented as either sexual gratification or as 'ladettes': parodies of men without the economic power. The tabloids of the day even featured surreptitious paparazzi 'upskirt' shots of female celebrities.

And yet it was also true that the pickup community could take the leering masculinity of the day and turn it into something worse.

*

Nobody is entitled to sex; however, it is not unusual to wonder why some men have it while others don't. This felt like an especially pertinent question when I was in my early twenties. Aged twenty-three, it had become clear to me that an urgent change of course was necessary. The alternative – of rotting away at home until I finally expired in a mouldy armchair – was too horrifying to contemplate. This was probably me catastrophising a bit. But still, I shuddered at the prospect of going through life having to deal with scorn or pity for want of a girlfriend.

In societies conforming to traditional dominant male stereotypes, sex and romance were usually seen as the domain of women. Moreover, as a man, there was a tawdriness about asking for help. It is true that both men and women are judged on how much sex they have, albeit rather differently and on an unequal footing (women have it significantly worse). Whereas it can be socially lethal for a woman to be having lots of it, the sexless man by contrast is usually treated as an object of mirth. Indeed, the 'forty-year-old virgin' is a stock comedic character whose lack of potency is thought to betray some Darwinian inadequacy. Complaining only risks compounding this unenviable social position. Better instead to resign oneself to the fact that some have it – whatever *it* is – and others do not.

Even the relationship advice given to me by well-meaning friends was questionable. People told me to *be myself* when what they really meant was 'be attractive'. Things would 'work themselves out in the end', they reassured me – but why would they? Confidence was said to be attractive but what was that when you broke it down into its component parts? It was a sort of faith that things would go well because they had gone well before. But what if they hadn't gone well before? From where was this magical property supposed to spring? In truth, the pickup artist adage – that if we kept doing what we were doing we would keep getting the same results (or lack of) – sounded more realistic to me than the soothing bromides I was constantly hearing from the people who loved me.

Of course, women are not interchangeable robots with predictable psychologies. They are not algorithms or pieces of computer coding. A man cannot simply roll up, say certain things and expect to elicit responses on repeat. But pickup was designed to appeal to someone like me: a 23-year-old mouldering in a prolonged dry spell who is willing to overlook this elementary point. Indeed, we – for I became one of them

– were happy enough to deploy our scrupulously rehearsed, prefabricated routines on unsuspecting women if we thought it might result in sex. It was so bad that even Neil Strauss would eventually come to denounce the industry. 'The techniques, let's face it, are so objectifying and horrifying,' Strauss told *The Atlantic* in 2015:

> Why did I really stop writing for the *New York Times*, hang out with all these kids running around, you know, the Sunset Strip like a maniac in stupid clothing? I see those photos and I vomit in my mouth a little bit. Even when I wrote it, I didn't think it would be a guide. I thought it would be a book about male insecurity. I even knew then that it was about low self-esteem.[5]

*

And yet there was a tantalisingly meritocratic appeal to pickup. Mainstream society tended to put people in fixed categories. You were an introvert or an extrovert, shy or outgoing, the life of the party or a social hermit. By contrast, the pickup industry presented itself as the start of a proactive journey of self-improvement. It instilled in us the belief that we too could transcend our unflattering former identities and rise agreeably up the social pecking order. Those outside the community might laugh at the scripted lines but these were a temporary gambit; they were like the stabilisers we once relied on when we were learning to ride a bike. Eventually it would become effortless. We just had to put in the work. The process would be long, arduous and frequently nerve-wracking. The instructors were clear about that. We should be under no illusions: most guys weren't cut out for the opportunity that we had been given. We had uncovered the hidden code and, through its dutiful study and application, even men like us could go 'from loser to lothario'. Even. Men. Like. Us. Reading those words for the very first time gave me goosebumps.

It certainly recommended itself to me more than some of the tried and tested alternatives – buying the latest designer aftershave or resigning myself to the vicissitudes of 'fate'. The community had given me a sense of hope about the future. This was yet to translate into worldly results to be sure; but I felt like I was on the right track. For a long time I had been grappling with this most embarrassing and vexing of issues. And now, here I was with all the answers at my fingertips.

It wasn't that I had abandoned all of my moral scruples. It was more that I'd rationalised my misgivings away. I wanted to learn some basic conversational scaffolding and escape the knot of tangled emotions: outgrowths from a fractured childhood. I couldn't see what all the fuss was about. Did men outside of the community not also have their own social routines? (*'Hey'*; *'What's up?'*; *'Can I buy you a drink?'*). By the time I found pickup I had grown tired of hearing that I should 'be myself'. What I wanted was an *honest* (i.e. unvarnished) appraisal of where I was going wrong. The pickup community found me at a point in my life where I was ready to pay good money to be told that my haircut was shit, my mannerisms weird and my air of desperation incredibly off-putting.

I was a pickup marketeer's dream. The industry preyed on men like me – men who believed that in order to be successful with women we needed to efface our personalities. I'd briefly had a girlfriend when I was sixteen. I hadn't exactly been the protagonist in that one: she'd taken an interest in me and I'd more or less gone along with it. She was more experienced than I was and made all the moves. We eventually had sex. It didn't last long – the sex or the relationship – and for the next six years the only action my bedroom saw was dusting and hoovering.

My social skills steadily atrophied after that. I had left school and was living in the countryside with my grandmother. I had a dial-up internet connection and a cannabis dealer on speed dial. I worked in a petrol station two days a week but besides that I barely even needed to leave the house. I gradually became more isolated. A few drunken kisses occurred at the dwindling number of parties I was still invited to, but that was about it. On the rare occasions that I did go on a date I always blew it by failing to move things forward. At the crucial moment I would clam up and shut down out of some lingering fear of being rejected. Even outside of a romantic context I was afraid of raising my voice or taking up space in the world. Men hadn't played a particularly impressive role in my life and I was, on some level at least, ashamed of my masculinity.

Attending a pickup artist boot camp was hardly my proudest moment. And yet at the time, feelings of frustration, rejection and thwarted romantic ambition were weighing more heavily on my shoulders than any ethical considerations. What was the harm in going to a nightclub and trying out some scripted lines? After all, I was what the pickup artists called an 'average frustrated chump', or AFC for short, and since I'd learned that I had gradually allowed them to convince me that I needed their help.

*

Every weekend, Real Social Dynamics, or RSD for short, takes men like me – anxiety-ridden, gauche and socially awkward – into 'the field', a term pickup artists use for the bars and nightclubs they frequent.

The pickup artists cribbed most of their theories from evolutionary psychology. According to Mystery, the most famous of the 2000s pickup artists, we were 'biological machines' whose sole purpose was to survive and replicate.[6] Every pickup artist has a talismanic alter ego. There is Tux, Playboy, Juggler, Badboy, Adonis, Matador, to name but a few. They are a psychological device to free men from social conventions and a way to avoid exposure while documenting their salubrious exploits on the community's sprawling forums and newsgroups. Following a date or a night out at the club, members of the community will sit at their computers and record every gesture, comment and brush-off for their peers to dissect. Naturally they don't want their family, colleagues and friends – nor the women they are writing about – to know about any of this.

In 2006, the biggest online pickup forum has thousands of members. Many of the men who use it are able to draw on an encyclopaedic knowledge of seduction theory. They write long detailed posts about how to behave around women, about what the perfect opener is, about who history's greatest seducers were. Women are viewed as machine-like and programmable by a subculture that is made up disproportionately of engineers and computer programmers. *Say this and she will do that; do this and she will respond in this way; follow these steps and she will have sex with you.* There is a preponderance of men in the community who struggle to communicate with people (and women especially) outside of a problem-solving context.

They spend most of their time on the sprawling forums engaging in one-upmanship, pointless flame wars and throwing themselves into hair-splitting dissections of pickup theory. It is Warhammer for the sexually frustrated. So-called keyboard jockeys (KJs) are treated with contempt by Tux and the other instructors. 'The game is played in the field,' Tux says during his introductory preamble in Starbucks. He warns us that if we get caught trying to slope off at any point during the night, we'll be made to approach the most intimidating sets (i.e. groups of women). I feel a tightening sensation in my stomach as I listen to the instructors say that by the end of the weekend, each of us will have learned how to take an interaction with any woman 'from open to close'. Cowering behind our computer screens is no longer an option.

*

On the short walk over to the two women that Ox has sent me hurtling towards, I scramble to locate a piece of paper. I have placed it inside my trouser pocket earlier in the evening; written on it are two opinion openers I've cribbed from the internet. One is the classic 'Who lies more, men or women?' The other is another conversation starter that goes something like, 'Hey, did you guys see that fight outside?' It's not exactly Oscar Wilde but hopefully enough to get my foot in the door.

Yet when I manage to locate the slip of paper, I'm so nervous the words look like hieroglyphics.

My pulse quickens; I'm now almost over the shoulder of one of the brunettes. I've been told not to approach from directly behind because it's creepy. Getting here wasn't as difficult as I expected it to be, mainly because I had somebody literally pushing me into the conversation. The fact that Ox sent me here is psychologically reassuring somehow, perhaps because I can blame him when I have Martinis thrown in my face and my eyes gouged out with little paper umbrellas.

I linger for a moment and a strong whiff of perfume passes my nostrils. This must be the closest I've been in months to a woman who isn't a direct relative. I take one last surreptitious look at the brunette standing closest to me. She has her hair tied back; the ringlets tumble endearingly down each side of her face. My heart stirs with the gold of her laughter. Perhaps she's 'The One' and we just don't know it yet. I look at her and then I remember who *I* am; the prospect of our union seems unlikely. Then, coming out of my dream, I realise that I'm almost directly in front of them. Faithful to the teachings,

I place my body at an angle so it looks as if I'm ready to leave at any moment. I lurch forward and emit a shaky 'Hi'. Then I wait. The word hangs limply in the air for what feels like a very long time. Meanwhile the brunettes have continued talking, oblivious to my hovering presence. I feel like a piece of furniture, awkwardly fixed to the spot like one of the bar stools. I need to take action before my momentary burst of courage deserts me. According to the pickup artists, you have to approach within three seconds of seeing a target to stop your brain from chickening out. It has the added bonus that you won't be seen as another lurker, the bane of women in nightclubs and a phenomenon to which their social radar is highly attuned.

Ten seconds elapse. My face feels like it's on fire. 'Love Generation' by Bob Sinclar is blasting out of the sound system. A loud whoop ripples around the club and the floor starts once again to vibrate. 'Right here, right now,' I murmur softly to myself. And here goes. I tap-tap one of the brunettes gently on the shoulder. 'Hey, did you guys see that fight outside?' I deliver the line with as much mock enthusiasm as I'm able to muster; it can't be obvious that I've rehearsed the line at home in the mirror. This time they do hear me. 'No,' says one of the women with a hint of curiosity in her voice. I continue with my opener while I can still remember it. 'Oh yeah it was crazy, these two women fighting over this one little guy.' They laugh politely while looking me up and down with a sceptical look. It's a bumpy landing but I have their attention. No drinks have been thrown in my face. The bouncers haven't been summoned. I haven't been placed on a register. I chalk my first approach down as a success, exchange a few 'nice to meet yous' with the two women before heading triumphantly back to Ox who is standing next to the dance floor talking animatedly with Dan. I feel fantastic. Ox, though, is frowning. 'Why did you leave?' he asks me pointedly. I say I don't know. 'Think about it; why did you leave?' I think a bit harder and tell him that I ran out of things to say. 'Go back and run the train,' he says. I ask him what this means. He tells me I shouldn't leave until I get a kiss or a phone number. 'You gotta close, man, or it's nothing.' *'Run the train!'* Some schools of pickup say you shouldn't leave a set until you are ejected from the club or a rival male is threatening you with violence. Ox had his own view of the matter: you had to go in and 'run the train', which meant staying in every interaction until the bitter end. 'The girl that is acting bitchy to you and giving you the *face*, that's the one you're going to take home at the end of the night, but you don't know it yet.' I had my doubts but nodded along compliantly.

Ox's words are swirling around in my head as I trundle back over towards the two women. One of them catches sight of me and says something to the second woman. They both then glance over at me before looking at each other and rolling their eyes. I arrive in front of them and robotically reel off my back-up opener, this time with slightly less energy. I go with 'Who lies more, men or women?' The DJ has turned up the sound system and the crowds are getting drunker, *'Oh baby when you talk like that, you make a woman go mad...*

Shakira Shakira. Something else has changed too: the faux sympathetic smiles that had greeted me ten minutes ago are gone, replaced with looks of cold contempt. The women are doing the robot act, answering all of my interview-style questions with surly monosyllables. They are giving me what pickup artists call the 'bitch shield', a tactic women use to repel unwanted attention from men like me. They aren't really 'bitches'; I'm just being a nuisance. I linger there uselessly for a few seconds. I want to leave but I can see Ox out of the corner of my eye gesturing with his arms and saying something I can't quite make out. 'Kino. Do the kino!' Kino is short for kinaesthetic, a term the pickup artists use to mean physical touch. Aware that Ox is watching me, I drape a limp arm across a shoulder of one of the women. It hangs in the air like the branch of a tree. I assume the pale and fleshy intrusion isn't welcome because almost immediately the woman with the ringlets extracts herself from under it. The women look at each other as if some secret signal is passing between them and disappear into the no-go zone of the bathroom.

I solemnly walk back to Ox with the failure cutting me like a knife. My place in the social pecking order has been revealed by a contemptuous visage of mascara and red lipstick. Any Hollywood-inflected notions of finding true love on the dance floor have gone up the spout. I'm expecting Ox to chastise me for bad game or for failing to deploy my 'kino' at the appropriate moment. Instead, he raises an arm triumphantly. 'High five!' he yells. 'Good job sticking in there, man,' he says. 'You did great. You nearly ran the train!'

Despite Ox's enthusiasm, I struggle to shake off the feeling that I've done something wrong. But before I get a chance to probe what it could mean, Ox is pointing me in the direction of another group of women. 'Next set,' he says. I obediently spin around. 'Look, the fatty over there, go – go now.' At this point, Ox gently shoves me in the back and I start to make my way over. I'm just as nervous as the first time – perhaps more so now that I have a rejection under my belt – but I end up having a relatively enjoyable conversation with the woman. Her name is Claire and she's travelled from Chelmsford in Essex. She's a dental nurse and to our mutual surprise and astonishment, we discover that we both share the same birthday. I feel good but later on, one of the instructors will admonish me for staying in there for too long: Claire is merely an 'obstacle' when I should be talking to the 'hotties'.

Things are already starting to feel rather bleak and I've only been in the club for an hour. On a more encouraging note, my outfit has already got me into several conversations. According to the pickup artist theory of 'peacocking',[7] the best way to attract a mate is to stand out. Aspiring pickup artists were easy enough to identify with their fluorescent shirts, leather trousers, feather boas, top hats and silk cravats. In any major city on any given night, as soon as the sun went down they would descend on the nightlife like a plague of luminescent insects. Tonight is my first time peacocking. I'm wearing a dark blue blazer with a striking fuchsia pink interior that has the word 'Staff' emblazoned in gold lettering across the back. It seems to be working. Several revellers approach me during the course of the night to enquire as to the location of the toilets.

*

My own transformation was getting off to a less than auspicious start. The rejections were coming thick and fast, even if they were mostly gentle rebuttals: a wrinkling of the nose here or an irrepressible urge to use the bathroom there. Most people, and women in particular, don't generally make a point of seeking out confrontation. Partly because a lot of men don't take rejection especially kindly. And so women are obliged to tiptoe around them, mindful not to deflate any fragile egos lest it trigger a mercurial response. By the end of the weekend I was certainly making progress, albeit in the sense that I was now familiar with a wide repertoire of withering facial expressions.

I was also slowly coming to realise that a lot of my fears were overblown – that plenty of women were happy to engage in a conversation with me – so long as it didn't seem like I had an ulterior motive. My interactions had steadily improved over the course of the weekend. I was still using scripted openers but they were no longer the crutch they had been on the first night of boot camp. Back at my hotel on the Sunday night, I flushed the 'cheat sheet' that had nestled reassuringly in my pocket down the toilet. I never did try to neg a woman or impress her with a 'demonstration of higher value'. But I was learning to *let go*. It was when I managed to do that that I started to find myself in the really rewarding interactions. For the first time in my adult life, I was being myself – with all the potential risks to the ego that it entailed. I caught glimpses of the extrovert I'd always wanted to be – fraternising with people for the sheer hell of it – and importantly, not expecting anything in return. It was fine if somebody didn't like me; I would wish them well and be on my way. Rejection wasn't the paralysing, heart-stopping bogeyman that I'd built it up to be. In fact, nothing bad had really happened at all. Or at least nothing that I couldn't shrug off.

Did I need to spend an entire weekend with members of a bizarre underground subculture to figure this out? Perhaps not. Perhaps, in falling for their salacious marketing, I was simply another one of their gullible marks.

Either way, with time I would come to realise that the seduction community wasn't for me. I didn't need a taxonomy of womankind; I just needed to put myself out there more and work on my sensitivity to rejection. The penny had started to drop on the boot camp itself – a boot camp that I would subsequently try to pretend never happened. I could see the irony in that. However, the solutions proposed by the pickup gurus involved effacing one's personality and creating a new one based on dubious pseudo-scientific theories about what women were supposedly 'hard-wired' to want. To be a pickup artist wasn't to be free at all; instead, you simply ended up chained to a cartoonish, hyper-masculine husk.

In truth, a part of me had always blanched at the reconfiguration of love and romance into a cold and clinical 'game'. Whatever my early setbacks in that department, there never came a time when I wanted to demystify love altogether – to turn it into another frigid outpost of evolutionary science. I was a rational person (or so I thought) but I wanted to be more than a 'biological machine' intent on maximising its reproductive value. Men who hung around pickup for an extended length of time tended to develop a robotic and salesy way of dealing with people. I didn't want to start treating other people as scientific variables; I didn't want to be a scientific variable.

That said, there was clearly *something* unhealthy about the way I viewed women, or else I suspect I would have recoiled from the pickup scene immediately, like putting my hand on an electric fence. The fact that I was able to look past some of the teachings was damning enough. But I also knew in my bones that it would be impossible to create a bond with another person without allowing them to see the parts of me that I was ashamed of – parts of me that were as real and as human as my better qualities. By contrast, the manosphere encouraged men to appear *invulnerable*; to transform themselves into one-dimensional objects who had lobotomised the parts of them that contained vulnerability and tenderness and irony too. Men were encouraged to keep anything that hinted at sensitivity hidden from the outside world (and especially from women). Yet genuine self-esteem is impossible without revealing yourself in some way. If the message you put out to the world is inauthentic, you will inevitably distrust the feedback you receive since it won't really be a response to you. And who wants to play a character all the time? What happens if you meet somebody you like – do you have to stay in the role for the rest of your life?

Maturity and the march of time undoubtedly played a role for me. A man invariably grows out of his adolescent fixation with 'getting laid' – or at least he probably ought to. My own epiphany – that I didn't need to swathe my personality in a contrived assortment of tricks and techniques to get a girlfriend – occurred gradually over time and was expedited by going out and making an effort to talk to people and a genuine effort to, well, be genuine. My social skills improved and my confidence with it. The more time I spent around women, the less I felt the need to leave the *perfect* impression. People didn't want artificial smoothness; they wanted connection. In this regard, having female friends did more for me than the advice of any self-appointed pickup guru. I was finally able to express my personality without hiding behind the scripted patter of some pseudo-authority figure from the internet.

2

RETURN OF THE BRUTE

Minnie Lane is a dating and personal development coach for men based in London. She briefly became involved in the seduction community in 2007 when she was twenty-two. 'I joined the industry by complete fluke or serendipity, depending on which way you look at it,' she tells me over Zoom.

It all started when she was out at a bar. A man was hitting on her and she recognised some of the things he was doing. She had read *The Game* and proceeded to call him out on it. As it turned out, he'd not only read *The Game* but was a pickup coach. They then had a long conversation about the industry (Lane had recently completed a psychology degree and was interested in social dynamics). She was 'fascinated by the whole [pickup] world' but also not as 'appalled by it' as she 'probably should have been'. The pickup instructor invited her along to one of his workshops and, her curiosity piqued, she accepted. Perhaps unsurprisingly she was the only woman present on the boot camp. 'Some of the students would come and ask my opinion on things. And then one of the trainers was like, "Why don't you have a go helping some of the guys with their conversation skills?" And it turned out I was very good at it, so they asked me to stay.'

Lane ended up going out with the instructors and their students to bars and clubs in London every weekend for several months. 'It was a fun Saturday job. I'm getting paid cash in hand to go out and chat to people and go to bars.' Almost two decades on, Lane is candid about the fact that she 'got sucked into' the pickup industry. 'I think I justified it to myself by saying, "I'm not going to teach anything that I wouldn't want done to me,"' she says, before adding that at the time she had 'very low standards about how people should or shouldn't treat me'.

Lane describes the industry as full of 'gateway behaviours' that can escalate over time. 'It's the small things, like asking a client to rate a woman's attractiveness on a scale of one to ten. At the time, I would just be like, that's efficient and helps me to quickly learn his type. Now I would never do that because I can see how it affects the way people are thinking. You're making the woman into an object and a statistic rather than a human being.'

A lot of men in the community and beyond it – and I include myself in that – tended to view sex transactionally. It was a reward that women bestowed on men who followed the correct steps. We were told that the lines and techniques we were learning worked on *all* women. Perhaps unsurprisingly, some men felt a sense of outraged entitlement when sex wasn't forthcoming. They would verbally lash out, dehumanising the women who had rejected them as 'sluts' and 'whores'.

And yet I also met lots of men who just needed a few pointers. The mainstream didn't seem to know how to talk about dating from a male perspective. Men were supposed to instinctively know how things went down. When they didn't, they sometimes went looking for answers in spaces where they wouldn't be ridiculed for not knowing.

'I think a lack of genuinely helpful, practical, good advice in the mainstream is one of the problems,' says Lane. 'Sometimes someone just needs a bit of encouragement and being pushed into taking action, and then you'd see that kind of guy really gain something from the industry.'

But over time you would often see men who joined the community embracing a cartoonish caricature of masculinity. 'Pickup essentially teaches people to create a character, a persona that they can act in, that will get results and be more attractive to women,' says Lane. Pickup teachers would often preach 'authenticity' – i.e. reconnecting with the carnal urges blunted by social conditioning – while simultaneously making students even less true to themselves.

Pickup could be addictive because some of the advice could sometimes work – not that anybody outside of the community would ever admit it. And when that happened you started to wonder what else the mainstream might be keeping quiet about. 'It works because it's not what girls are used to,' says Lane in *The Pickup Game*, a 2019 documentary she featured in about the pickup community.

Few in the industry consider the long-term effects of what they are doing. 'It becomes like this echo chamber of toxic masculine energy that grows exponentially because it's feeding itself from the inside,' says Lane. 'And because it's all underground there's no women getting involved, there's no authorities getting involved. It just cascades in these horrendous directions. I think the main problem with the industry is the way it's run and unregulated and hidden. Like any underground thing, it can go to very dark places very quickly [because] there's nothing outside to stop it from happening.'

In 2015, two 27-year-old pickup instructors – Alex Smith and Jonas Dick – together with one of their clients – 28-year-old Jason Berlin – were charged with raping a 31-year-old woman.[1] The crime had taken place in 2013 in San Diego, California. Smith and Dick worked for a company called Efficient Pickup and were charging large amounts of money for seduction boot camps. The three men were also active members of the Real Social Dynamics forum RSD Nation. They got caught partly because one of them posted a 'field report' of the rape on a different pickup forum. The three men saw nothing unusual in bragging about their horrifying actions online. The judge in the case imposed eight-year sentences on all three men – the maximum term available under the law, though Berlin's sentence was later reduced to six years because of his testimony against the other defendants.

'You don't see yourself as ending up at the bottom of that slide; nobody does,' says Lane. 'What you don't realise is how subtle some of the gateway behaviours are, and how manipulative and brainwashing the industry is, so your idea of what's right and wrong can get very blurry.'

Seduction guides for men long pre-date *The Game*, even if the book's commercial success saw a glut of self-appointed gurus emerge to try to cash in on the 'science' of pulling women. In the late twelfth century, a man named Andreas Capellanus had written a guide for upper-class men on grooming and conversation tips. *De Amore,* about the art of courtly love, encouraged readers to cultivate jealousy and if they wanted a love match to look outside of marriage (most marriages at the time were arranged by parents). Later on, *The New Academy of Compliments* (1799) instructed men to make a dramatic entrance and impress women with their meat-carving skills. Curiously, the book also featured several pickup lines – 'I have a long time been broiling on the flames of ardent affection towards your dear self,' was one example. In a precursor to negging, the book also advised readers to 'catch her off guard by insulting her first'.

It was in the 1970s that men's dating advice came into its own, largely thanks to classified ads in top-shelf magazines. Published in 1973, Eric Weber's *How to Pick Up Girls!* sold over three million copies and was translated into twenty languages. In 1978, the book was even made into a film for ABC. Strauss described Weber – a 22-year-old student when he wrote *How to Pick Up Girls!* – as the author of 'the book that started it all'. It was ironic then that three decades before the pickup community emerged with its scripted lines and manipulations, Weber was advising male readers to 'let the real you emerge'.

And yet, if Weber had encouraged a more authentic approach than his spiritual heirs, he seemed to share their predilection for casual misogyny. At one point in *How to Pick Up Girls!*, Weber fantasises about sexually assaulting a woman. This imaginary woman is described as looking so 'downright delicious' that for a brief moment a man might 'even consider rape'.

Another innovator on the North American pickup scene was Ross Jeffries (real name Paul Jeffrey Ross). If Weber was the spiritual lodestone of the seduction community, then Jeffries was its 'Godfather' (according to Strauss). Jeffries was rumoured to be the inspiration behind Tom Cruise's character in the 1999 film *Magnolia*. In perhaps the most famous scene in the film, Cruise strides out onto a stage in front of a baying audience of male followers before instructing them to 'Respect the cock and tame the cunt'.

Jeffries, who would charge $3,000 for pickup seminars, self-published his first book in 1992. *How to Get the Women You Desire into Bed* was promoted as 'A Down and Dirty Guide to Dating and Seduction for the Man Who's Fed Up with Being Mr. Nice Guy'. Jeffries himself featured on the book's cover, dressed in a silk kimono and hovering over a bed on which a young blonde writhed in her underwear. Jeffries' method involved subliminal messages using suggestive words and hand gestures. Heavily influenced by neuro-linguistic programming (NLP), a pseudoscientific theory of persuasion – the mental health equivalent of homeopathy – Jeffries called his techniques Speed Seduction.

Advice included hooking your thumbs inside your trouser pockets and subtly pointing at your crotch when standing in front of a woman. The phrase 'below me' (i.e. 'blow me') was then supposed to be slipped into the conversation. The woman seeing and hearing this would then feel a strong compulsion to perform fellatio. That was the theory at least. When the journalist Louis Theroux visited Jeffries in 2000 for an episode of his *Weird Weekends* series, Jeffries proudly demonstrated his techniques while the two men rode exercise bikes at a Los Angeles gym. 'If I start talking about moving in a new direction, am I saying nude erection or new direction?' Jeffries asked a puzzled Theroux.

I had at one point in my life owned an 'inner game' audio series by Jeffries. It promised to give me 'unstoppable confidence' through the recital of 'power attitudes'. These included: *'I radiate a natural, easy self-acceptance that women find irresistibly attractive'; 'being with me is the best possible choice that any woman can make'; 'I never get rejected. I only discover if a woman has good taste.'*

I tried the tapes for a while before throwing them out. The only change I noticed was Jeffries' nasal voice ringing in my head for about a week after.

Even if the techniques resulted in few sexual encounters, the jaundiced tone of the material resonated with men who were tired of being rejected. 'Flushing a chick down the toilet of humiliation is almost as great a kick as scoring!' Jeffries had written in *How to Get the Women You Desire into Bed*. In 2019, Jeffries would admit that he had been a 'misogynist' with 'a lot of anger' back then.² At this point he was a 65-year-old living alone with two cats.³

If the 1980s in the West were characterised by macho geopolitics, then the emerging masculinity literature of those years was animated by a desire to take women down a peg. Surveying the new self-improvement literature aimed at men, the *Los Angeles Times* columnist Robin Abcarian noticed 'a brewing meanness'.⁴ She referenced *A Bartender's Guide on How to Pick Up Women* (1991) and *How to Cheat on Your Wife and Not Get Caught* (1990) as examples of this 'harsh '90s twist on the war between the sexes'. The author of one of the bestselling men's books of the era, *Fire in the Belly* (1991), captured the mood of the genre when he described men as resentful and angry at 'being blamed for everything'.

There had been an earlier backlash against the women's liberation movements of the 1960s. As women chalked up further incremental material gains over the proceeding decades, the counter-revolution would in turn marshal its cultural shock troops. The writer Susan Faludi skilfully documented this backlash in her influential book of the same name (1991).⁵ 'Women are told they are unhappy because feminism has "gone too far", giving [women] more independence than they can handle,' noted Faludi. 'At the same time they are asked to dismiss [feminism] as a well-meaning experiment doomed to founder on the rocks of biological difference.'

One such example was the bestselling book *Men Are from Mars, Women Are from Venus* (1992). In it, the relationships counsellor and self-help author John Gray characterised men and women as inhabiting entirely separate mental planets. Women lived in their emotions whereas men withdrew to their 'caves'.

Beating a retreat from the emerging field of neuroscience, whose findings did not always accord with the dogmatic assertions of pop science 'just so' stories about 'female brains', some decided to cleave instead to woo-woo and mysticism. In *The Way of the Superior Man* (1997), the men's spiritual guru David Deida depicted men and women as inhabiting mutually incomprehensible 'polarities'. Too many men and women had supposedly lost touch with their respective male and female 'energies'.

Also present alongside what Faludi described as a desire to 'reverse women's quest for equality' was a growing hostility towards the newly popular metrosexual style. It was strongly hinted that these effete and 'feminised' men were letting the side down. He was a 'new age wimp, all spineless, smiley and starry-eyed', as Deida phrased it. Deida was no pickup artist; however, his book was widely read and admired in the community for the transcendent quality it seemed to give to some of their ribaldrous theories.

The loudly asserted urge to reconnect with a subjugated and *authentic* masculinity – and the desire to reassert authority that often accompanied it, albeit in *sotto voce* – was also making itself felt in less libidinous forms. The most impactful of the self-consciously *rugged* masculinity books of the period came courtesy of the poet Robert Bly. *Iron John*: *A Book About Men* (1990) is intended as a male initiation story and a piece of anthropological speculation. The book was widely popular, sitting stubbornly on the *New York Times* bestseller list for almost a year and inspiring an emerging cottage industry of men's retreats. The story of Iron John was intended as a metaphor for male initiation rituals, told through an allegorical telling of a Brothers Grimm tale.

Bly was adamant that his work did not 'constitute a challenge to the women's movement' which he 'supports tremendously'. He also acknowledged the limitations of the unreconstructed male – the 'fifties man' who was 'supposed to like football, be aggressive, stick up for the United States, never cry, and always provide'. Bly said he found 'something wonderful' in the way men had become 'more thoughtful, more gentle' in the subsequent decades.

And yet a reactionary yelp was audible beneath Bly's high-flown perorations on the 'deep male'. For all of its supposed accommodation with a softer and more enlightened age, Bly's *deep male* still exhibited a tendency to recoil from what the author described as an increasingly 'feminised' world. According to the poet, young men were spending too much time in the 'female realm' – and it was turning them into ineffectual 'soft males, eager to please and emotionally full of light'.

Bly's vision instead was of a 'positive patriarchy'. Men were encouraged to channel the energy of warriors and kings – while still assenting to do the washing-up. Yet for all its accommodating nods to the feminist movement, Bly would occasionally slip up. 'Zeus energy is male authority accepted for the sake of the community,' he had written in *Iron John*. Beneath the opaque mythology and supercharged Jungian banalities, Bly had burrowed down to the crux of the issue. Pseudoscience had been replaced by 'Zeus energy'. Men were to remain on top – albeit as more introspective and joyful patriarchs than in the past. And all for the sake of 'the community'. Handy, that.

The self-help section wasn't the only place where besieged men were formulating new stratagems to halt the slide. The nascent internet was about to become the newest frontier in the battle to reanimate a primal machismo. As men lost ground in the boardroom and the bedroom, they gathered on sprawling internet forums and plotted how to wrestle it back.

*

Journalists frequently adopted a tone of bafflement when reporting on the subculture popularised by *The Game*. In some quarters, pickup artists were depicted as an eccentric curiosity – a phenomenon to be laughed at for their elaborate antics. Over time, this mocking scepticism hardened into outright hostility. In a 2015 research paper on the London-based seduction community, the academic Rachel O'Neill observed that the men who participated in it were routinely depicted by the media as 'pathetic, pathological or perverse'.[6]

It wasn't hard to see why so many feminists were horrified by *The Game*. Every woman in the media seemingly had a story of being clumsily negged by an aspiring pickup artist. Male journalists too began tripping over themselves to denounce the industry and proclaim themselves good feminist allies.

The transformation in the mainstream perception of pickup artists – from oddballs and misfits to the predatory bane of bars and nightclubs – coincided with a cultural shift that took place around the early 2010s. In the summer of 2013, the R&B singer Robin Thicke and the singer-songwriter Pharrell Williams released the song 'Blurred Lines'.[7] Ostensibly about hitting on another man's girlfriend, the track was panned by feminist critics who claimed it glorified 'rape culture'[8] due to Thicke's repeated use of the line 'You know you want it'. More than twenty British universities banned the song from being played at student events.

The reaction against the song would be a portent of the changing cultural climate. Feminist websites such as Jezebel brought a more uncompromising feminism into the mainstream, popularising terms like 'toxic masculinity', 'mansplaining' and 'manspreading'. There were also a number of social media-driven campaigns to 'take down' misogynistic content creators.

In the summer of 2014, the British comedian Daniel O'Reilly was given his own show on ITV2 on the back of his act – a mixture of student union humour and jocular contempt for women. Yet what had previously been considered 'banter' by television executives was soon deemed to have gone too far, mainly thanks to noisy protests by users of social media. In November of that year, following an incident in which O'Reilly had been caught on camera telling a female audience member at a live event that she was 'gagging for a rape', ITV pulled the plug on the second series of his show.

2014 would also be the year that RSD pickup instructor Julien Blanc was hauled into the CNN studios and branded as the 'most hated man in the world' by *Time* magazine. Blanc was one of the most popular instructors at RSD, which at that time was the biggest pickup company in the world. Much of RSD's success in the earlier 2010s came as a result of their early adoption of YouTube. The company's two main channels had hundreds of thousands of subscribers. Channels belonging to the company's instructors – who would upload weekly unscripted monologues to camera – had thousands more. Increasingly, RSD was also uploading 'live infield' recordings of instructors picking up women in bars and clubs. Following the runaway success of *The Game*, pickup was a competitive industry, with new gurus and companies constantly emerging. One controversial way to prove that their instructors were the real deal (though it wasn't especially controversial in the community) was to deploy hidden cameras and film instructors out in the field. The footage would then be uploaded to YouTube and used as a teaching aid. Infield was hugely popular with RSD's client base. The company could point to it as evidence that their instructors weren't just talking big for the internet.

Aside from picking up women, Julien Blanc was renowned in the community for his dark and puerile sense of humour – a style of comedy that thrived on sailing close to the edge.

By this point, RSD had already begun to sensationalise their content to stand out and generate traffic. They started to do more audacious pickups and say more outrageous things. They went from *teaching* their clients to *entertaining* them. And women were the props.

As audience capture did its work, RSD seemed steadily to realise that a segment of its audience wasn't necessarily tuning in to watch textbook pickups. And so they upped the ante. RSD instructors started being filmed making derogatory comments to women in bars and clubs (in one video, RSD founder Owen Cook, who played the role of the heel in *The Game*, could be heard calling a woman a 'dog' and a 'slut'). Unsuspecting women became the butt of an in-joke that was shared between the company and its audience. Those who raised concerns on the RSD forum about the direction things were going usually got piled onto by other forum users who were eager to curry favour with their pickup idols. Students began to film themselves swaggering around a club insulting people, throwing drinks and grabbing women. This was what being 'self-amused' and 'not giving a fuck' looked like, they claimed. Being alpha became synonymous with 'not asking for permission', which was something that 'betas' and 'chodes' (a variation on AFC) did. The industry had devolved into a cult of puerile bullying and misogyny.

Meanwhile, videos uploaded to Blanc's YouTube channel were given increasingly dark and offensive titles. One video was captioned: 'My Girlfriend Passed Away: The Twisted Humour That Inevitably Knifes Through To Her Panties'.

Blanc was candid about why he was doing it: to boost traffic. Where the algorithm led, the seduction industry followed. 'It's offensive, it's inappropriate, it's emotionally scarring, but it's damn effective,' he said.

And it was frighteningly effective for a while. Until it wasn't – because change was in the air.

*

I first saw it in early November 2014. Blanc had uploaded the video to his YouTube channel with the title 'White Male Fucks Asian Woman in Tokyo (And The Beautiful Methods To It)'. He then presumably thought nothing of it. Another weekly video to keep the students happy. What's more, because it was recycled footage from a live event, it saved him the trouble of making a video from scratch. Presumably he never imagined it would be the most impactful video RSD had ever released. Thousands watched it. Then hundreds of thousands. Then millions.

In the video, Blanc is at the front of a seminar room holding court before a room full of men. He is talking about picking up women in Japan when he gives the following advice. 'At least in Tokyo, if you're a white male, you can do what you want... I'm just romping through the streets, just grabbing girls' heads, just like, head, pfft on the dick. Head, on the dick, yelling, "Pikachu" [a character in Pokémon].' Blanc also told students to 'Just grab her... To take the pressure off, yell Pikachu or Pokémon or Tamagotchi or something.' An 'infield' video that was broadcast during the workshop showed Blanc with his hand around the throat of a woman in a Japanese nightclub.

Pickup instructors often put on a bombastic show during their live events. Their narcissistic personalities were replenished by the applause of an audience that viewed them like rock stars. The men in the crowd lived vicariously through the outrageous antics of their favourite instructor. Both sets of participants egged each other on, constantly upping the ante. Minnie Lane had described the 'ego trip' that certain pickup coaches went on, fuelled by this escalatory dialectic with the crowd. 'The way they stand, the way they talk in front of the audiences. It's like the enjoyment of feeling that they've got all the power and control.'

Maybe Blanc was feeding off that. Or maybe he was serious – jokes had a habit of morphing into core beliefs. Either way, the backlash was swift and grew precipitously. A petition started by the feminist activist Jenn Li – on the back of the hashtag 'TakeDownJulienBlanc' – quickly gathered over 300,000 signatures. The petition described RSD as 'a group of sexist and racist "pick up artists", who have made a living by teaching men how to violate women through physical and emotional abuse'.[9] It called on hotels and venues where RSD events were scheduled to take place to cancel them and for web servers to stop hosting their content. Blanc cut a timorous figure when he was grilled by Andrew Cuomo on CNN – a stark contrast to his overblown pickup persona. He said the images from Japan had been 'taken out of context' and that he had been 'hanging out with' the women prior to the footage being taken. Longer versions of the videos did appear to show the women involved playing along with Blanc and in good spirits. But it was RSD that had originally spliced the scenes in the most sensationalist way possible, presumably with the titillation of its audience in mind. That was to say nothing of the racist tone of the video: Blanc was seemingly encouraging his audience to take advantage of a culture that placed a high premium on politeness to the point of timidity.

The scandal prompted activists to comb through Blanc's historical social media content. In doing so they unearthed an old Instagram post in which the RSD instructor had captioned a graphic of the 'Power & Control' wheel used to tackle domestic violence with 'May as well be a checklist... #Howtomakeherstay'. Activists uncovered other troubling RSD content, including a video in which co-founder of the company Cook appeared to boast about raping a stripper[10] who was 'just totally not in the mood':

> The last way I fucked her too, it was in the morning, she was taking a shower, and I didn't think she wanted to have sex again, but I just threw her on the bed and I put it in her, and I could barely even get it in because she was just totally not in the mood. And I was like, 'Fuck it, I'm never seeing this bitch again. I don't care.' So I just like, jam it in, and it's all tight and dry and I fuck her, and I'm like, 'I'll just make this quick because she doesn't even want it.' But then she starts to get into it, and once she gets into it I came prematurely.

By 6 November 2014, Blanc and RSD had been banned from holding events in major cities around the world. Blanc's Australian visa was revoked and he was barred from entering the UK and Singapore. Ticketing website Eventbrite removed all RSD events from its website and Blanc's content was taken down from YouTube or set to private. A large number of pickup artist channels on YouTube would subsequently be demonetised or pulled down. By 2016, RSD was described in the *Guardian* as running workshops that 'teach men strategies and techniques to deceive and manipulate women into sex, using both force and emotional abuse'.[11]

Perhaps unsurprisingly, I wasn't overly keen to draw attention to the fact I had once solicited advice from a company that employed the 'most hated man in the world'.

*

According to the American writer Rebecca Solnit, 2014 was 'a year of feminist insurrection against male violence: a year of mounting refusal to be silent, refusal to let our lives and torments be erased or dismissed'.[12] As well as the campaign to take down Julien Blanc, it was also the year that Malala Yousafzai, the Pakistani female education activist who two years earlier had been shot and wounded by the Taliban, was awarded the Nobel Peace Prize. Women were also finally allowed to become bishops in the Church of England. At the VMA Awards, Beyoncé, the world's biggest pop star at that time, performed in front of a giant luminous 'FEMINIST' sign. *Slate* magazine would describe it as a 'banner year for feminism'[13] with 'the clamour of female voices demanding respect, autonomy and equality... getting louder'. Another popular hashtag that year – along with #TakeDownJulienBlanc – was #YesAllWomen, which women used to share their personal stories of sexual abuse and harassment. What would officially become the MeToo movement in 2017 – whereby at least some powerful men in Hollywood would be held accountable for sexual assault and harassment – was steadily gathering momentum on social media. 'If #MeToo has made men feel vulnerable, panicked, unsure, and fearful as a result of women finally, collectively, saying, "Enough!" so be it. If they wonder how their every word and action will be judged and used against them, welcome to our world,' wrote the feminist author Soraya Chemaly in her 2018 book *Rage Becomes Her: The Power of Women's Anger*.

And yet, as Gore Vidal once wrote of the resurgence of the far-right in the United States, the 'muddy depths' were being 'stirred by new monsters from the deep'. Also discernible in 2014 were signs of yet another reactionary backlash.

In the pickup community, a more toxic and abrasive type of influencer was emerging. Roosh V (Daryush Valizadeh) was one of the most vile and misogynistic pickup artists to emerge at that time. Roosh would author more than a dozen self-published books, including a series of libidinous travel guides titled *Bang* that discussed how to pick up women in different countries around the world. 'Poor favela chicks are very easy, but quality is a serious problem,' Valizadeh wrote in *Bang Brazil*. He said that, given a free choice, women would always prefer 'an exciting man who treats her poorly and does not care for her well-being'. In 2015, Roosh wrote a blog post called 'How to Stop Rape', in which he argued that rape 'should not be illegal if done on private property'.[14] He would later claim that the article was 'satirical'.

Moreover, while social media had proved an effective tool in taking down Julien Blanc and Dapper Laughs,[15] it would also be the preferred medium for an angry, meme-driven counterblast. 'Gamergate' – named after a Twitter (now X) hashtag – was novel in several ways, not least as an online assault on progressives that couched itself in the language of the tech-savvy culture it was attacking.

The spark for Gamergate was an incendiary blog post by Eron Gjoni, a 24-year-old man who accused a female indie game developer, Zoë Quinn, of cheating on him with a gaming writer in the hope of getting a positive write-up of her game. The central accusation wasn't true; however, an army of online trolls quickly decided they would like it to be. Here was an avowed social justice advocate exchanging sex for positive reviews. Progressive hypocrisy! Gamergaters claimed to be standing up for 'ethics in video games journalism' and to be protecting the 'gamer' identity. Yet the claim became less persuasive as the onslaught of harassment and trolling gained momentum. Gamergaters viciously trolled and threatened anybody who criticised them. Particular vitriol was directed at female gamers and journalists.

The defining characteristic of the movement seemed to be resentment at the encroachment of women into male-dominated spaces, including the push for more female characters in video games. Gamergaters began to present themselves in snivelling and whining tones as besieged victims of politically correct 'social justice warriors'.

In this sense, Gamergate was 'a mutant variant of the traditional American grievance movement, a rearguard action marching under the banner of high-minded media critique',[16] as the *Gizmodo* writer Kyle Wagner noted at the time. 'There are notes here... from a hymn book that predates the internet: self-pity, self-martyrdom, an overwhelming sense of your own blamelessness, the certainty that someone else's victimhood is nothing more than a profitable pose.'

Gamergate would ultimately be characterised by gendered cybermobs trying to publicly silence women: a modern-day witch-hunt to drive women from online spaces, just as they had once been driven out of other public spaces. As the academic and author Jack Z. Bratich wrote of the harassment campaign, 'Geek masculinity (betas)... joined in tentative alliance with declining hegemonic patriarchs (alphas) in a war to re-establish a gender order, after which they will work out their treaties and spoils among themselves'.[17]

Others have since likened Gamergate to a trial run for the movement that would propel Donald Trump to the White House two years later – a 'debutante's ball' for the rootless males who would form Trump's electoral base. Tactics that were pioneered during Gamergate would subsequently be used to intimidate critics of Trump and his Make America Great Again (MAGA) movement. One involved releasing the private information of ideological enemies – known as doxxing. During Gamergate, Zoe Quinn received death and rape threats from anonymous online accounts. Her home address, phone number and passwords were all shared widely on social networks along with private photos. Several of her colleagues had their emails hacked.[18] Brianna Wu, the founder of a Boston-based game studio, had to flee her home after anonymous attackers published her address and sent graphic threats to rape and kill her. The feminist game critic Anita Sarkeesian was forced to cancel a talk at Utah State University after the school received an anonymous email promising 'the deadliest school shooting in American history'. The sender said he wanted people to know 'what feminist lies and poison have done to the men of America'.

For many mainstream journalists, Gamergate was their first brush with the pestilential loser culture of anonymous forums such as 4chan – subterranean internet worlds where white male grievance politics went to stew and fester. Gamergate contained in embryo some of the features of an ascendant right-wing populism. This included an exaggerated anxiety about 'political correctness' (later redefined as 'wokeness'); a style of discourse meant to disorientate rather than persuade; and the laundering of old hatreds under the guise of irony and humour. Gamergate was also characterised by an inverted rendition of the conventional oppressor-oppressed narrative. Men (white men in particular) were taught to think of themselves as victims – not of the capitalist system, but of a progressive culture that was trying to take away what was rightfully theirs. Simone de Beauvoir once remarked that 'the most mediocre of males feels himself a demigod as compared with women'. For a downwardly mobile constituency of men, sexist and racist trolling functioned as a repository of self-worth in a world where their right to take up the most space was felt to be under threat.

At the head of the Gamergate mob were a philistine vanguard of internet personalities. 'Gamergate is remarkable,' trilled Milo Yiannopoulos, editor[19] at the time of the far-right Breitbart website. Yiannopoulos, a flamboyant provocateur who had once dismissed video gamers as 'pungent beta male bollock-scratchers', saw in Gamergate a resentful energy that could be harnessed to attack the left. Yiannopoulos had initially got his job at Breitbart through Steve Bannon, Trump's future White House aide. During a brief stint owning a gaming company, Bannon himself had discovered the 'monster power' of 'rootless white males'. In Yiannopoulos he saw someone who could 'connect with these kids'. Gamergate had given them someone to blame and now they were looking for someone to follow. As Bannon would tell the journalist Joshua Green in 2017,[20] 'They come in through Gamergate or whatever and then get turned on to politics and Trump.'

3

ANGRY MEN ON THE INTERNET

Me: *'Somebody should write a book about angry men on the internet.'*

My editor: *'Why don't you write it?'*

Me: *'Why would I want to do that?'*

By 2018, I was looking for a topic for my next book. The subculture I had dipped my toe into back in 2006 wasn't at the top of my list of things to write about. As far as I was concerned, the boot camp was firmly in the past, memory-holed together with other unflattering reminiscences. We've all done things that we look back on and squirm; and paying a stranger to teach me how to talk to women was right up there. I wasn't keen to dwell on the subject in my own time let alone broadcast it to the world. If I ever did think about the boot camp, it was mainly to wonder how many men had blown it with women because they'd taken the advice of companies with names like 'Alpha Male Dating Systems'.

Looming large was the fear that in writing about the manosphere I would have to confront my own flirtation with it. It would be discombobulating. But most of all it would be humiliating. It would be like recovering from some terrible illness only to reinfect myself all over again. I could only hope that my body had generated enough antibodies the first time around. Most of all I was wary of inadvertently parroting the credo of the community I would be investigating. To spend time immersed in a culture to which you do not belong – to 'go native' as it were – requires a certain amount of adaptation. You must mix with people who speak a different language to yourself, who possess a sense of humour that is subtly at odds with your own and whose values you don't necessarily share. Certain social tics that you encounter will be incomprehensible at first. In order to accurately translate what you are seeing you must go deeper still. You begin to learn the language and eat the local food. You laugh along with the jokes that those outside of the community would struggle to comprehend. You plant one foot down firmly inside this new community. Yet although you might feel like a local by this point, if you drink the tap water you're still going to get ill. In other words, you must hold a part of yourself back at all times as an obligation to your reader. The last thing I wanted to do in taking on such a project was go *full Neil Strauss*.

The risks associated with immersion are heightened considerably if the community in question is in any way cult-like. Cults deliberately extract themselves from the mainstream so that the minds of their followers can remain sealed against the heresies of the outside world. The manosphere's various subdivisions – pickup artists, red pill ideologues, male separatists, involuntary celibates, lifestyle gurus – all clung to various cult-like propositions. The world beyond their little community was depicted as a hostile place that was steered recklessly by the gullible masses. By contrast, only they – an enlightened few – had grasped the essential truths.

I wasn't sure I would even recognise the subculture any more. Indeed, a lot had changed while I had been busy forgetting. Some of the old faces were still around; however, a darker energy seemed to be in the ascendant. The new masculinity influencers that had emerged in the mid-to-late 2010s preferred three-hour diatribes about women (shallow, manipulative, 'hypergamous') to getting off with them. Gone was the black eyeliner, top hat and scripted openers. Instead it was all about being 'dominant' and 'alpha' and 'high status'.

For all of their toxicity, the early pickup artists had been less inclined than their successors to blame women for the choices they made. They tried to drum it into their students that it was 'never her fault' but 'always yours'. Instead of complaining about women it was incumbent on clients to mould themselves into what she desired (albeit in an extremely narrow sense). 'She's not a bitch,' as Mystery used to say; 'she's just a bitch to you.' Over time, this would descend into total solipsism – self-development becoming self-obsession.

When I revisited this world, I found men who were preoccupied with getting back at women in some cosmic way. I'd open YouTube and it wasn't Mystery I'd see, telling men to perform a DHV or a magic trick. It would be influencers warning their audiences that the dilution of traditional gender roles was precipitating the collapse of Western civilisation. Men in eyeliner were now part of the problem, apparently a sign that society was putting the 'weak' and 'effeminate' before the strong.

There are *degrees* of harm. The old pickup scene had been a conveyor belt to more extreme ideas. Men who found it were taught to believe that women were fundamentally *different* from themselves: that they were ruled by a fluctuating tide of emotion; that they didn't know themselves; and that they were *lesser* and more disposable in some way. Perhaps most disturbingly, there was a cavalier approach to women's free will. Men were told by their gurus and guides to 'disregard' what women said and to 'push through' what was characterised as 'token resistance'.

I had deliberately chosen to ignore much of this stuff back in the day – that, I was obligated to admit to myself, had been selfish. And yet, despite the abundance of evidence that the seduction community could turn men into worse versions of what women were already putting up with, there was no question that things had taken a darker turn since I'd been away.

*

The world I was setting out to investigate was also starting to find its way to me. A few months before the meeting in London with my editor, a Canadian psychology professor was causing a storm a few miles down the road. In January 2018, Jordan Peterson had sat down for an interview with Cathy Newman for Channel 4 News. A clinical psychologist and lecturer at the University of Toronto, Peterson already had a cult following in certain corners of the internet. His YouTube lectures on topics ranging from The Gospels to Soviet totalitarianism had racked up millions of views. However, his popularity was about to go to another level.

Peterson had first hit the headlines in 2016 following a series of YouTube videos in which he criticised an amendment to the Canadian Human Rights Act and the Criminal Code (Bill C-16). The Bill's stated aim was to introduce 'gender identity and expression' as prohibited grounds for discrimination in Canadian law. According to Peterson, the proposed amendment represented a grave danger to free speech. He threatened to go on hunger strike rather than use 'the words that other people require me to use, especially if they're made up by radical left-wing ideologues'.[1] The resultant videos clocked up over 400,000 views and resulted in a spate of appearances on Canadian television. Peterson hit the headlines again the following year when Lindsay Shepherd, an English graduate teacher at Wilfrid Laurier University, Ontario, played her class two short clips of him discussing the gender pronoun controversy. The clips were taken from a 2016 episode of *The Agenda* with Steve Paikin, a TVO (known at the time as TVOntario) current affairs programme. Following a complaint by one of her students, Shepherd was hauled before administrators and accused of creating a 'toxic climate for some of the students'. Shepherd's actions were compared by one of the faculty's professors to 'neutrally playing a speech by Hitler'.[2] The episode was jumped on by sections of the media as an example of censorious students trying to shut down free speech.

Yet when he arrived in the UK, Peterson was still relatively unknown here outside a small but devoted following on social media. He was in the country to promote his newest book, *12 Rules for Life: An Antidote to Chaos*. His previous book, *Maps of Meaning: The Architecture of Belief* – an ambitious work that brought together mythology, morality and psychoanalysis – had been published in 1999. Some of the hallmarks of Peterson's mature style were already discernible back then, including a penchant for verbosity, fluffy Jungian speculation and obscure academic language.

Peterson appeared on BBC Radio 4's flagship *Today* programme and then three days later sat down with Newman. During the subsequent thirty-minute interview, Peterson would take questions from Newman about his latest book as well as several other topics, including the purported 'crisis of masculinity' and the gender pay gap.

A trap appeared to have been set for Peterson by producers of the show. During the interview there were repeated attempts to cast Peterson as the curmudgeonly white guy railing against progress. However, his calm demeanour contrasted favourably with Newman's indignant questioning – a method of interrogation that strayed several times into misrepresenting Peterson's answers and attempting to bait him into saying disparaging things about women.

Cathy Newman: *So you don't believe in equal pay? ... You're saying women aren't intelligent enough to run top companies?*

Peterson: *No, I'm not saying that at all [laughs].*[3]

The interview went viral on YouTube, clocking up over four million views in a few days.[4] Peterson's composure as he batted away Newman's insinuations lent itself well to social media virality. Instead of debunking Peterson's book, the interview helped to propel it up the bestseller lists. Its author became an overnight celebrity and his scheduled talks quickly sold out. Peterson was soon being hailed by conservative commentators in gushing tones. The economist Tyler Cowen described him as 'the most influential public intellectual in the Western world'.[5] The heterodox feminist Camille Paglia anointed Peterson as 'the most important and influential Canadian thinker since Marshall McLuhan'. For the Fox News host Tucker Carlson, Peterson's head-to-head with Newman was 'one of the great interviews of all time'.[6]

For existing fans of Peterson – and for many others who were hearing him for the very first time – the interview seemed to confirm that the mainstream media had been captured by progressive orthodoxy. The scandalised attempts at a 'gotcha' moment (and the hostile treatment he received from liberal journalists in its aftermath) were presented by conservatives as evidence of a broader drive to delegitimise certain points of view. 'They' had tried to 'cancel' Peterson by placing him outside the purview of acceptable opinion. To be sure, some Peterson fans clearly resented the fact that a woman had possessed the effrontery to challenge their hero. Following her dust-up with Peterson, Newman was subjected to a barrage of misogynistic abuse, including death threats. Things got so bad at one point that Channel 4 had to call in security specialists.[7]

The row encapsulated a dynamic that would become wearily familiar. Clumsy progressive overreach was ferociously exploited by right-wing actors and cited as evidence of cultural capture by the left. Peterson – the folksy, tweed-wearing professor from Canada with a voice that sounded vaguely like Kermit the frog – had been vaulted to the front lines of the culture war.

And there he would remain. Polling carried out in May 2020 by anti-extremist charity Hope not Hate found that two in five young men had read, watched or listened to material by Peterson.[8] The Christianity-tinged, up-by-the-bootstraps guidance contained in *12 Rules for Life* (tidy your room, make your bed, stand up straight with your shoulders back) wasn't all that different from the advice of washed up motivational gurus such as Tony Robbins. And yet a groundswell of men seemed to be finding something revelatory in Peterson's work. They devoured his books, binge-watched his YouTube lectures and turned up in droves to hear him preen cerebrally about lobsters and the 'burden of being'. With his sprawling lectures, Peterson made it seem possible to master all of politics and theology without ever having to study either. There were countless testimonies on websites such as Reddit and YouTube from men who claimed that Peterson had endowed their life with purpose and, in some cases, had even saved it. Peterson himself claimed to have received more than 35,000 letters of appreciation.[9]

During a 2017 interview with *The Spectator,* prior to the viral interview with Channel 4 News, Peterson had been asked why 90 per cent of his audience were male. 'I'm telling [these men] something they desperately need to hear – that there are important things that need to be fixed up,' he replied. 'I'm saying, "You guys really need to get your act together and you need to bear some responsibility and grow the hell up."'

At this point, Peterson began to weep. 'Every time I talk about this, it breaks me up,' he confessed. 'The message I've been delivering is, "Find the heaviest weight you can and pick it up. And that will make you strong. You're not who you could be. And who you could be is worthwhile."'

Peterson was casting himself as the stern (if teary) father figure extolling tough love to a directionless male audience. My first impression of Peterson was of someone who was making a simple but important point: that the path of least resistance isn't always the optimal one. In this sense he was conveying a difficult – and in some ways a countercultural – truth: that discomfort is a necessary by-product of growth. It may feel good to assuage feelings of anomie and stagnation with distractions – computer games, reality television, pornography – but Peterson challenged his audience to 'accept the terrible responsibility of your life'. In other words, there was a price to be paid for taking the easy option. It was an unusual message in a society that had become preoccupied with the avoidance of pain. 'If you don't feel ennobled by your porn-related masturbation, then perhaps that means it's of questionable utility,'[10] Peterson warned his young viewers. He was issuing them with a challenge: were they fulfilling their potential? For some, he was the first person in their lives who had seen any potential. He believed in them even if nobody else did. Peterson's earnest conversational style made him an easy target of mirth. Yet the sniggers merely reinforced the sense among his fans (many of whom were autodidactic, lower-middle-class men) that liberals were sneering at them. They took him seriously because he seemed to take them seriously. Peterson knew they didn't feel like they had won the lottery by being male. He knew that not all men were flourishing. Indeed, one older fan of his told me that Peterson's YouTube lectures had 'captivated' him at a time when he was struggling to navigate a mid-life crisis:

> Existential anxiety was ever-present, triggered by various situations, particularly my work at that time. My career path was becoming increasingly unclear, and I felt trapped by recent decisions that seemed to be backfiring. This external situation (an unfulfilling job) spiralled into deeper existential doubt – I felt like I wasn't building anything meaningful, like I was wasting my life. My efforts to change this situation were failing, and I felt stuck. Then, Peterson appeared. What drew me in was his ability to articulate valid points on controversial topics. His use of psychological language and metaphors was compelling and he seemed to genuinely understand the struggles men face – issues often overlooked by broader society. I was captivated by Peterson's arguments about men's roles in society and the psychological approaches he suggested for leading a fulfilling life.

Yet beneath Peterson's loquacious rhetoric and spongy mythological abstractions, a righteous anger was burning away. This would grow more pronounced in the ensuing years. The Canadian-Hungarian physicist Gabor Maté observed[11] that Peterson's distinctive voice could sometimes sound as if it was literally choking with rage. For some of his fans, the jaundiced energy was very much a part of the appeal. Peterson's stern fatherly advice also came with a stridently conservative message. His was a creed of single-minded personal responsibility. Inequalities of class and gender were innate and ineradicable. Readers must set their 'house in perfect order' before venturing to criticise the world. Capitalism was 'not the fundamental cause of inequality'.[12]

As time went by, Peterson became a celebrated figure among the political agitators of the 'anti-woke' right. His sentiments were also increasingly in tune with the growing underground men's movement. He rubbished the gender pay gap, railed against 'radical feminists' who had an 'unconscious wish for brutal male domination', and claimed there was 'not a shred of evidence' that Western society was 'pathologically patriarchal'.

Peterson had a warning too: if society pushed men too far to 'feminise' they would, he said, become interested in 'harsh, fascist political ideology'.

For somebody whose work came marinated in the gospel of personal responsibility, this sounded like an abdication of it. Was Peterson saying that men – indeed, the sort of men who might watch his content – were easy marks for fascist propaganda? There certainly seemed to be a link between feverish hyperbole about society being 'feminised' and the rise of militant ideologies of the radical right. But that wasn't the point Peterson was trying to make. It was not a point he necessarily could make, considering he was guilty of dabbling in the same hyperbole himself.

4

THE 10 COMMANDMENTS OF GAME

'Helping guys drown in pu$$y is what [Derek] enjoys doing most'.

September 2018. The email had just landed in my inbox. It was from a man named Derek Moneyberg, a pickup artist and wealth coach who was coming to London. He would be in town to promote his new course, 'The 10 Commandments of Game', the accumulated wisdom from fifteen years as an RSD instructor.[1] Moneyberg – real name Dale Buczkowski – would also be showing us how to get rich.

I decided it would be useful to go and try and make some connections. I put my name down for the event and cancelled any plans I had that weekend. A short time later I received another email which contained the following warning:

'***DO NOT*** approach females in and around the seminar location as venues have not wanted to host us again as a result of attendees doing this previously.'

*

I wasn't sure what to expect on the first day. I arrive to find perhaps thirty to forty men milling around gingerly in the lobby of the hotel. I stand with them as we wait to be given our blue wristbands. The audiences for RSD events have dwindled since the heady days of *The Game*. Hard-core followers of the company – and you had to be hard-core to still be turning up to live events in 2018 – could be like xeroxed photocopies of each other. At events like this they would be ham-fisting their contrived personalities on to you under the guise of networking or 'offering value'. However, before that can happen, we are told to place our phones in plastic containers provided by the event stewards. They assure us we will get them back at the end and we will. The phone thing has become de rigueur at RSD events ever since the Julien Blanc scandal. The last thing they want is for something inflammatory to go viral on social media.

Several warm-up acts take to the stage before the main event. Unpaid RSD interns in their early twenties regale us with stories of how RSD is helping them to live out their wildest fantasies (which frequently involve arranging threesomes through Tinder). They go into rhapsodies about their 'personal transformations' since purchasing RSD products and boot camps. Every RSD instructor has an origin story like this: they were losers until they discovered RSD; now they are winners.

A personal trainer and bodybuilding influencer called Brandon Carter takes to the stage as the final warm-up act before Moneyberg. His is a hard knock story of rugged self-reliance. As Carter tells it, he went from being a poor black kid selling drugs on the mean streets of Chicago to flying around the world as a wealthy fitness entrepreneur. Stories like this are the white wallpaper of the self-help circuit. Following a series of trials and tribulations, Carter managed to clamber his way to the top. And without any help from the government. So what was our excuse? Before we have time to think of any, Carter gives us the answer. 'Nobody gives a fuck about your excuses,' he says.

It makes for a rousing if unoriginal speech which has an implicit no refunds policy. With responsibility for success placed firmly on the shoulders of the students, they can also be blamed if success fails to materialise. They obviously did not want it badly enough. The possibility that a client's failure might be attributable to bad advice – advice obtained at an event like this one perhaps – is conveniently closed off beforehand.

Pickup events nearly always shared the up-by-the-boot-straps ethos of the wider self-help industry. The idea that looks and money didn't matter – that what mattered was 'game', which could be learned – was simultaneously part of the subculture's appeal and a source of resentment among its male detractors. It placed the burden of responsibility for success or failure entirely on the student. In other words, when an expensive pickup programme failed to live up to its preposterous sales pitch ('MAKE HER EMOTIONALLY ADDICTED TO YOU IN JUST 15 MINUTES') it was blamed on you, the client. Over time, this would generate a backlash that would occasionally turn violent. Indeed, the misogynist incel (involuntary celibate) community would initially emerge out of an anti-pickup artist website that first appeared online in 2009. PUAHate.com was envisioned as a place for men to vent about being ripped off by pickup hucksters. In his 137-page manifesto, Elliot Rodger, a self-described incel who in 2014 would murder six people and injure fourteen others in a misogynistic killing spree in Isla Vista, California, was a poster in the forums. PUAHate was 'full of men who are starved of sex, just like me'. It was, he said, a resource that 'confirmed many of the theories I had about how wicked and degenerate women really are'.

*

Moneyberg was charging $3,000 for a three-day nightclub boot camp. For this he promised to furnish clients with 'an abundant sex life with high-calibre women'. Buczkowski was a self-proclaimed expert in this regard, though at the risk of sounding judgemental, he didn't necessarily look like someone who was 'drowning in pu$$y'. He had greasy unkempt hair and piggy eyes that looked out blearily from a bloated face. The scruffy polo shirt he had on was a size too big even for his oversized frame. As he held court at the front of the room, I scanned the faces of the men staring saucer-eyed and asked myself: do they really want to be like *that*? The intermittent bursts of whooping and hollering suggested to me that they might well want it.

The 10 Commandments programme consisted of boilerplate self-help patter with a smattering of pickup advice.

THE 10 COMMANDMENTS OF GAME

'*You are in charge of your life, not anyone else*'; '*Build a life that she would want to be part of*'; '*Thou shall always be building your value*', etc.[2] It wasn't exactly Moses receiving the stone tablets on Mount Sinai. Yet many had plainly come here for the vibe as much as the practical content. Moneyberg began his talk by telling the audience – made up overwhelmingly of twenty-something men in V-neck T-shirts (it was September and still relatively warm) – that anyone who didn't know what their gender was could 'leave now' and 'go fuck off'. The laughter started and never really stopped thereafter. Anyone who didn't want to hear about 'threesomes' and 'fucking hot young women' was also advised to 'fucking leave right now'. The audience erupts when Moneyberg says he refuses to date women older than twenty-four. They approve because Moneyberg is forty-one; by refusing to date women his own age he is seen to be getting one over on the women who turned *us* down when we were twenty-four. Moneyberg has an unmistakably bullying demeanour; but then, people will often gravitate to that if they believe there is some advantage in it for them.

By 2018, pickup companies were finding it harder to operate in a rapidly evolving cultural climate. Even some of the more popular pickup instructors[3] no longer wanted to be associated with the industry. The RSD forums were being taken over by 'incels' and were awash with nihilistic rants. Julien Blanc, at one point the 'most hated man in the world' for his behaviour, was still working for RSD but had stopped teaching pickup; he refused even to talk about the subject in public. Not that he was full of palpable regret for his previous transgressions. Blanc's personal rebranding saw him become a 'trauma release' coach. His expertise in this area came from all the trauma he had purportedly suffered during his 2014 scandal.

RSD's emergence as the largest pickup company in the world was driven to a significant degree by YouTube. Their channels had hundreds of thousands of subscribers, their videos millions of views. Students gravitated to them because their free content was better than most of what their competitors were charging for. The coaches they employed were young, charismatic and compelling public speakers. RSD's Inner Circle groups – a peer-to-peer global network – had tens of thousands of members, helping men arriving in a new city to find places to go out as well as wingmen to go out with.

A slew of policy changes would be introduced by social media platforms in the 2010s as they sought to fall into line with the cultural mood and launder their social justice credentials. For YouTube, this involved a shift towards more advertiser-friendly content and a focus on preventing pickup artists from profiting from their videos. By 2019, pickup videos were still available on the platform but were increasingly demonetised. Following a BBC Scotland investigation that year, over a hundred pickup videos were removed from YouTube[4] for violating its rules on nudity and sexual conduct. Some of the channels (though not RSD) were accused of hosting secret recordings of women having sex.

Over time, pickup artists pivoted to new topics to avoid deplatforming. RSD started calling itself Self-Mastery Co and became a boilerplate self-help channel. Most of RSD's pickup videos gradually disappeared from YouTube and the company parted ways with some of its popular instructors.[5] Others in the industry sought to rebrand themselves by becoming more political and conspiratorial. This in turn could act as a further conduit to extremism. As the authors of a 2021 academic study of the manosphere concluded, 'Many of the individuals involved with the PUA community went on to participate in more extreme anti-feminist communities.'[6]

*

The pickup artists had followed a two-step process when it came to marketing their products. They would discredit the mainstream before presenting themselves as oracles of forbidden knowledge. *They* were going to reveal what powerful elites didn't want *you* to know (for a price, obviously). They broke down reality and then presented their audiences with a way to stitch it back together. It was a highly effective formula: I had first-hand experience of how easy it was to be taken in by alluring promises of 'insider' wisdom.

It was also an ominous portent of the future information landscape: before long, a myriad of online actors would be trying to discredit the mainstream in order to sell their followers an alternative version of reality. The so-called red pill movement was at the centre of it. That was where I was going to go next. I thought I knew why men like me had fallen under the influence of charismatic dating coaches. But I wanted to know what made this new movement tick. What was their beef with women about? Why was the so-called red pill gaining in popularity? And did they really call themselves 'alpha males'?

PART 2

The Red Pill

'Fascism was a counter-revolution against a revolution that never took place.'

Ignazio Silone, *The School for Dictators*, 1938

5

ORIGINS OF THE RED PILL

RSD had been co-founded by a pickup artist teaching under the handle of Tyler Durden. The name was lifted from *Fight Club*, a novel by Chuck Palahniuk. Made into a film in 1999, *Fight Club* was wildly popular in the manosphere. The film's narrator, played by Edward Norton, is a depressed white-collar insomniac who is undergoing an identity crisis. His personality begins to split and at night he becomes Tyler Durden, a messianic soap salesman played adroitly by Brad Pitt. Durden is charismatic, sexually promiscuous and, most importantly, unconstrained by social conventions. 'All the ways you wish you could be, that's me,' Durden tells the Narrator at one point in the film. 'I look like you wanna look, I fuck like you wanna fuck, I am smart, capable, and most importantly, I am free in all the ways that you are not.'

Pitt's character represented a return to a primal authenticity that was venerated in the manosphere. For a subculture of men who expended a great deal of energy constructing elaborate masculine facades, this attachment to 'authenticity' might sound paradoxical. However, it was about breaking free from the oppressive strictures that were separating men from a self-balancing, naturalised order. To be truly authentic meant listening to the 'ancient wisdom' and 'timeless truths' found within. In *Not All Dead White Men: Classics and Misogyny in the Digital Age* (2018),[1] the classicist and author Donna Zuckerberg noted that the men of the manosphere 'would have their readers believe there is a straight line from antiquity to today, a continuity of male and female behaviour.' She described this 'illusion of continuity' as an 'ideologically motivated strategy to resurrect ancient norms in the present day'.[2]

Masculinity entrepreneurs imbued their life hacks, workout routines and entrepreneurial strategies with the 'wisdom of the ancients'. Marcus Aurelius's *Meditations* and other Stoic works were selectively read and promoted as an alternative to emotional introspection and therapy. Infowars conspiracy theorist Alex Jones had a line of 'Caveman' products that supposedly drew on the 'ancient traditions and practices that our ancestors held dearly'. Brian Johnson, an American fitness influencer known by his alias The Liver King, promoted the 'ancestral lifestyle' to over six million followers. This 'primal way of life' would 'put back what the modern world has left out.' In 2022 it was revealed that Johnson had left out the most important 'ancestral tenet' of his lifestyle: his chiselled and muscular physique was less the product of a 'raw organ meat diet' than an $11,000 a month anabolic steroid habit. Ancient wisdom, indeed.

ORIGINS OF THE RED PILL

Another popular film in the community – a film ostensibly about the future rather than the past – was *The Matrix*. Released, like *Fight Club*, in 1999, it was where the metaphor of the red pill was first coined. Humanity is trapped inside a computer simulation – the Matrix – and its life force is parasitically farmed as a power source by artificial intelligence. The film's protagonist, Neo, is offered a red pill as a gateway out of the Matrix by rebel leader Morpheus. Alternatively, he can continue to live in blissful ignorance. This is the blue pill. Morpheus offers Neo two choices. 'You take the blue pill, the story ends. You wake up in your bed and believe whatever you want to believe. You take the red pill... and I show you how deep the rabbit hole goes.' Neo chooses the red pill and begins his struggle against the Matrix.

The rabbit hole for the manosphere involved the biological truths supposedly being concealed from men by a 'gynocentric social order' (a society designed for the benefit of women). Men outside the manosphere would come to be contemptuously referred to as 'blue pilled'. By contrast, to have taken the red pill was to have discovered the true nature of reality. Exponents of the red pill claimed that female oppression was a myth and that men (rather than women) were disenfranchised by modern society. Moreover, feminists were accused of being more interested in misandry (contempt for men) than gender equality. To be 'red pill aware' was to be cognisant of these unvarnished 'truths' about society and 'female nature'.

The red pill had an eschatological flavour. It involved a break with a past, a descent into hell and the arrival of salvation. By reading the approved books, watching the approved videos and attending the approved workshops by the approved gurus, it was possible for a man to develop his own strategy in the struggle against the feminine Matrix.

*

Since its founding in 2005 as a radical and anonymous free speech platform, Reddit, the self-proclaimed 'front page of the internet', has come to encapsulate both the democratic potential of the internet and its dark underbelly. With over 330 million users today, the platform began life with an absolutist conception of free speech. Yet the site was soon facing criticism for its lax content moderation policies. In *We Are the Nerds*, her book about the social media company and its origins, Christine Lagorio-Chafkin described parts of the site as 'filled with hate, harassment, bullying and a lot of behaviours that when taken as one individual post might not seem that bad, but once a community forms around it... clearly showed a picture of a kind of depravity'.[3] By the mid-2010s, Reddit was facing similar challenges to those that platforms such as Facebook and YouTube were trying to navigate. As an article for the Australian news agency ABC put it:[4] 'Reddit was being swept up in the growing pressure for social media companies to regulate hateful material on their platforms, and an increasing reliance on advertisers – who weren't thrilled to be associated with such ideas.'

Many men first encountered the red pill on Reddit. Created in October 2012, the red pill subreddit (/r/TheRedPill) had over 250,000 subscribers by the time it was quarantined six years later. It is a 'difficult pill to swallow, understanding that everything you were taught, everything you were led to believe is a lie', read the forum's sidebar. 'Men who are still growing up from the '80s, '90s, and even the last decade, they're starting to realise that what their parents taught them, what television and chick flicks taught them, what church and Sunday school taught them... *it's all wrong.*'

The red pill arose partly out of a schism in the seduction community. Though undoubtedly animated by sexist ideas, the pickup artists had seldom expressed over-hostility towards feminism. They were above all pragmatists whose main concern was the utility of the tactics and techniques they were using. To be sure, discussions on pickup forums were frequently couched in reductive assumptions about women. Yet users were mainly concerned with things like how to ask a woman out, how to create a good online dating profile, or how to tell if a woman is interested. This apparent lack of concern about a global feminist conspiracy would ultimately lead to accusations of surrender to the 'feminine imperative'. Soon after its inception, the founder of /r/TheRedPill would accuse the rival /r/Seduction subreddit (172,473 subscribers) of being 'politically correct' and trying to 'feminise the discussion'. He disparaged them for dealing in 'self-improvement tips' that 'purport to make you a better man'. By contrast, followers of the red pill saw themselves as rational, objective and scientific, bravely resisting feminism in a world where 'we [men] no longer run the show'.

Over time, the red pill would come to consume the manosphere, culminating in the emergence of a new and even more extreme type of pickup artist. Red pill gurus who moonlighted as dating coaches would claim that women held all the cards in relationships – that they were the 'gatekeepers' of sex. It didn't take long for this to then morph into the broader claim – that society itself was controlled by women.

*

The primary concern of red pill forums was to breathe life back into older patriarchal theories. Men were also urged to devise their own sexual strategies – primarily as a response to feminism, which was viewed as women's version of that.

According to /r/TheRedPill, feminism and egalitarianism have little to do with genuine equality. Instead, these are merely a smokescreen to legitimise women's desire to 'locate the best DNA possible'.[5] Women are described as 'Machiavellian in nature' and only interested in the genetic or material benefits they can derive from men. Women are said to be sexually attracted to only a small percentage of men. These are the 'alphas'. The majority of men are 'betas'. In a society where women are free to choose, the majority will ruthlessly pursue the alphas at the expense of the majority.

The idea is lifted from a theory about feeding patterns among captive wolf packs – a theory that has been widely debunked. Posters on /r/TheRedPill have a tendency to treat feminism as a proxy for their romantic failures. It is feminism's fault that men have lost their role as 'breadwinners'; feminism's fault that there was a sexual revolution giving women a wider suite of romantic and sexual opportunities; and feminism's fault that men are brainwashed to be 'weak' and 'effeminate'.

The red pill is thus envisioned as a way for men to 'flip the script' and take back from women what is rightfully theirs. Proponents of the red pill share with the seduction community a belief that men should learn from society's alphas. As the sidebar of /r/TheRedPill explains: *'Game is a facet of The Red Pill's sexual strategy. Determining good game is impossible... without first understanding the context given by The Red Pill's framework.'*

The feeling among consumers of the red pill that they are privy to dangerous or subversive truths is amplified when their critiques occasionally land. The red pill draws on evolutionary psychology to give a patina of 'science' to its theories about men and women. As a field of investigation that seeks to identify psychological traits that have evolved in the same way as biological traits (i.e. by evolution and natural selection), evolutionary psychology can occasionally yield interesting results. It is true that human beings (women not excepted) do not always choose sexual or romantic partners on a strictly egalitarian basis. Moreover, it is not unreasonable to suspect that there might be *some* evolutionary basis for this. It is logical to suppose men and women may (on average) show distinct romantic preferences because evolution has furnished them with distinct reproductive priorities. It is certainly a worthwhile line of enquiry that in no way obliges one to accept the naturalistic fallacy (that because something exists in nature it is the best way to organise society).

And yet there has been a tendency among *some* evolutionary psychologists to make sweeping generalisations based on untestable hypotheses. This arises from the habit of seeing every human behaviour as an evolutionary adaptation. This 'adaptationist' bias is then spread via 'just so' stories that chalk off a wide range of inequalities (usually based on sex, ethnicity or class) as 'natural' and 'hard-wired'.

The red pill combines cherry-picked research with emotionally inflammatory anecdotes. One example is its depiction of women as 'biologically programmed' to be hypergamous (i.e. to only seek out men of a higher social rank than themselves). Such claims are usually supported by research from evolutionary psychology, which has hypothesised that women tend on average to 'marry up' because they want to pass the same 'successful' traits down to their offspring. According to the red pill, this is the nature of reality – it is *just so*. Yet there is evidence to suggest that hypergamy, where it persists, may be less an outcome of genes than a product of history, which is rich with examples of women being prevented or discouraged from engaging in economic activity on an equal basis. When the only way to obtain economic security is to marry into it, hypergamy becomes a *social* rather than a *biological* imperative. The behaviour may persist as a hangover from the recent past; something that has been *consciously* baked into the structure of society rather than transmitted *unconsciously* by genes; a question for sociologists rather than evolutionary psychologists. Even in relatively egalitarian countries such as Sweden and Norway, substantial gender differences in pay and employment persist. Hypergamy might properly be thought of as a rational response to the persistence of economic inequality. Tellingly, at least one study suggests that privileged groups are more likely

ORIGINS OF THE RED PILL

to endorse findings that come from evolutionary psychology.[6] If it's all in the genes then any attempt to disrupt the status quo is doomed to failure. Equality is always a chimera.

Socio-economic explanations are given short shrift by the red pill, which prefers to ram every square peg through an evo-psych-shaped hole. 'All of us have been taught how women have supposedly been oppressed throughout human existence... In reality, this narrative is entirely fabricated,' reads an introductory post on /r/TheRedPill. Elsewhere on the subreddit, moderators describe the gender pay gap as a 'myth that gets lip service because if you don't you're a misogynist!'

*

One of the most influential red pill gurus is Rollo Tomassi (real name George Miller). Tomassi calls himself the 'Godfather of the red pill'; his book, *The Rational Male,* is sometimes referred to (frequently by Tomassi but also by others in the manosphere) as the 'Bible of the red pill'.

Tomassi styles himself as a sceptical observer of the human condition, coolly doling out red pill wisdom to an audience of men who are bamboozled by the 'gynocentric order'. He started to gain popularity after publishing his first book in 2013. Today his YouTube channel has over 224,000 subscribers. Tomassi is especially popular among an older demographic of men – in particular, men who have been chastened by acrimonious divorces or been cheated on. Reading *The Rational Male* one begins to understand why: a hostile and antagonistic tone emanates from every page like steam billowing off hot tarmac.

If *The Rational Male* was written with an audience of embittered men in mind, it also provides the 'newly unplugged' with advice on how to 'flip the script' on the opposite sex and escape the 'feminine matrix'. In common with other red pill influencers, Tomassi makes repeated references to *The Matrix* in his work. 'You have to understand, most of these people are not ready to be unplugged,' he writes in *The Rational Male*, quoting from the film.

Tomassi was in a small-time metal band in his younger days (Tomassi is fifty-six) before joining the SoSuave forum (an early pickup community) in the 2000s and becoming one of its self-appointed experts. These days he charges $1,000 an hour for one-to-one coaching on 'sussing women out'. His only qualification for claiming a monopoly of insight in this area is the monogamous marriage he has been in since 1996.[7] And the fact he adopts former racing greyhounds at his home in Reno, Nevada. 'Everything I ever needed to learn about life I learned from my greyhounds,' he has said.

In case this CV fails to reassure, he endows his work with a scientific patina, routinely falling back on obscure graphs and charts and quoting (selectively) from evolutionary psychology and behaviourism (the idea that behaviours are acquired through conditioning). At other times he tries to sound like an anthropologist by making references to 'hunter-gatherers', 'lizard brains' and 'tribalist beginnings'.

Garden variety sexists have long been known to say that men and women are *different but equal*. However, Tomassi is a purist. At the core of his work is the assumption that 'men's and women's brains are wired differently'. He views men and women as different *and* unequal. Men are dominant and women are submissive. Men are the 'idealistic' sex whereas women are 'opportunistic' and 'innate solipsists'.[8] Men age like wine whereas women age like milk.

The 'science' that Tomassi draws on for his sophistries is consistent if nothing else. Men, it turns out, are 'hard-wired' to do the things they have always wanted to do: play the field, chase women half their age and lord it over the wife back at home. Women on the other hand are programmed by their 'evolved mental firmware' to smile and put up with it.

But the good times are under threat from feminism and rampant 'social engineering'. According to Tomassi, the MeToo movement was a 'moral panic inspired by outrage brokers'.[9] Meanwhile, feminists are seeking to 'remove all constraints on female sexuality while maximally restricting male sexuality'.

Considering his own phallic obsession with 'notch counts',[10] this sounds like Tomassi's goal, albeit with the sexes reversed. Despite being married for twenty-eight years,[11] Tomassi encourages his readers to be promiscuous and 'spin plates' – i.e. date multiple women non-exclusively. By contrast, if a woman behaves similarly then according to Tomassi she risks frying her neurological circuits and nuking her ability to form a loving relationship. Tomassi advises male readers contemplating a relationship to 'vet' her sexual past as an 'absolute imperative'. Men on the other hand are warned to 'never, under pain of death' reveal their own.[12]

The idea of hypergamy is central to Tomassi's work.

According to Tomassi, women are motivated by little more than the cold and calculating pursuit of 'alpha' genes. 'Women's only agency is their sexuality. Their first reflex isn't insight, humility, or coming up with new ideas; it's withholding sex until men change the world to their liking.'[13] It is this lowly view of women that leads Tomassi to say that he could never vote for a female politician – perhaps because he thinks she would try and exchange sex for the nuclear codes.

Unfortunately, Tomassi occasionally says some reasonable things; and it is unfortunate because this is what can lure men into consuming red pill content. He cautions men against developing 'an unhealthy romantic obsession with a single person' (one-itus) and rubbishes what he calls the 'soulmate myth' (the idea that a single predestined love match is out there for everyone). Rather than succumbing to this 'romanticised mythology', Tomassi says it is healthier to recognise that one can be both happy and compatible with many people. This is not altogether bad advice; however, in Tomassi's telling it only applies to men.

When Tomassi does occasionally address women in his writings[14] he frames his complaints in the language of faux concern. The sexual revolution is described as 'giving women the impression that they have an indefinite window of time in which to find their optimal Alpha man'.[15] However, women cannot 'have it all'; nor can they be the 'fiercely independent women the sisterhood demands'. He pleads with them to reject 'the sisterhood über alles' and instead to submit to a man who will 'lead' them and 'mould' their relationship. In other words, they should settle down early, have kids, and be cognisant of their subservient role in the home. 'You are not his equal, you are his complement,' Tomassi disclaims.

When these overtures fall on deaf ears, Tomassi resorts to dire warnings. The 'clock is ticking' before women 'hit the wall' aged thirty, signalling 'the inevitable decay' of their sexual appeal (presumably he doesn't talk to his wife this way). Men by contrast can go on and on. 'Women's sexual marketability declines with age, while men's (should) increase,' crows the 56-year-old.[16,17,18]

If this doesn't convince there is always circular reasoning to fall back on. Women are accused of deceiving themselves. After all, 'reason is always downstream from emotion in women's mental firmware'.

The red pill's preoccupation with 'cat ladies' – older women who mistakenly believed they could 'have it all' – is the redemption arc that's baked into the ideology. For an audience of angsty divorced boomers worn down by rejection, it is comforting to be told that the object of their woes – the women who once turned them down for 'the hot guy in the foam cannon party' – is destined to end up depressed and alone. The Godfather of the red pill is on YouTube four hours every week. However bad his audience might be feeling, Tomassi is on hand to reassure them that[19] a 'growing undercurrent of mid-life women [are] questioning and regretting their past decisions to remain single into spinsterhood'.

*

Now that I had got some of the theory out of the way, I wanted to see where the action was at. I made a few connections at the Derek Moneyberg event that would furnish me with some relevant introductions in the United States. Most of the red pill gurus had built their followings in America so it made sense to take my investigation over there. The US was also where most of the relevant programmes, conferences and workshops took place. And so I embarked on what would turn into several lengthy trips. In the middle of which everything shut down for Covid and I couldn't travel.

When flights to America resumed again, Orlando, Florida, would be my first stop. A four-day red pill summit was happening in the city.

The manosphere had fizzed with excitement when Donald J. Trump announced his first run for the Republican nomination in 2015. /r/TheRedPill grew from 138,000 members in early 2016 to over 230,000 by early 2018. An analysis of the forum by academics at the University of Chicago found an 'abrupt shift' in the tone of the subreddit in 2016. Moderators and elite users 'celebrated the ascendance of alpha male Donald Trump in the presidential race and argued that forum participants needed to take advantage of this unique political opportunity to undercut feminists'.[20] Once Trump was confirmed as the Republican nominee, the election was seen as an opportunity to put a 'real man' in the White House.

One former user of MGTOW ('men going their own way', a branch of male separatists) forums told me that pro-Trump sentiment was ubiquitous following Trump's announcement that he was going to run for president. 'There would be a lot of posts talking about what an amazing person Trump is and how Hillary Clinton was attracted to him because of what a powerful and intelligent leader he was,' he said. He left the manosphere soon after, partly because he didn't like Trump ('a sociopathic narcissist') but also because of how 'angry and obsessive' forum users were about women. 'I thought MGTOW was supposed to be men pursuing their own lives,' he said when we spoke over Skype. 'They said they were men *going their own way*; yet all they did was complain about women.' He was also put off by an uptick in the number of conspiracy theories being circulated on the forums, some of which contained antisemitic themes. 'People would talk about "Jewish control of the media" and "international globalist agendas",' he told me.

Trump's rhetoric frequently echoed that found in the manosphere. He was recorded boasting that he could 'grab [women] by the pussy'. Trump called the Fox News anchor Megyn Kelly a 'bimbo' during a televised presidential debate and implied that she was menstruating. The fact that Hillary Clinton – a self-proclaimed feminist – was Trump's opponent gave the election added significance and Trump accused Clinton of playing 'the woman card'.[21]

In 2017, the American journalist Trevor Martin found a significant crossover between users of /r/TheRedPill[22] and pro-Donald Trump subreddit /r/The_Donald. And it went all the way to the top. A short time later it was revealed that the /r/TheRedPill was founded and run by Robert Fisher, the Republican representative for New Hampshire. He had posted on the subreddit himself at times, describing women[23] as having 'sub-par intelligence' and 'lacklustre' personalities.

*

I had been at home in England, waiting for the world to open up again after Covid, when a mob of Donald Trump supporters had stormed the US Capitol building on 6 January 2021. Almost a year and a half later, I was about to attend my first red pill conference. I was leaving the damp and cool tranquillity of autumnal London and heading out to the heat and humidity of Orlando, where the self-appointed alphas and patriarchs of the manosphere were gathering for their annual convention. According to the glossy brochure I had in front of me, they were going to 'Make Men Great Again'. By 2022, Donald Trump was no longer the American president; however, in Orlando I would see how influential he still was in the movements I was tracking. Although I didn't know it yet, I was also going to get a much better sense of just how easily some of the rhetoric I was seeing online could translate into violent political action.

6

MAKE MEN GREAT AGAIN

Orlando, Florida

A man with a closely cropped Mohawk hands me a rectangular box and gives me a bone-crushing handshake that bends my fingers back until they nearly break. This is an assertion of dominance. I've just arrived and somebody is already trying to win a cock fight.

The box emits a pungent aroma. Soap – three bars of it – are inside, each named after an iconic masculine cultural figure, in this case *Bond*, *Durden* and *Maverick*.[1] The soap comes infused with a potent pheromone kick that promises to 'enhance alpha status, masculinity, charisma, mischief and attractiveness'. I want to test this claim out but when I look around all I see are burly white dudes with Ned Kelly beards, tight-fitting T-shirts and scrunched up facial expressions. I make a mental note to splash myself with Bond before I head downtown to the bars tonight.

I am at the Avanti Palms Resort and Conference Center on International Drive, a popular vacation spot a short distance down the freeway from the famous Walt Disney World. It's October but the weather remains hot and muggy. Outside the front of the hotel, rods of sunlight slip between the tall and slender palm trees and land on the dew-glazed verges. Meanwhile, in the hotel lobby sunburned tourists melt into faux leather armchairs and crane their necks at iPhones, their white flab turned a shade of tandoori red by the blazing October sun. Conference attendees arrive in a steady stream, heavyset men in T-shirts emblazoned with uncompromising slogans – 'Barbarian', 'Freedom not Fear', 'Give Violence a Chance' – who zigzag through the scattered fortress of suitcases and human flesh.

In the conference suite itself a selection of merchandise is spread out on a trestle table. Vendibles include quasi-MAGA (Make America Great Again) trucker caps. Priced at $37, they come in red, white, blue and black – plus a pink one for the women back at home (preferably in the kitchen). The caps feature slogans that are variations on the same theme. 'Make Women Great Again', 'Make Women Sexy Again', 'Make Men Alpha Again' and 'The Future is Patriarchy'. There is something for the kids too: a brown and white teddy bear wearing a little vest that says 'FEMINISM IS CANCER'.

This is the 21 Convention, the self-proclaimed Woodstock of the manosphere now in its sixteenth year. For four days every October the alpha males of the internet come together to rail against the feminist conspiracy which they believe runs the world. The long-time organiser of the event, Anthony 'Dream' Johnson, describes the four-day event as 'TED Talks for men' – albeit with a misogynist twist.

MAKE MEN GREAT AGAIN

The turnout in Orlando is relatively small compared to some of the other workshops I've attended: I count forty men in total. This probably has something to do with the ticket price: it costs $2,000 to be here. Only diehards come to live events; most choose to engage with the recordings at home: the 21 Studios YouTube channel has over half a million subscribers.

Together with the violent smell of perfumed soap, an air of anticipation is discernible as Johnson gets up on stage to deliver his opening address. I take my seat alongside the other attendees. A diminutive man with a closely cropped beard and a MWGA (Make Women Great Again) trucker cap that sits permanently on his head, Johnson is the self-proclaimed president of the manosphere. He started the 21 Convention in 2006 when he was twenty-one years old and claims to have 'helped over 100 million men'. Johnson is an 'Objectivist' (a libertarian philosophical school of thought inspired by Ayn Rand who, appropriately enough, described herself as a 'man worshipper'). He refers to himself as 'beachmuscles' on social media and takes beta males and turns them into 'apex red-pilled alpha males'. Prices for one-to-one consulting begin at $500 an hour.[2]

My first encounter with Johnson took place in early 2020 when he appeared on breakfast television. He'd been invited on to the popular television show *Good Morning Britain* to talk about the 22 Convention, a spin-off from the regular franchise: a conference aimed at women that was run by men. The event promised to be the 'mansplaining event of the century' and was almost guaranteed to make headlines; in fact, some might say that was its entire purpose. The convention[3] promised instruction in how to be an 'ideal woman' and avoid 'toxic bullying feminist dogma'. An email from Johnson promoting the event said that women needed to stop going against their 'ancient, biological nature' and instead have 'unlimited babies' before '90 per cent of their eggs die aged 30'.

This was catnip for TV producers whose job it is to see controversy as synonymous with ratings. It worked for Johnson too, because ever since he has been able to put an 'as seen on TV' logo on his website. He had patiently explained to presenters Piers Morgan and Susanna Reid why he was waging a 'war on feminism'. He appeared nervous and stony-faced as the two presenters openly mocked the things he was saying ('I'm a community organiser, a bit like [Barack] Obama'). He then beat a retreat to prefabricated phrases and heavily rehearsed stock answers. None of it was quite landing. What did for him the most was his arrant humourlessness. It was a self-seriousness that was easy to laugh at. He certainly wasn't the apex alpha male I had been expecting.

Nevertheless, three years on, Johnson is still proud of his eight-minute cameo on British television. Standing on stage in Orlando, ruddy-cheeked and wearing black, he boasts of 'getting on the news'. Controversy is Johnson's business model, though in that he is hardly alone. The trick is to say something outrageous – perhaps something like 'We need a lot less women in power and a lot more women in the kitchen' – and then sit back and wait for the producers to call you up. Johnson says the 'media criticism' he received in the aftermath of his TV slot 'helped get our message out to 100 million people', though this is impossible to verify. What's clear is that Johnson is a troll. He proudly declares from the stage that he 'loves being hated'. That's not to say he doesn't mean any of it. In her 2020 book *Trust Me, I'm Trolling: Irony and the Alt-Right's Political Aesthetic*,[4] the academic Julia DeCook points out that trolling itself has become a political aesthetic in extreme right-wing circles. 'Hiding behind hoaxes, irony, edginess, and trolling, members of the alt-right and other extremist internet subcultures then engage in a kind of subversion that allows them to avoid taking any responsibility for real and violent attacks that occur as a result of their discourse.' Edgy jokes and provocations allowed for plausible deniability, creating room for extremists to accuse progressives of seeing ghosts. Anybody taking offence was accused of being hysterical.

The rest of Johnson's opening preamble is a long complaint about how the West is being flushed down the toilet by feminists, weak men, radical leftists, liberals, transgenders, globalists, Antifa (a loose-knit network of anti-fascist activists), communists, and so on. He describes America as 'a shit hole ruined by feminism' and a 'matriarchy'. Men, he says, need to 'alpha the fuck up'.

Most of the speakers in Orlando contend that society is waging a 'war' on all things masculine; that courts and institutions are working in concert for the benefit of women; that false rape accusations and paternity fraud are rife; and that modern women are out of control.

Tech companies are frequently objects of the manosphere's ire, despite being responsible for an internet landscape that is broadly hospitable to the spread of extremist ideas. Johnson likens YouTube – where several controversial manosphere influencers have recently been demonetised or banned altogether – to a 'gulag'. One influencer who had recently fallen foul of the tech giants was self-proclaimed misogynist Andrew Tate. A 36-year-old former kickboxer, Tate's public notoriety had begun years earlier. In 2016 he was removed from the *Celebrity Big Brother* house by Channel 5 bosses after a video emerged appearing to show him attacking a woman with a belt and slapping her across the face.[5] In the video, Tate threatens to 'f***ing kill' the woman if she messages other men and tells her to say she loves him. Tate claimed that the footage was from a 'kinky sex video' with a Ukrainian ex-girlfriend and had been edited to make him look bad. The woman in question subsequently backed him up, describing the incident as 'just something we used to do'.[6] It was later reported that Tate was removed from the *Big Brother* house because the show's producers became aware of a more serious investigation by Hertfordshire police into allegations of rape.[7]

Until 2022 Andrew Tate was just another a minor celebrity – one Z-lister among many, all desperate for their big break. And then suddenly he was everywhere: at one point during that summer he was reportedly the most googled person on the planet. Distinguishable by his bald head, muscular physique and large cobra tattoo across his torso,[8] short motivational videos of Tate talking about making money, working out and how to treat women had by August of that year racked up more than 11.6 billion views on TikTok. Many of the videos were posted not by Tate himself but by an army of copycat accounts. An investigation by the *Observer*[9] revealed that Tate's burgeoning following were deliberately manipulating the algorithm to boost his controversial content. In one clip that was watched 2.5 million times, Tate, who styles himself as the 'king of toxic masculinity', says that women should 'take some degree of responsibility' to prevent rape.[10] In other videos, Tate claimed that 'virgins are the only acceptable thing to marry' and that women who don't want children were 'miserable stupid bitches'.[11] Tate was banned from what is now X in 2017 for similar comments, though his account would be reinstated in November 2022 following the tech billionaire Elon Musk's takeover of the platform.[12] Tate's own TikTok account was banned in August 2022 on the back of similar bans by Instagram and Facebook.[13]

'There are high-school kids talking about Tate,' Johnson proudly exclaims to the audience in Orlando. Which there are. By 2023, 84 per cent of British boys aged from thirteen to fifteen had heard of Andrew Tate and nearly a quarter (23 per cent) of that age group claimed to have a positive view of him, prompting teachers at UK schools to warn that young boys were idolising Tate and internalising his sentiments about women. 'Men are superior. We're better, we're stronger, we're smarter than women. That's just the way it is,' a teacher at a school in Edinburgh reported one eight-year-old boy as saying. Johnson tells the 21 Summit that he finds it 'hilarious' that people are 'freaking out' about Tate. A photo of him with Tate[14] takes pride of place on the 21 Studios website and Johnson refers to him as 'my buddy', a 'great guy'.[15]

Tate is the red pill's breakthrough act, the chauvinist pig who reaches new audiences because he possesses a blunt charisma and speaks with the force multiplier of conviction. Other red pill influencers can only dream of achieving his level of clout. They wear a mask – the sum of their accumulated red pill wisdom – whereas Tate is a method actor. He is more fully in the role than they will ever be.

Anthony Johnson's personality does not provide the same pop as Tate's – nor the gleaming-eyed preacher-in-the-pulpit qualities of Jordan Peterson. His speaking style is flat and inexpressive, his southern drawl animated by a pugnacious timbre of resentment even on the rare occasions he tells a joke.

*

Johnson's origin story was not unusual in the manosphere. In fact, it was similar to my own. He discovered the pickup community in 2005, a couple of months before *The Game* came out. He had taken a girl from his school to a dance. However, when it came time to actually get up and dance he didn't know how; he didn't have the moves. And so he went online to look for them. That was when he found the seduction community. 'My mind was blown. [I] was like, "Holy fuck, this is magic,"' he would tell me.

He started going out to bars and clubs to ply his craft (i.e. trying to have sex with as many women as possible using scripted routines). 'Dream' was Johnson's pickup artist pseudonym. Eventually, having done thousands of approaches, in 2014 he got married (in Vegas no less). Sadly, the marriage failed. Within two years he discovered that his wife had been cheating on him. Not only that; she was a prostitute and had continued to turn tricks after the wedding. His marriage fell apart in February 2016. He considered suicide at one point. Years later, he would tell anybody who listened that he had 'married Medusa'.[16]

Johnson had vetted his first wife based on the teachings of the red pill. 'She didn't have any nose rings. She didn't have any piercings,' he would tell me when we had a short conversation over Skype in the summer of 2024. And yet – with a note of surprise still in his voice as he retold the story – he discovered that these weren't necessarily the best criteria on which to judge a romantic partner (let alone a marriage).

There were men in and outside of the manosphere who flashed a lifestyle so loudly that it attracted a certain type of person. Similarly, when it 'worked' the pickup material tended to attract women who were low self-esteem, emotionally damaged or craving validation. Eventually, like a war veteran with PTSD who thinks everywhere is dangerous, the pickup artists decided that women could not be trusted. This helped to fuel one of the paradoxes at the heart of the manosphere (there were many): a generalised hostility towards women existed alongside a desire to mould themselves into the thing that women desired. The writer Jane Ward called it the 'misogyny paradox': a 'simultaneous desire for and hatred of women – all wrapped together into one dysfunctional sexual orientation'.[17]

When we chatted, I asked Johnson if he thought something similar might have happened to him; if his sample of womankind had been skewed by the manipulative techniques he was using.

'There's truth to what you're saying,' he said, before trying to derail the question into a conversation about 'crazy' American women. 'I mean, something like 25 per cent of American women are on psychiatric medications,' he said.

Antidepressant use is high across the board in the United States, and higher among women. But didn't that rather undermine Johnson's claim that the United States was some sort of matriarchy – that men were squirming 'under the boot of feminism'? If women have everything their own way, why are they so unhappy?

There was a grim inevitability to what Johnson would say next. I had heard the same argument a dozen times already. Statistics showing the number of male suicides or 'deaths of despair' were regularly bandied about in the manosphere as 'proof' that men were the oppressed gender. By contrast, harms to women were taken as evidence that feminism had failed. In Anthony Johnson's words, women are 'highly destructive creatures when they're not given instruction'.

Now in his mid-thirties, Johnson has bounced back from the failed marriage and sells private coaching on how to be an alpha male. He boasts of sleeping with more than 130 women.[18] Vis-à-vis his marriage, he got unlucky. Of all the gorgeous women throwing themselves at him, he unknowingly picked an escort. He was presumably helping men to avoid the same mistakes during his $500-an-hour coaching calls.

At one point during our conversation, Johnson had berated Jordan Peterson for being 'way too fucking beta'. 'You've never once heard Jordan Peterson talk about dominating his wife,' he said.

Johnson recently got married again and his wife had a baby. How is that relationship going? 'We're on the same team, and there's a hierarchy to it. I'm the decision maker, I'm the King, the Emperor, the God, the Alpha and the Omega. And I think that's how women operate best.'

Yet the story of Anthony Johnson's own childhood would suggest otherwise. He grew up in Florida, in a violent and abusive household. His father was an alcoholic who would 'drink twenty beers' and 'beat my mom bloody and then drag her around on the floor like an animal down the hallways, [with] my sisters screaming and crying,' he told me.

It seems strange then to hear Johnson extolling the virtues of 'dominant' men. Had he not grown up with a man who wanted to dominate everyone around him?

It made me think about my own background. I never went through anything remotely like that. But for a while growing up I did chafe under a stepfather for whom I was never quite tough or manly enough. And a funny thing can happen in a situation like that. First you rebel against it. You want to get out from under it, to escape the despotic pressure to conform to a rigid ideal you feel no affinity for. And yet when you do manage to prise yourself out from under it, you notice that the feelings of inadequacy haven't gone away. And so slowly but surely you start trying to live up to the impossible masculine standard all over again. You steadily become the thing you hated in the hope that it might drive the feelings of unworthiness away. When I first discovered the manosphere I thought I was free from all that. Only later did I realise that I was still taking instructions from some unwanted ghost from the past. Following our brief conversation, I wondered if the same was true of Anthony Johnson.

*

Men floated around the conference rooms at the 21 Summit flaring their latissimus dorsi muscles and tensing their arms. Derogatory terms – 'faggot', 'soy boy', 'beta cuck' – were regularly affixed to anyone or anything deemed to be lacking in the approved masculine qualities. Anthony Johnson's go-to insults all draw on the theme of homosexuality. The things he doesn't like are either 'gay', 'totally gay' or 'totally fucking gay'. This is in contrast to Andrew Tate – a man whose videos feature him wearing tiny trunks, his sculpted torso smeared in baby oil as he berates the 'beta males' in the audience – whom Johnson describes as a 'pure-blooded alpha male'.

In a world where masculinity is bound up with the sexual conquest of women – not to mention an exhausting, round-the-clock assertion of dominance – homosexuality is seen as undermining male hegemony. In contrast to other red pill teachings, it is also treated as a cultural choice rather than a biological inevitability. Some speakers blame the 'rainbow community' for women's sexual liberation and everything else they consider defective about the contemporary world. Indeed, the ubiquity of anti-gay rhetoric at the conference is such that I will feel short-changed if none of the speakers ever shows up in the news under a heap of male prostitutes. 'Stop being gay, that's bad for you,' declares Jeff Younger, a thrice married man who says he likes his women 'chaste and obedient'. Younger, fifty-six, was once discharged from the United States military following an 'admission of homosexuality'.[19] Yet these days he purports to follow traditional Christian teachings on sexuality. 'We live in a profoundly decadent age,' he tells the room. In 2022 he ran as the Republican candidate for the Texas House of Representatives on a ticket campaigning against gender-affirming treatments for children (he lost in the primary runoff).[20] Younger[21] has also been involved in a custody battle with the mother of his biological son over whether the child should be allowed to change gender. It isn't just gender transition he opposes but gender non-conformity: the men in his family are forbidden even from growing their hair out.

At least four of the speakers at the 21 Summit are former pickup artists. Red pill spaces are brimming with former hard-partying womanisers who are suddenly all about conservative values – the teachings of Genesis supplanting those found in *The Game*. 'The gay community has brought a lot of these things in and women have piggybacked on it,' says Greg Adams, a YouTube influencer who coaches men in what he calls the 'free agent lifestyle'. Predictably enough, the free and easy life is off limits for women. 'You can't turn a hoe into a housewife,' says Adams, who evinces some implausible concern that 'women will end up single and old'. Anthony Johnson, a self-confessed former playboy, had used his speech to bemoan a 'complete decline in female modesty'. The sexual double standard is treated as a given. Men are encouraged to 'spin plates' – which is to say, to date multiple women at the same time – whereas women who do the same are diminished as 'sluts' and 'whores' who are 'run through' and 'ruined'.

Being a red-blooded alpha male seems to co-exist alongside a gnawing sense of sexual inferiority. The importance of a woman's body count is emphasised ad nauseam in Orlando, albeit with different connotations to the way I'd encountered the term sixteen years earlier in Starbucks (thankfully nobody in Orlando wants to know my body count). What keeps the men here up at night is the prospect of women 'riding the cock carousel'. Restrictions on the male libido are minimal. However, according to red pill 'science', women who want a piece of the action risk losing their ability to 'pair bond' – i.e. to form a romantic emotional attachment.

It is a tale as old as time. Throughout recorded history, men have sought to maximise their own reproductive success by controlling the sexuality of women. However, in Orlando the familiar stories about men and women being 'wired differently' co-exist alongside what can only be described as a form of performance anxiety. After all, if she's had *more* then there's always a chance she's had *better*. It's an unnerving thought, especially for those who are susceptible to fantasies of being the dominant alpha – a rank that demands a certain thrust and potency. This tension feeds into an uptight machismo that feels mortally threatened by party girls, rainbow flags and Andrea Dworkin. Sitting at the back of the air-conditioned conference suite listening to this stuff, I was tempted to laugh. There *was* something undeniably comic about the brutal handshakes, the tensing of muscles and the conflation of strength with brute force – not to mention the arrant humourlessness of it all. Laughter is unavoidable when confronted by such a taut and inflexible aesthetic. Whether turning people like that into figures of fun diminishes them or not is another matter. In any case, the jovial mood soon gives way to something darker.

7

'WAR IS COMING':
THE STORY OF LYNDON MCLEOD

The most bizarre speech I sit through in Orlando is given by a man calling himself 'Ivan Throne'. Not surprisingly this is a pseudonym; the speaker's real name is Robert Haggerty Teesdale. For a short time in 2019, Throne was a 'lieutenant' in Andrew and Tristan Tate's 'War Room', a global network that allegedly teaches participants how to abuse and sexually exploit women.[1]

Anthony Johnson introduces Throne to the stage as a 'very good friend', an 'amazing man' and 'one of the most savage motherfuckers I've ever met'. The dark and cool conference suite fizzes with excitement following this effusive introduction. Throne then bounds on to the stage wearing a well-tailored black suit, a tightly knotted yellow tie and perfectly polished shoes. Copies of a slim, white, laminated volume adorned with a golden eagle – *Age of Militants* – have been handed to each of us on the way in. The book's contents are a mixture of apocalyptic rhetoric and impenetrable corporatese. 'Survival, momentum, and triumph in the new age demands full delivery of manhood,' it says on one of the pamphlet's slippery pages. 'You must find your brothers, and you must go to war,' it says on another.

Throne went deaf at the age of four after contacting meningitis. This has furnished him with an unconventional speaking voice. Yet he is also playing a character. His speech is a doom-laden harangue featuring the usual bugaboos. Western society is going down the tubes because of feminists, Antifa and (this is one I hadn't heard about) 'people who bring rainbow dildos into libraries'. Johnson in his preamble had compared Throne's speaking style to that of a Viking. The language is certainly striking. 'My God is the God of famine, war, pestilence and death!' Throne thunders above an audience of tattoos, paunches and androgenetic alopecia. 'And maybe ultimate victory on the other side.' The speech goes on like this for around an hour, Throne's basso voice unleashing a torrent of brimstone and resentment against 'decadence' and 'Globohomo' (a portmanteau of globalism and homosexuality). Shadowy forces are plotting to bring down Western civilisation; it is always five minutes to midnight. 'Children destroyed, educational institutions perverted, houses of knowledge turned into dens of degeneracy.' Throne is stoking a residual paranoia which, from my own so-far limited interactions, seems to be present in above average quantities in the audience. 'They are coming for you… They do not care for you. You are to be stripped, mind exterminated… I was not born to be a slave and neither were any of you.' Throne believes another American Civil War is imminent. 'What will the winter of 2025 be like in January?' he asks. 'Collapse is inevitable, whether it's this election or the next.'

*

Throne was banned from X back in 2020. He has since migrated to Gab, a microblogging service popular with white supremacists and the far right. According to researchers at[2] University College London, Gab has been 'repeatedly linked to radicalisation leading to real-world violent events'. Andrew Torba, the founder of Gab, has written of his intention to create 'a parallel Christian society on the internet'. Torba has also promoted the so-called Great Replacement Theory, a conspiracy popularised by the French author Renaud Camus. I'd also heard it espoused in the manosphere. It claims that Western politicians are trying to replace white populations in Europe and America with non-white peoples. Commenting on the mass shooting in Buffalo, New York, that took place on 14 May 2022 in which a white man murdered ten Black people after citing replacement theory, Torba said: 'The best way to stop White genocide and White replacement, both of which are demonstrably and undeniably happening, is to get married to a White woman and have a lot of White babies,' he wrote.

During his speech in Orlando, Throne makes multiple references to 'Throne Dynamics', ostensibly a Wall Street company which, according to its website, offers to help businesses to prepare for a Third World War. He also announces a quasi-militaristic initiative from the 'company' called Project Rome, which sounds a lot like a private militia. 'We go to war. That's project Rome,' Throne bellows. He compares his movement to Hezbollah, the Iranian-sponsored Lebanese terrorist group. 'Look at their troops, as professional and equipped as ours. They have hospitals, they have schools, they have courts. They are the legitimate state,' he says before segueing into a recruitment drive. 'There are many of you here who are strong, capable leaders,' Throne tells the men gathered in the conference suite. 'Each and every one of you has a role to play in this future. You will live or you will die. You will fight or you will submit, you will win or you will lose – and soon.' The soaring rhetoric reaches its apogee as the men are encouraged to join Throne in 'fourth generation warfare'. 'We understand that there is a terrible fear involved in the decision to do something like this, to be part of something like this... It is frightening because it is urgent and imminent and the time is now, and I tell you, get up and walk with us.'

Even war comes with a hard-sell in America. 'Go to Project Rome, sign up, pay us,' Throne says as he departs the stage; though he declines to say if this is tax-deductible.

A ripple of applause travels around the room as I hop out to the cafeteria for a coffee. When I return, the barracks-like atmosphere has slackened. Throne's glossy pamphlets remain scattered about the place, reflecting the image now projected onto the stage: a photo of the pop star Christina Aguilera wearing a green-bejewelled strap-on dildo. 'THE STATE OF AMERICAN WOMEN', the caption reads.

'WAR IS COMING': THE STORY OF LYNDON MCLEOD

*

Despite the effusive introduction from the president of the manosphere, three days after the 21 Summit is over, Anthony Johnson apparently wants to distance himself from Ivan Throne. In a statement sent out to all 21 Studios subscribers, Johnson describes the latter's speech as 'alarming and extreme'. He also bans him from speaking at or attending any future 21 Studios event. The Dark Triad Man, who had spoken at every previous 21 Summit bar one, had officially been 'excommunicated' by Johnson.

> The content of Ivan's speech was alarming and extreme, and I believe is not protected (free) speech, by state law or federal law, including the 1st amendment. Had I been in the conference room during the speech I would have ended the presentation immediately and had Ivan escorted off the property by law enforcement.

Johnson's claim that he was outside the room[3] was plausible enough: I hadn't seen him at all after his laudatory introduction. In his statement, Johnson also disavowed Throne's *Age of Militants* pamphlet, which he described as 'extremely alarming' while warning his audience against interacting with it 'in any way'. Perhaps he had noticed the defence of Patriot Front within its pages, a blood and soil neo-Nazi group who claimed their ancestors conquered America and bequeathed it to them (and no one else). Around the time of Throne's speech, an online conspiracy claimed that Patriot Front were, alternately, a sting operation set up by the FBI / a 'false flag' operation by Antifa. Throne clearly disagreed. 'This criticism is an impressively incandescent display of stupid,' he wrote in *Age of Militants*. 'Men must take action beyond mere words,' he added. Patriot Front were certainly doing that: according to the ADL, the group was responsible for the majority of white supremacist propaganda distributed in the United States.[4]

*

I had never heard of Ivan Throne prior to landing in Orlando, though I now had a copy of his hate sheet in my possession. Back at my hotel room that night I figured I should probably look him up. The first thing I learned was that he is fifty-two years old. He also claimed to have aristocratic ancestry. On his social media he had posted photos of himself straddling motorcycles in tight-fitting leather outfits. These moody catalogue shots were frequently accompanied by apocalyptic captions such as 'War is coming'.[5] I found out that Throne was the author of a previous book called *The Nine Laws* (2016), a jabbering self-help manual whose floral prose gurgled with tendentious Nietzschean rhetoric and incomprehensible spiels about battles, sword fights and other historico-mythological events. The mental atmosphere of the book – which, as of 2025, remains on the recommended reading list for Andrew Tate's War Room – is as if motivational guru Tony Robbins decided to write a *Warhammer* novel. My imagined audience for this doltish fare were 5'7"

'WAR IS COMING': THE STORY OF LYNDON MCLEOD

computer programmers with statue avatars who liked to compare themselves to Chinese generals and Roman centurions.

It doesn't take me long to discover that Throne is getting in on a familiar grift: he sells self-help courses. One is called 'Ninja Survival Secrets To Keep You Alive During Ethnic Civil War'. Another is titled 'Ninja Plague Warfare: an aristocrat's coronavirus survival guide' – and is priced at $300.[6] Throne is hawking the courses with a difficult to verify claim: that he trained as a ninja in Japan. He also offers 'ruthless mentoring for a dark world', which appears to be a meet and greet at a hotel in Denver, Colorado, costing $90. Throne liked to refer to himself as a 'Dark Triad' man. However I was reminded more of Roderick Spode, otherwise known as Lord Sidcup, a recurring character in the *Jeeves and Wooster* novels by P. G. Wodehouse. Spode is the leader of a fictional fascist group in London that calls itself the Saviours of Britain. His 'general idea... is to make himself a Dictator'.[7] Throne even bore a physical resemblance to Spode as played by John Turner in the BBC adaptation. Like Spode, Throne's lofty rhetoric seemed inversely proportional to the weight of his influence. Or so I thought at the time.

*

Eventually I found a relevant video on Reddit. Moreover, the user who posted it had mentioned Throne so I pressed play. Grainy footage at first. Some kind of bar or the lobby of a hotel. I see Throne; I can see the fitness and masculinity influencer Alexander Cortes too. They are sitting around, drinking, smoking cigars and listening to a hirsute and heavy-set man talk about his book.

Are you ready for the hate mobs? Throne asks the author.

Bearded Man: *Yeah, I'm surprised they haven't come earlier.*

Throne: *They'll get you, especially when some of them read what you've written.*

Bearded Man: *Yeah, it's an offensive book.*

Throne: *You need that, that's why it's gonna get big.*

The book, called *Sanction*, was a sprawling three-volume novel set in a dystopian future. The author was Roman McClay, the nom de plume of a man named Lyndon McLeod. Curiously, the protagonist in the book was named Lyndon MacLeod and had a nearly identical backstory to the author. On the page he was described as 'an extraordinarily gifted boy born into an average family' and a 'Supreme Sigma' (another type of alpha male). As the story unfolds, the MacLeod character metes out violent retribution on the people who have wronged and betrayed him, culminating in a six-month killing spree in which he murders forty-six people. He also makes plans to start a war on American soil.

Sanction bristled with victimhood and resentment: it wasn't so much a novel as a primal scream of indignation. The main character justified his decision to kill by falling back on Nietzschean rhetoric. It was the natural right of the 'strong'

'WAR IS COMING': THE STORY OF LYNDON MCLEOD

to rule over the 'weak'. And yet the world the protagonist inhabited was dominated by inferior types driven by spite and envy. 'The strong men have been sidelined, jailed, killed, told to sit down and shut up by harpies and millions of virtue-signalling betas,' wrote McLeod in his apocalyptic vision of murder, societal collapse and civil war. The author had created a fictional world where the only principle worth anything was raw masculine power. 'This whole society is sick, and it needs [to be] healed or euthanised. And you [Lyndon MacLeod] are the man to do it.'

*

Sanction had garnered more than fifty reviews by the time it was pulled from Amazon in late 2021. One reviewer described it as 'an epic, visceral journey into the dark heart of every man broken by society'. Another saw the book as giving 'full vent to the sexism, racism, and every other -ism kept out of mainstream discourse'.[8] McLeod was also selling *Sanction*-related merchandise, including T-shirts, mugs and Zippo lighters. Some fans even got *Sanction* tattoos, inspired by the book's esoteric imagery.[9]

Sanction turned McLeod into a minor celebrity in the manosphere. Masculinity influencers lined up to promote the book on their social media channels. These included the podcaster Hunter Drew, the former heavyweight boxer Ed Latimore and Mike Cernovich, a far-right conspiracy theorist who gained prominence during Gamergate and was a key promoter of the Pizzagate conspiracy theory.[10] Invitations to manosphere podcasts and events (including a meet-up with Ivan Throne in Denver) soon followed.

It was clear from the book's content that McLeod shared many of the manosphere's obsessions. 'Alpha males', 'tyrannical females' and 'dominance hierarchies' were all mentioned in the text. As was Jordan Peterson's name, at least fifteen times. Hovering over it all was a prurient obsession with women's sexual morality. Women were described as 'promiscuous people who only think with their heads in the clouds'.

In November 2019, McLeod appeared on the podcast of right-wing YouTuber Nzube Olisaebuka Udezue, a British self-help influencer of Nigerian descent who described himself as the 'Jordan Peterson of rap'.[11] Zuby – the name he went by on social media – was an associate of Andrew Tate[12] and a Covid vaccine conspiracy theorist.[13] He also had a large and influential online following: in 2023 the tech billionaire Elon Musk would appear on his podcast.

By 2019, Lyndon McLeod was sleeping in a shipping container up a mountain in Colorado. His life consisted of 'books, guns and meat' – and none of that 'modern bullshit'. McLeod had never had many close friends. Yet thanks to the online popularity of *Sanction*, in the manosphere he had found his 'new tribe', as he told Zuby. His host seemed keen to corroborate this. Zuby claimed to have heard 'ringing endorsements' of *Sanction* from his X followers; 'a whole ton of people' had mentioned McLeod to Zuby and told him 'you need to speak to this guy about his book'. McLeod said he was grateful for the 'big help' in promoting his apocalyptic novel. 'I had forty-nine [X/Twitter] followers... and guys like Hunter Drew and Alexander Cortes picked me up and said, "This book is great; I want my readers to see this and read it,"' he told Zuby. 'Then what happened was their followers bought the book, read the book and were contacting me all the time in DMs.'

McLeod had written *Sanction* over a ten-month period in 2017. His tattoo business had recently failed and he accused various people — including his former business partners — of betraying him. 'The people I trusted in life, [it] turns out they didn't like me that much,' he told Zuby. Following the collapse of the business venture, McLeod went to 'a very dark place' and had 'all kinds of ideas' of how he was going to make things right. One option was to channel the anger and pain into something creative. The author said the book had 'madness baked into it'[14] and even spoke of hearing voices from the ether: he said the contents of *Sanctio*n were relayed to him by God, a claim his host treated in earnest. The book was 'Plan B', as he told Zuby. 'I said [to myself], "Look, if this book thing doesn't work out, you can go back to plan A."' Zuby didn't think to ask what Plan A was. Perhaps he took it for granted that the initial scheme, whatever it was, had been duly aborted.

A little over two years later it would become terrifyingly apparent that Plan A had been left firmly on the table. McLeod hadn't merely channelled his 'madness' into a paranoic and primitive literary canvas. He had acted it out; now it was something corporeal; and five people were dead.

LOST BOYS

*

At around 5 p.m. on 27 December 2021, police in Denver were called to the Sol Tribe Tattoo and Piercing shop. Reports had come in of a shooting. Police arrived to find the bodies of Alicia Cardenas, forty-four, a Chicana feminist artist and tattoo artist, and Alyssa Gunn-Maldonado, thirty-five, a jewellery manager who also worked at the shop. Maldonado's husband Jimmy Maldonado was injured in the shooting. Soon after, local police received reports from an apartment complex three miles away. They arrived to find Michael Swinyard, a 67-year-old local builder and former associate of the suspect, lying dead of gunshot wounds. The suspect had gained entry to the building wearing a police logo and badge.[15] Denver police officers arrived at the scene and exchanged gunfire with the gunman, who disabled their vehicle. Officers then received reports of another incident at the Lucky 13 Tattoo Parlour on nearby Kipling Street. They arrived to find 38-year-old tattoo artist Danny 'Dano' Scofield dead inside the shop. The assailant proceeded to enter the lobby of the nearby Hyatt House hotel, shooting and killing the 28-year-old employee working on the front desk.

By this point, five people were dead. Two others were injured, one of them Lakewood police officer Ashley Ferris, who had been wounded in the abdomen and right leg after confronting the shooter and telling him to drop his weapon. Ferris had then fired back, the female officer killing the self-declared alpha male with a single precision shot to the chest.

'WAR IS COMING': THE STORY OF LYNDON MCLEOD

*

In *Sanction*, McLeod had mentally rehearsed the murders he would later commit. Two of McLeod's five victims – Alicia Cardenas and Michael Swinyard – were named in the book.

Others who had been murdered in the fictional realm managed to survive. In 2013, McLeod had opened a tattoo studio in Denver with several others, including local tattoo artist Jeremy Costilow. Yet by 2016 the All Heart Industry tattoo studio had failed due to McLeod's poor financial management and abusive behaviour towards colleagues. McLeod had alluded to the business venture during his interview with Zuby. He blamed his business partners for the company's failure and claimed that he had been 'fucked over' and 'betrayed'.

On the night of the murders, McLeod called at Costilow's apartment disguised as a delivery man. His partner Chelsea answered the door while Costilow together with a friend and the couple's three-month-old daughter were in an adjoining room. Suspicious, Chelsea informed[16] the visitor that her partner wasn't home. 'Normally, mail people just say I have a delivery. [But] he was aggressive,' she told CBS News.[17] 'And he pressed me to see if Jeremy lived there. I said, "Maybe try around the front," and he said, "Oh the tattoo shop?" A random person wouldn't know that because it doesn't say tattoo shop on the building.' McLeod wasn't a random person; indeed he knew the place well; in *Sanction* his alter ego had slain a tattoo artist named Jeremy there and beheaded his girlfriend.

Undeterred, McLeod went away and came back with a sledgehammer, which he then used to try and break into the apartment. When that didn't work, he fired six shots through the door and walls; some of the bullets passed close to the baby's crib. Luckily the family managed to get out of the property and take cover in a neighbouring business. McLeod then set the family's van on fire and fled the scene.

*

Once news of the murders started to spread online, McLeod's online 'tribe' quickly moved to disown him. Zuby denied having read *Sanction* at all and put out a belligerent statement railing against those employing 'guilt by association' ('screw anybody trying to implicate me in this', he wrote).[18] Others, including Anthony Cortes and the self-proclaimed relationship guru Adam Lane Smith,[19] scrubbed their interactions with McLeod from the internet. A week after the murders, on 3 January 2022, Anthony Johnson put out his own statement. It had come to light that the president of the manosphere had invited McLeod to speak at the 21 Convention eighteen months earlier (though in fairness he had subsequently retracted the invite). 'Through the standard vetting process leading up to [21 Summit in 2020], I rescinded Roman's invitation from our event,' Johnson said. He called McLeod a 'lunatic' and described the murders as 'personally motivated'. He also categorically denied that McLeod's actions 'in any way reflect the manosphere men's movement or the men and fathers in it'.[20]

'WAR IS COMING': THE STORY OF LYNDON MCLEOD

And yet in the months and years leading up to the killings, nobody in the manosphere had seen anything averse in McLeod's apocalyptic ravings. Instead he was indulged: toured round the podcast circuit and invited to conferences as some sort of rough-hewn literary genius.

Meanwhile, outside of the manosphere, at least one person was sounding the alarm to the authorities. In 2019, McLeod had started a Telegram group where fans of *Sanction* were encouraged to donate towards an audio version of his book. A German citizen named Andre Thiele had been invited to the group chat. Thiele was interested in McLeod's self-published novels and began interacting with him directly. By late 2020, however, the German was becoming concerned. On social media and in the Telegram group, McLeod had been recommending neo-Nazi pamphlets and talking about 'starting a war on American soil'. Thiele's first contact with Denver police took place on 3 January 2021. 'It may very well be that the accused is a typical case of a literary genius and a petty thug who runs his mouth and talks too much. I would from my personal experiences say that this might be a 90 percent chance,' Thiele wrote in an eight-page report he sent to the authorities.[21] He continued: 'But there is a 10 percent chance that he has – at least in his own mind – created the perfect storm of right-wing terrorism. I cannot in good conscience say that he will act with certainty. But I can say that IF he should act, the result would be devastating.'[22] Thiele used an online form to contact the FBI; he also sent a letter in the mail. McLeod[23] had been briefly investigated by the bureau several months earlier for threatening to murder a man on social media, though the authorities said there wasn't enough evidence for charges or monitoring. A detective emailed Thiele back the following day, promising to look into his concerns. Thiele replied with a nine-page document setting out the various threats McLeod had been making, though he never heard back.

*

There was no shortage of evidence to suggest that McLeod was an emotionally unstable person whose sense of reality had completely unravelled. As well as the failed tattoo business, *The Denver Post* reported that McLeod had been fired from a cannabis farm in 2012 after pulling a gun on co-workers.[24] He was also kicked out of a house in Louisiana in 2020 because roommates found him 'unhinged'.[25] 'We lost our son and brother years ago,' a statement from McLeod's family said following the shootings.

Sanction – a wrathful and rambling text – was plainly the work of a psychotic mind. In addition, McLeod had acted alone, which made it easier to posthumously cast him as something less than compos mentis; his actions were the rotten fruit of a misfiring neurotransmitter, making him one more 'lone wolf' propelled along his bloody course by an accident of brain chemistry. And yet, as the sociologist Naomi Braine has written, 'a decision to act alone does not mean acting outside of social movement frameworks, philosophies, and networks'.[26]

It wasn't as if McLeod was the first right-wing extremist to write a book intended to inspire terrorism. *The Turner Diaries*,

'WAR IS COMING': THE STORY OF LYNDON MCLEOD

a racist dystopian novel published in 1978, has reportedly inspired more than 200 murders, including the Oklahoma City bombing in 1995, the worst act of domestic terrorism in American history.[27]

McLeod's rationale for carrying out what he had previously called 'retributive violence'[28] drew heavily on the grievances, obsessions and ideological currents found in the manosphere. He viewed masculinity as synonymous with expansion and imposition; women as a resource that belonged to a warrior clan of elite males.[29] 'I want a return to Alpha Kings and their harems,' he wrote on his blog. 'We are sexually dimorphic and that means the alpha – the badass – gets all the women and the other 90 per cent don't get any at all.'[30]

He ranted about 'insouciant women' and celebrated male honour violence. According to the whistleblower Thiele, McLeod 'hated women'. 'I never experienced a man who openly showed that he held no respect whatsoever for women,' Thiele told the media following the shootings. Those who declined to affirm McLeod's frangible (not to say pitiable) self-image as an alpha warrior were marked out for retribution. Former romantic partners told of McLeod's physical and emotional abuse.[31] Between 2012 and 2016, the authorities were called eleven times to his then residence – four times over allegations of physical abuse.[32] One former girlfriend described[33] McLeod as 'super volatile, angry, throwing stuff, and very emotionally abusive'.

McLeod shared this penchant for tyrannical domestic behaviour with other mass shooters. According to a 2021 study, in more than two-thirds (68 per cent) of mass shootings that took place in the United States between 2014 and 2019, the perpetrator either killed family or intimate partners during the shooting or had a history of domestic violence.

Far from being a rudderless outsider, McLeod's violent impulses were nourished by the ideological waters he immersed himself in. He was fixated on the idea of tribalism, exalted the primitive, and fantasised about waging war on a country that had 'feminised' its menfolk. He was obsessed with the idea of societal failure and believed that a 'revolt against the modern world', characterised by savage violence, was both imminent and necessary. He saw himself as a Nietzschean Übermensch, enthusing about the cathartic power of right-wing terror to 'cleanse' a society that had been subverted by weaklings and failures. 'The only thing that can save America is a [Pinochet] purge,' he wrote on X in April 2020.[34] 'The weak better buckle up... shit is about to get real.'[35] According to a former roommate, McLeod had discussed attacking buildings with flamethrowers as a prelude to the bloody conflagration he hoped to ignite.[36] *Sanction's* three-word slogan was 'War is Coming'.

*

In the manosphere, the would-be killer believed that he had found his *tribe* – the allies and collaborators who would march alongside him in the looming battle against a decadent and *feminised* world. That the manosphere decided to welcome McLeod as a brother in arms should hardly come as a surprise. Despite the furtive attempts by masculinity influencers to

'WAR IS COMING': THE STORY OF LYNDON MCLEOD

posthumously distance themselves from the mass murderer, you didn't have to look far to find a subculture fizzing with violent rhetoric and authoritarian appeals to a 'natural order'.

Eight months on from the killings in Colorado, a press release from 21 Studios landed in my inbox. It was from the president of the manosphere himself, Anthony Johnson, and was dated 20 August 2022. Public interest in Andrew Tate was exploding at the time. However, Tate's accounts on Instagram, Facebook, TikTok and X had recently been taken down for violating the platforms' terms of service. Johnson accused the 'feminist establishment' of trying to censor Tate. 'The people who want to silence Andrew are the same people who want to silence me, silence the legitimate President of the United States [Trump], and ultimately silence you personally,' he wrote in the email. The 'deep state', he said, was trying to 'control' men and turn them into 'slaves'. According to Johnson, this was 'Orwellian' and 'evil'.

But it was something else too. In the email titled 'Feminism will die', Johnson described the decision by the tech platforms to go after Tate as 'extremely dangerous'. He then quoted the person he would 'excommunicate' from the manosphere two months later:

'As my good friend Ivan Throne likes to say, "When the talking stops, the shooting starts," referring to the next American Civil War.'

The August email was hardly consistent with Johnson's more measured tone following the McLeod murders. He had said at the time that the manosphere 'universally denounces violence across the board'. Now the incident had seemingly been forgotten. War *was* coming after all.

I was genuinely confused. I also started to wonder whether Johnson had been genuine in his disavowal of Throne's speech. Was the president of the manosphere trolling us again? In light of the earlier email, his subsequent statement 'excommunicating' Throne from the manosphere seemed out of character, not least in its detail and theatricality. Of Throne's glossy pamphlet, Johnson had written:

> For any attendees, volunteers, staff, or other participants who obtained a free copy of this book, I strongly recommend against interacting with the book in any way including but not limited to the "QR code" displayed towards the end of the book.

Was it all a publicity stunt? A form of reverse psychology to encourage the very engagement with the booklet that was ostensibly being warned against? Though I couldn't prove anything – and Johnson would denounce Ivan Throne again during our private conversation – I was moving through a world where elaborate hoaxes and inside jokes were often used to disorientate outsiders. The absurdity of the discourse acted as a nod and a wink to other extremists – while telegraphing plausible deniability to the wider public. Having been in and out of the manosphere for several years, I thought I was finally getting to grips with the vernacular. Yet there were times when even I felt like I was passing through a hall of mirrors.

8

WAITING FOR CAESAR

Alexander Reid Ross is an expert on the radical right and the author of the book *Against the Fascist Creep* (2017). He describes Lyndon McLeod as a 'good example' of the 'overlap' between the manosphere and white nationalism. For him, McLeod epitomises what he calls 'the cult of male dominance' – the idea that men should always be dominating those around them. This idea is central to the manosphere's admiration for Donald Trump. Ross points out that Trump 'actively seeks to dominate people's lives'. When Trump was first elected president in 2016, Russian state media lauded him as an 'alpha male'.[1] Vladimir Putin is another leader who treats every interaction as a petty power play (and who is similarly revered in the manosphere for his ability to 'hold frame'). The Russian dictator is a living embodiment of 'the man who is always on top', and not only because he likes to be photographed riding shirtless on horseback. 'You see more Putin memes than you see Trump memes in a lot of [far-right] Telegram,' Ross tells me.

Putin was widely admired in the more overtly political sections of the manosphere. In 2024, a manosphere YouTuber who posted under the alias Coach Red Pill[2] died of pneumonia in a Ukrainian detention centre after being arrested in the country's eastern city of Kharkiv. Gonzalo Lira,[3] fifty-five, a dual citizen of the United States and Chile who had been living in Ukraine since 2010, was arrested in May 2023 for spreading propaganda justifying the Russian invasion to his 300,000 followers. In one video, Lira described the Russian assault as 'one of the most brilliant invasions in military history'.

During our conversation over Zoom, Ross highlights an interview Putin did with former Fox News presenter Tucker Carlson in February 2024. The day after the interview, Putin told a Russian state journalist that he had been expecting Carlson to ask sharper questions. 'You could see this as a petty power play, but it's not petty at all,' says Ross. The purpose of Putin's seemingly offhand comment – not to mention his liquidation of political opponents – is to demonstrate that 'there's never a consent relationship in an equal way. It's always about re-establishing hierarchies'.

The idea of dominance hierarchies – that each person dominates someone below him in exchange for submission to somebody above – is central to the idea of patriarchy. Moreover, you do not need to go all the way to Russia to find it. In his book *12 Rules for Life*, Jordan Peterson – who reveres masculine 'order' as opposed to feminine 'chaos' – describes dominance hierarchies as a 'mechanism that selects heroes and breeds them'. Peterson has also claimed that feminists have an 'unconscious wish for brutal male domination'.[4]

Of course, the macho Russian leader is more explicit in his defence of untrammelled masculine authority than Peterson. Putin has justified his military assault on Ukraine as part of a crusade against 'gender freedoms' and has accused the West of heading towards a 'spiritual catastrophe'. And yet Peterson — who like the Russian leader blames NATO for Russia's invasion of Ukraine — has openly pondered whether Putin may be on the right side of the civilisational struggle against 'wokeness'.

'All the way down the line, Putin dominates everybody, nobody questions that,' says Ross. 'Who's under Putin? Well, they can dominate anybody under Putin.'

Men who find themselves on the lowest rungs of the ladder can dominate their families. In 2017, Putin signed a law that partially decriminalised domestic violence in Russia, a country where a woman is killed by a man in a domestic setting every forty minutes. Patriarchy thus confers even the lowest ranking males with a sense of domiciliary lordship and dominion. In a liberal democracy this cult of patriarchal dominance is '[no longer] really supportable,' as Ross points out. 'Socially, women want to be treated as equals… And so that increases the need to dominate society and turn it into a patriarchal one. Because otherwise, in this liberal society — and you see [the manosphere] complaining about this all the time — women have options.'

*

Sanction can easily be read as the superheated ravings of a mad man. Nevertheless, the sulphuric effect of the prose – not to mention the complete failure of the book as a cogent literary endeavour – should not obscure the political nature of the book's message. You do not even need to read the thing to get an inkling of what the message might be. For a start, the front cover of the book is adorned with the *Wolfsangel,* a runic symbol used by a notorious panzer division in Hitler's Waffen-SS.

Warrior masculinity is a frequent theme in fascist ideology. As is violent societal rebirth. Lyndon McLeod's goal was to instigate a war on modernity: to bring down liberal democracy, sweep away the iterations of degeneracy – the 'weak men and tyrannical females' – and return society to a more tribal and hierarchical footing.

McLeod shared this interest in countercultural fascism with the masculine philosopher Jack Donovan. McLeod was a 'fan' of Donovan's work which he described as a 'big influence' on *Sanction*.[5] Donovan was also mentioned in the book's opening pages. In 2020, McLeod was a guest on Donovan's *Start the World* podcast, where the host described *Sanction* in the episode's description as 'a massive work of masculine fiction that's caught on with a lot of men I respect.'[6]

At the 21 Summit in Orlando, Anthony Johnson had introduced Donovan to the stage as the 'best masculine philosopher in the world'.[7] Donovan, fifty, has advocated what has been termed 'gang' masculinity; he has also previously embraced the term 'anarcho-fascism'. A theme that runs through all of Donovan's writings is the supposedly cathartic power of violence. His self-proclaimed magnum opus is a 2010 book titled *Violence is Golden*[8] and his website even sells merchandise with 'Violence is Golden' on it.[9] 'People are violent, and that's OK... It's time to quit worrying and learn to love the battle axe,' he has written.

The charismatic Donovan is unusual in the manosphere for being openly gay. Yet he rejects 'effeminacy' and the 'gay identity' in favour of the idea that 'men can have sex with men and retain their manhood'.[10] He considers himself an 'androphile' and frames his sexual proclivities as an expression of his own version of male separatism. 'When it comes to sex, homos are just men without women getting in the way,' Donovan has said.

Between 2014 and 2018, Donovan was a member of the Wolves of Vinland (WoV), a bucolic fascist group based in rural Virginia. Founded in 2006 by the fitness coach and white supremacist Paul Waggener (who also appeared as a character in *Sanction*), WoV has branches in the USA, Russia, Germany, Norway, Spain and Serbia. Fixated on racial tribalism and survivalism, WoV members take their aesthetic inspiration from outlaw biker gangs such as Hells Angels, Norse pagan imagery and the black metal music scene. They frequently wear patched-up leather jackets and pose for ghoulish-looking photos. They also paint their faces and hang out in the woods, roughhousing, taking part in pagan blood rituals, and congregating around roaring fires (city life and materialism are viewed as decadent realms of female domesticity).

The group's materials quote liberally from *Fight Club*[11] and members are expected to engage in violent male camaraderie. These macho initiation rituals include fist fights with other members and animal sacrifice. Prospective members of the group are expected to follow a rigorous weightlifting regimen and become proficient at homesteading. WoV ideology also adopts some of the film's crude anti-consumerist messaging, railing against what it calls the global 'mono-culture' and the 'Empire of Nothing'.

WoV's materials describe the group opaquely as a 'group of folkish heathens'. However, the Wolves are more accurately described as a 'crypto-fascist' group – i.e. their brand of folkish and bucolic fascism is designed to be 'harder to spot and confront than some buffoon marching around with a swastika flag', as one anti-fascist blogger has memorably phrased it.[12] The Italian *squadristi* (the paramilitary wing of the Italian Fascist Party) and the German storm troopers both started out as street-fighting movements; and to those well acquainted with the Wolves' historical antecedents, the group's propaganda quickly gives the game away.[13] The WoV have a feeder organisation for new recruits called Operation Werewolf,[14] which also happens to be the name of the guerrilla resistance organised by Hitler as the Nazis lost control of Germany.

An unfortunate happenstance perhaps. Or maybe not. In 2012, a member of WoV[15] was jailed after setting fire to an African American church in Virginia.[16] And in 2020, two men linked to WoV were arrested in Pennsylvania and charged with plotting to rob a bank. According to Katie McHugh, a former Breitbart editor who dated Wolves member Kevin DeAnna before subsequently renouncing what was then called the 'alt-right' in 2019,[17] 'They [WoV] hate Black people.' McHugh also said the group regularly used racial slurs, including calling Black people *'Unters'*, a diminutive of the Nazi word *Untermensch*, meaning sub-human.

In *Sanction*, Lyndon McLeod had quoted from the work of Julius Evola, a self-proclaimed *'superfascista'* (superfascist) who moved from Italy to Germany in 1943 following the fall of Mussolini. Born in Rome in 1898, Evola was a militant anti-egalitarian and esoteric elitist who believed that healthy societies were masculine whereas 'decadent' societies were feminine. A rabid antisemite, Evola's obsession with virility and manliness fed into his prejudicial view of Jewish culture, which he considered to be overly intellectual and 'effeminate'.[18] Evola's work drew on the Hindu cosmological cycle, which divides history up into four cosmic time cycles. Each cycle is called a *'yuga'*. For Evola, the West was corrupt and degenerate and therefore in the *Kali,* or final, *yuga*. This stage would be characterised by an apocalyptic transformation in which the old order would collapse and be replaced. Destruction and regeneration.

Like Evola, McLeod rejected 'modernity' and instead viewed history as a grand saga in which the task of superior peoples was to return history to a social Darwinian 'state of nature'. Characters in *Sanction* suggest the world is ready for a 'revanchist movement' which can bring about a 'Great Return' (concepts lifted directly from Evola).

The Wolves of Vinland founder Paul Waggener has also cited Evola (along with Nietzsche) as one of the inspirations for his *völkisch* group. In recent times, Waggener has developed a line of self-help businesses, including workout programmes, self-published books of his writings and branded Operation Werewolf clothing. One of these is called 'Total Life Reform', a programme marketed at men who wish to develop physical strength, spiritual vitality and become more financially free. As the writer and filmmaker Shane Burley has observed, these self-improvement programmes have been known to funnel customers to far-right ideas.[19] Burley has noticed parallels with the trajectory of some who fall into the manosphere:

> Just as happened in the 'pickup artist' community, where lonely men were introduced to the anti-feminist ideas of the manosphere when tuning in to learn how to pick up women, Waggener's programs build on the appeal of strength and loyalty to connect self-improvement with far-right ideas about racial tribalism.

*

Following the shootings in Colorado, Jack Donovan posted a public statement on Instagram in which he said that McLeod's ideas on masculinity were 'simplistic and cartoonish' (presumably unlike his own).

While masculinity influencers were trying to wash their hands of McLeod, others were anointing him a saint and a martyr. White supremacist and militant accelerationist

Telegram channels (the so-called Terrorgram) lit up with messages celebrating the killer.[20] McLeod was anointed an accelerationist 'Saint' and added to the white supremacist 'Saint Calendar', which glorifies murders by extremists.

Militant accelerationism is a tactical framework that can be bolted onto different ideologies, though it has mostly been adopted by neo-fascist organisations. Militant accelerationists seek to 'accelerate' societal collapse through acts of violence, sabotage and terrorism. The goal is to 'spark chain reactions of social upheaval and violence',[21] as Matthew Kriner of the Accelerationism Research Consortium has put it. Not to unleash chaos for its own sake, but to hasten the collapse of civilisation so that fascists can emerge and ascend to power, restoring tradition, patriarchy and racial segregation.

McLeod's writing had echoes of the accelerationist vision promoted by James Mason, a Canadian neo-Nazi who authored *SIEGE*, a 1993 anthology of influential white supremacist essays. Mason, the 72-year-old former associate of the cult leader Charles Manson,[22] has argued in favour of the collapse of American democracy as setting the stage for fascist rule. White supremacists, he argues, should *accelerate* the process by destabilising society[23] through random attacks and murders. In the months before he attempted to ignite his own conflagration, McLeod had made a short film called *War Horse*, in which he documented his planning of the murders. He described the film as depicting 'a future wherein the most aggressive and grudge-holding males are engaged in full-on war with modernity'.

Multiple terrorist attacks in the past two decades[24] have been inspired by militant accelerationist ideas. At least ten of the insurrectionists of 6 January 2021[25] wore skull masks signalling adherence to the ideology. The perpetrator of a 2019 attack on a mosque in Christchurch, New Zealand – in which fifty-one people were murdered and forty more were injured – titled a section of his manifesto 'Destabilization and Accelerationism: Tactics for Victory'.[26] On 14 May 2022, a mass shooter murdered ten African Americans in Buffalo, New York. The killer had lifted the same line from the Christchurch shooter and included it in his own declaration. The perpetrator of an anti-Hispanic attack in 2019 which killed twenty-three people and injured twenty-two others in a Walmart in El Paso, Texas, also cited the New Zealand killer as inspiration. All three killers referred to the white supremacist 'great replacement' conspiracy theory, which claims that Jewish 'elites' are trying to replace white European populations with immigrants from the Middle East and North Africa.[27] All three acts of mass murder were widely celebrated on accelerationist Telegram channels.[28]

Meanwhile in the United Kingdom, a convicted child sex offender and member of the militant accelerationist and neo-fascist organisation National Action was convicted in 2019 of plotting to murder a female Labour Member of Parliament.[29] A former member of the BNP's youth wing, Jack Renshaw, had railed against 'cultural Marxism', 'militant homosexuals' and multiculturalism. He also called for the Jews to be 'eradicated'. National Action, which was proscribed by the British government in 2017, publicly celebrated the 2016 murder of Labour MP Jo Cox by far-right activist Thomas Mair.[30] In its 2022 report[31] looking at terrorist trends in the European Union over the previous year, Europol (the European Union Agency for Law Enforcement Cooperation) noted that 'SIEGE and Accelerationism, both with significant potential for inciting violence, were the most prominent ideologies in 2021, especially attracting young people radicalised online.'[32]

For Alexander Reid Ross, the idea that society is about to break apart and descend into war allows hypermasculine men 'to constantly maintain [an] active role as a fighter, a hunter, something carnal'. Indulging this 'primal urge', he says, makes them 'feel free of modern strictures'. Alpha warrior kings are supposed to be above everyday vexations. As Ross puts it, they are 'tired of queuing up and want to break free of the fact of living around other people and having to abide by conventional norms'. They also want to be the pack leader, which is not always compatible with the drudgery and obeisance of a typical nine-to-five job. Hence the fixation with tribalism and Viking or warrior masculinity. 'They want to be in leadership roles. They feel like life is going to pass them by or has passed them by. They feel like this is the way they can dominate and feel powerful, because they don't feel powerful,' says Ross. '[But] it's not a healthy feeling. And that's why most people aren't like that. It's also why it's such a dangerous urge.'

Both male supremacists and white nationalists agree that the entrance of women into public life will precipitate the collapse of Western civilisation. Anthony Johnson described masculinity and femininity as the 'oldest forces in our species' and said that 'disobeying nature' would lead to 'the fall of [the United States]'. The American neo-Nazi Richard Spencer said women should 'never be allowed to make foreign policy' because their 'vindictiveness knows no bounds'. Aaron Clarey, a red pill YouTuber and author of *Enjoy the Decline* (a book whose supposition is that the West is in decline because of gender freedoms) told me that since gaining suffrage, women had 'voted for their best interests at the expense of men and society'. In *Bronze Age Mindset*, a self-published book written by the far-right internet personality and pseudonymous writer Bronze Age Pervert (BAP), the author described the liberation of women as the most 'ridiculous' thing that 'has ever been attempted in the history of mankind'. 'It took one hundred years of women in public life to almost totally destroy a civilisation,' he wrote.

Spanning 198 pages, *Bronze Age Mindset* is a supercilious and bombastic tome with a style that combines classical references with internet pidgin. It is racist, antisemitic and heavily parasitic on Nietzsche. Its author, a Romanian American immigrant named Costin Alamariu (the aforementioned Bronze Age Pervert), claims to 'believe in fascism or something worse'.[33]

None of this was an impediment to the book becoming an underground sensation among young, Trumpian right-wingers following its release in 2018. Nate Hochman, a former staffer for Republican governor Ron DeSantis who was fired in the summer of 2023 for sharing a video containing Nazi and white supremacist imagery,[34] told the *New York Times* that 'every junior staffer in the Trump administration read *Bronze Age Mindset*'.[35] Anti-feminism was a consistent theme in the book, perhaps explaining its appeal to right-leaning young men who chafed under politically correct HR departments at work and languished in the 'friend zone' outside of it.

In his writings, BAP exalted bodybuilding and a supremacist cult of 'higher specimens'. The fascist aesthetic has often lionised the male body as a symbol of virility and power – part of its cult of youth. Dreams of bloody ethnic violence occur against a backdrop of pastoral scenes, beautiful male bodies, and Greek and Roman statues. However, bodybuilding and fitness also serve a practical purpose. For BAP, his lifestyle advice was tied to 'above all preparation for struggle and war'. In this coming battle strong men would emerge and unleash violence on 'bugmen' (a reanimated version of the Nietzschean 'Last Man').

The prospect of an apocalyptic race war is, for most people, a decidedly unattractive vision. Not so for those who long to be at the front of the throng of onlookers when society hits the buffers. Predictably enough, Lyndon McLeod was keen on *Bronze Age Mindset*, sharing annotated extracts from it[36] ('great book') on his social media.[37] These included a paragraph in which the author called for the earth to be 'purified' of the 'human-cockroach'.[38]

Some more mainstream conservative commentators sought to imbue the pitiable hatreds contained in *Bronze Age Mindset* with an insurgent spin. The fact the author they were praising was openly fascist did little to discourage those whose existence seemed to revolve around 'triggering' liberals. If the book was *upsetting all the right people* then, to use an adjacent and comparably contemptible cliché, its author *must be doing something right*. The PayPal billionaire and Republican donor Peter Thiel spoke of being 'partial to a Nietzschean, Bronze Age Pervert-type perspective';[39] while the reactionary feminist writer Mary Harrington bizarrely described BAP as a 'genius'.[40] Others bleated in injured tones about how difficult it was to be a white man. The former Trump national security adviser Michael Anton[41] claimed to have located BAP's appeal in 'a youthful dissatisfaction (especially among white males) with… a hectoring, vindictive, resentful, levelling, hypocritical equality'.[42]

Reactionary propaganda has often sought to endow certain groups with illusions of superiority. And not only members of prototypical feudal or capitalist elites, who don't need much persuading to that effect. It is a strategy which assumes – to paraphrase Rousseau – that people will consent to wear chains if they may in turn give those chains to others. In the old American South, the poor white majority were compensated for their lowly material position by feelings of superiority over the enslaved black population beneath them. As the author John Ganz has astutely noted, BAP was particularly popular 'among the clerk class of the American right, as well as frustrated Bohemians, failed artists, political adventurers, and the online incel-tariat, all of whom are now increasingly bound together in one great [Republican] Party of Resentment.'

BAP was banned from X in 2017. His account was restored in 2022 along with hundreds of other white supremacist accounts following a takeover of the platform by the Trump-supporting billionaire Elon Musk. The other major change introduced by Musk (apart from renaming the company from Twitter) was to do away with legacy blue ticks – a despised symbol of the liberal cultural elite – and open up verification on the platform to anybody with $8 to spare. It was a move that went down well not only with fans of BAP, but with a wider constituency of men who felt like losers but believed it was their birthright to feel like winners. Their pretensions to elite status had previously been thwarted by what Musk called a 'lords & peasants system' of verification.[43] Now, thanks to Musk, they felt important too.

*

The control of women's reproductive rights is a frequent point of convergence between the manosphere and the far right. Gender and racial anxieties can also fuse. While modern women were resented for choosing careers instead of staying at home and acting as breeding stock for white patriarchs, 'pussyfied' men were accused of failing to 'protect' white female bodies (usually blonde and blue-eyed) from miscegenation and racial pollution.

Andrew Tate informed 'white men' that 'none of you are having children' because you've 'lost control of you're [sic] women'. Anthony Johnson was sending out emails to his mailing list encouraging subscribers to produce more 'white babies'. According to Stefan Molyneux, a Canadian philosopher and 21 Convention speaker, the white race would 'fucking end' because women 'choose the assholes'. Donald Trump was also casting himself as a defender of American women. 'I think women like me because I will be your protector,' Trump told supporters at a 2024 election rally in Aurora, Colorado, during a speech about illegal immigration. 'The women want protection. They don't want these people pouring in.'

It was a constant paranoic drumbeat. Docile Western men were failing to protect the wombs of *their* women. This had supposedly left society vulnerable to 'takeover' and 'invasion' by alien hoards. In *Sanction,* McLeod had complained that female teachers were indoctrinating boys to become weak and submissive. He also ranted about 'filthy Muslims and African freaks who are raping white women with impunity'. Another mass murderer who echoed these sentiments was Anders Breivik, the Norwegian terrorist who in 2011 set off a car bomb outside government buildings and opened fire on teenagers attending a Labour Party youth camp, killing seventy-seven people. In his manifesto, Breivik blamed 'feminist ideology' for turning society into a 'matriarchy' and reducing men to an 'emasculate[d]... touchy-feely subspecies'. Predictably enough, he claimed that Muslims were colonising Europe through 'demographic warfare'.

'Feminism is often seen as the starting point for where things started to go downhill for white men,' says Julia Ebner, who monitors extremist movements across the UK, Europe and North America and has written several books about far-right radicalisation. For example, those who subscribe to so-called Great Replacement Theory blame women for 'driving down the birth rates among whites and driving up the birth rate among non-whites'.

I meet Ebner at a café in central London. I can't reveal the exact location because Ebner has previously been targeted by far-right activists at her place of work. In 2017, after she wrote an opinion article for the *Guardian* newspaper about the mainstreaming of the anti-Muslim activist Tommy Robinson (real name Stephen Christopher Yaxley-Lennon), he turned up at the office where she worked.[44] As part of the research for her most recent book, *Going Mainstream: How Extremists are Taking Over* (2023), Ebner spent two years immersed in various extremist internet-based groups from across the ideological spectrum, including radical groups in the manosphere. She noticed the manosphere becoming more influential in the far-right ecosystem during the mid-2010s – and in particular in the lead-up to the 2016 American presidential election. 'It felt like that was really the turning point, or almost the beginning of the culture wars as we know them,' she tells me. Ebner sees the manosphere acting as a pipeline to the far right because the topics they discuss are closely related to some of the identity questions that men struggle with. An innocent-sounding question such as 'how do I ask a girl out?' can easily send someone down an algorithmic vortex of pickup artists, red pill gurus and, in some cases, neo-fascists who believed that changing gender norms are akin to the fall of Rome. Ebner points me to a study showing that men are increasingly adopting more anti-liberal and anti-feminist views, particularly men between the ages of fifteen and twenty-five. 'The youngest generations are now the most prone to radical, anti-liberal views,' Ebner says. 'There's a strong sense of wanting to go back in time, back to gender roles of the 1950s.'

Anti-feminist influencers tell men that society has been lying to them. That feminism is something omnipresent and threatening. It says that men, rather than women, are the primary victims of gendered social pressure. It is an ideological framework that seeks to reverse the conventional victim-perpetrator narrative. This can go on in perpetuity. 'It's easy to [then] apply the same argument to other minority communities who are allegedly now in more powerful or more privileged positions, like the black community or Jews for example,' says Ebner.

*

The existentialist philosopher Jean-Paul Sartre once remarked that antisemites like to view themselves as part of an alternative intellectual elite. Conspiracy theories – including conspiratorial antisemitism – can similarly endow believers with a sense of their own intellectual superiority. *They* have exclusive access to hidden information – information to hold over others and buttress their egos. Conspiratorial beliefs can also cross-pollinate. In Orlando, one 21 Summit attendee told me that the previous year's summit had been 'all about Covid' and the 'tyranny' of lockdowns and vaccines. Similar sentiments were still apparent a year later. Strolling around the hotel, I spotted several attendees wearing T-shirts boasting of their unvaccinated status. 'Proudly Unpoisoned' and 'Pure Blood', said the text on their clothing. The pandemic was supposedly a plot designed to make men soft and weak. Several of the speakers in the conference room repeatedly talked of 'globalist interests' acting 'behind the scenes' and 'globalist genocide'. The United States under Joe Biden was compared to Nazi Germany.

Prior to his killing spree, Lyndon McLeod had shared conspiracy theories about Covid-19, including a meme in which the Facebook and Microsoft founders Mark Zuckerberg and Bill Gates were shown discussing an 'injectable nanoworm'.[45] Jordan Peterson, who burst into public consciousness in 2017, was by 2024 insinuating that a new Covid-19 variant appeared whenever the share price of pharmaceutical companies went down.

Fitness communities were particularly prone to conspiracy theories about Covid. Some at the more extreme fringes took the view that illness was a form of Darwinian punishment for failing to be your 'best self'. Others had simply fallen into the slipstream of a wider cult of solipsism and self-regard. Either way, the newly shrunken horizons imposed during that strange interregnum were especially hard to accept for those who had grown used to refracting the minutiae of everyday life through a prism of opportunity costs. Personal development buzzwords were simply no match for a deadly pathogen.

As the Director-General of the World Health Organization told the assembly's first virtual gathering in May 2020: 'If this virus is teaching us anything, it's humility.'[46] Modern society, he said, had been 'humbled by a small microbe'. Surveying the online ecosystem of 'self-actualised' fitness and wellness influencers, 'humility' was not the first word that came to mind.

Indeed, one 21 Summit speaker attracted national attention in the US in 2020 after he and his business partner refused to close their gym during the pandemic. Ian Smith, a barrel-chested, hirsute man with a George Washington tattoo on his forearm, had kept his New Jersey gym open at a time when Covid deaths in the state had risen above 10,000.[47] 'My business partner and I decided that we were going to reopen our gym. And, well, I guess the rest is history,' he told the audience in Orlando. Smith would subsequently offer free gym memberships to anyone not vaccinated.

Smith and his business partner were fined thousands of dollars for every day they kept the gym open.[48] But the decision to ignore Covid restrictions was lucrative in another way. Smith was soon touring the right-wing talk show circuit (*Tucker Carlson Tonight*, *Fox and Friends* and *Newsmax*) telling the story of his fight against 'government tyranny'.

*

During my second day in Orlando, an Englishman named Richard Grannon had got up on stage. Introduced by Anthony Johnson as 'YouTube's number one psychology guru' (585,000 subscribers when I checked), Grannon initially reminded me of a timeshare salesman: gleaming white teeth, slicked-back haircut (part hipster, part Hitler) and slicker personality. Yet there was to be no high-pressure sales pitch for an apartment in the Seychelles. Instead, the 44-year-old 'Spartan Life Coach' launched into a bizarre rant about dastardly plots to transform humanity into genderless and androgynous 'worm people'. 'There will be no men. There will be no women. We will just be worms who consume,' he warned. Grannon recommended cold showers and NoFap (masturbation abstinence) as ways to fight this 'evil agenda'. 'Make your will strong... Everything inside the ideological soup you swim in is saying, "Don't be disciplined, indulge, indulge, indulge," because that's what makes you a good consumer.'[49]

Yet if anyone was lolling around a medley of ideological sludge, it was the Spartan Life Coach, who blamed humanity's descent into blissed out consumerist torpor on, of all things, communism.

More sinister was something that took place at a talk I attended by Elliott Hulse – a fitness YouTuber turned Trad-Catholic Nationalist. Hulse's presentation on the penultimate morning of the convention was mainly a variation on material I had heard perhaps half a dozen times already. The bull-necked and mohawked Hulse wanted men to 'reclaim their lost masculinity' by getting away from their mothers, leaving their sisters at home, and putting themselves through forms of good old-fashioned 'masculine initiation'. I was under the gruff auspices of Robert Bly again (even if Bly had not, as far as I was aware, been urging men to rid themselves of 'effeminacy' using 'semen retention'). Or at least I thought I was. Because it was then that Hulse started to ramble about 'the Js' acting 'behind the scenes'. The words barely had a chance to register before he smoothly segued back into his familiar macho-man routine. But there it was. He had sprinkled it in, like herbs on a pizza, hoping some of us would enjoy the taste.

9

INTERLUDE

From the pickup artists of Leicester Square to the red pill patriarchs in Orlando, the manosphere had long divided the world into rigid and distinct hierarchies. Women were rated on a scale from 1 to 10. Men would apply a similar taxonomy of social rank to themselves and each other. The pickup artists counterposed their own pursuit of *game* with 'average frustrated chumps'. There were alphas and betas; red pilled and blue pilled; high status and low status. I had encountered most variations of the theme during my dalliance with the manosphere back in 2006.

Yet with the advent of picture and video-based social media, the process of stratification had intensified. Dating was increasingly depicted as a winner-takes-all world in which a small percentage of men at the very top took the spoils. The rest were surplus men, condemned to a life of onanistic obsolescence.

In one sense the manosphere was reflecting wider market logic, which was continually pushing its tentacles into new areas of life. Instagram was launched in 2012; ten years later it was home to a billion users – around an eighth of the world's population. For some users of the app, life would steadily become a series of monetizable content opportunities. For others, the platform and others like it fostered subjective feelings of pauperisation. The more beauty and abundance on one side of the screen, the greater the sense of material and spiritual impoverishment on the other. Users were more keenly aware of what they didn't have; who their competition was; and how they were failing to market themselves correctly as consumable brands.

At around the same time, dating apps were injecting market logic into the intimate domains of love, sex and romance. The LGBT app Grindr went online in 2009, followed by Tinder in 2012. The *other* was becoming a two-dimensional object, marketed to potential consumers via these digital catalogues of flesh.

In the manosphere, these technological developments helped to spur the emergence of two contrasting – and mutually antagonistic – communities. Incels subscribed to an ideology they called the black pill. Followers of the black pill accepted most tenets of the red pill. Sex and relationships were viewed as rigid and hierarchical. Women, whom they depicted as shallow, deceitful and opportunistic, were said to be 'programmed' by their biology to sort men into desirable alphas and repulsive betas. Men outside of the community were viewed as 'blue-pilled' and brainwashed. Intimate relationships took place within a 'sexual marketplace' (SMP). 'High value' individuals had a greater sexual market value (SMV: exchange value) than 'low value' individuals.

INTERLUDE

If the blue pill was synonymous with ignorance and the red pill about understanding the matrix to manipulate it, the black pill was rooted in the decision to relinquish hope altogether. Incels viewed themselves as the unwanted detritus of successive sexual and social media revolutions. They were the underclass languishing at the bottom of the sexual marketplace, drowning in what the sociologist Zygmunt Bauman once described as the 'insipid mass of commodities'. They were condemned to social isolation because they lacked (or believed they lacked) the requisite marketable qualities in the dating *economy*. Refusing to compete with the torrent of perfect images, they stewed in nihilism and despair, denied access to the main currency of masculinity: women's bodies.

I wasn't in Vegas to meet incels. Instead, I had flown out to the city to meet the men who saw incels as a cautionary tale – the ultimate destiny of anyone who failed to mould themselves to the dictates of the digitised sexual marketplace. They subscribed to many of the same reductive theories as the incels. They knew all about 'SMVs' and – in common with just about every other faction in the manosphere – they frequently made men and women sound like eBay collectibles.

Yet they were *status-maxxers*. Instead of marinating in resentment on subterranean forums such as 4chan and Reddit, they were spending eye-watering sums of money in the hope of joining the digital sexual elite. And inevitably, a new generation of masculinity salesmen were on hand promising to make their dreams come true.

PART 3

The Black Pill

'There are millions of young men out there who just want to grow up, go to the gym, get strong, be respected, have a beautiful girl and a sports car.'

Andrew Tate, 13 September 2022

10

MEN OF ACTION

Las Vegas, Nevada

Michael Sartain is holding a student's iPhone. He brushes a thumb up and down the five-inch luminescent screen, pausing briefly so his eyes can take in the young man's Instagram grid. 'You need more danger,' Sartain says. 'Danger?' the student replies. '*Danger*,' Sartain repeats, looking up from the device. 'You need to look like more of a scumbag.'

The student is posting photos that are too safe, that won't attract too much attention or offend anybody. In other words, he is doing what everybody else is doing. There's a photo with his family on Thanksgiving; a bleary-eyed shot at a rock concert raising a beer in the air with male friends; and a picture of steak slathered in peppercorn sauce.

According to Michael Sartain there are three genders: high-status men, low-status men and women. When it comes to the digital sexual marketplace, the student is displaying all the hallmarks of low status. He is doing what everyone else is doing. 'The photos you have are comfort. Every guy is doing comfort. That's fine, but you need to have an edge. You want to look like more of a scumbag. You need more *danger*.'

Sartain is sitting cross-legged on the high-gloss floor of the basketball court. He has on a black vest, black shorts cut just above the knee and a pair of black and white Converse. A dozen men sit in front of him in a semi-circle along the three-point line, globules of sweat running down their flushed faces. 'When you have a solid social media profile, you're showing huge evolutionary signs that you are a high-status male,' Sartain tells the students. The basketballs have been put away and we are getting down to business. Sartain is breathlessly reeling off some of the glamorous women he has dated. The list includes swimsuit cover models, Playboy Playmates and adult film stars. Sartain is the first to admit that he punches above his weight thanks to social media. His Instagram profile is a case study in what being a scumbag entails. In almost every photo he is surrounded by scores of beautiful women, emblems of standardised physical immaculateness who spill out of cocktail dresses, lingerie and swimwear, their poreless skin, high cheekbones and lips congealing into pouts and coquettish smiles. A great deal of thought has gone into getting each composition exactly right. Sartain is positioned at the centre of the shots, usually dressed from head to toe in black.

The 46-year-old former US military officer – with over five hundred combat hours – has a bald fade haircut styled with a tall quiff on top. His arms flare out a little because he is on TRT (testosterone replacement therapy) and because he lifts heavy weights (he also takes caffeine pills to keep up with his 21-year-old girlfriend). He wears black pants because they make his legs look smaller, tight tops because they make his arms look bigger, shirts that go long because they make his waist appear slimmer. He keeps a single $100 bill in his wallet for when he wants to demonstrate financial abundance.

The students have flown in from around the world to be here, each paying as much as $10,000 to join Michael Sartain's Men of Action course, or MOA for short. One participant has travelled from Australia, another from Vancouver. The men listen attentively as Sartain lays out his rules for looking high status in social media photos. Women in the picture = attraction. Women + dog or cat = attraction + comfort. Kid in the photo = comfort. Bathroom mirror selfie = low status. Sports car, mansion, infinity pool = high status. Every photo must have a 4x5 aspect ratio. If a woman is standing or sitting next to you then you must not lean in. If she leans into you even better. Is she pointing her feet towards you or are you pointing your feet towards her? The students are taught to always monitor these variables.

Highlight reels at the top of Sartain's Instagram page show off his amazing lifestyle. There are videos of Michael on the red carpet hosting the *Maxim* magazine party; reels of him arriving at a glitzy Las Vegas nightclub trailed by seventy catwalk models; shorts of him compèring the Playboy bikini competition; photos of him partying with the pop star Jennifer Lopez, the actors Mel Gibson and Jeremy Piven, the Instagram influencer Dan Bilzerian, the heiress Paris Hilton and the reality television star-turned-DJ Pauly D. In one photo, Sartain has an arm draped around two glamorous peroxide blondes and another around Pro Football Hall of Fame running back O. J. Simpson, who in 1995 was acquitted of murdering his ex-wife Nicole Brown Simpson and her friend Ronald Goldman. Simpson is all smiles as he wraps his right arm tightly around Sartain's shoulder and raises a glass for the camera.

Apart from celebrities, men are mostly absent from Sartain's Instagram content, though they frequently appear in the comment section below. 'Wow, dime pieces once again. You lucky SOB,' writes one. 'Living the dream,' writes another. Other men resort to insults: they call the women silicone whores and brain-dead bimbos. Sartain isn't bothered though; jealousy is the price of admission when you broadcast a high-status lifestyle to the world. Being a hater is low status; one of the rules of MOA is *Don't talk shit about other people.*

Sartain is teaching the students how to create a 'high-status' lifestyle that resembles his own. They need to start treating social media as their own personal billboard, which means filling it with winning images. The average guy uses social media to be social when, according to Sartain, it's a place to market yourself, a vehicle for demonstrating access to scarce resources. 'You are going to be judged on your performance for the rest of your life,' he tells the students, most of whom have already accepted the basic tenets of red pill masculinity.

Sartain believes that Western society has a problem with what he calls 'surplus men'. If the students fail to show high status – and decline to curate their online personas to that effect – then their genes will be weeded out of existence by natural selection. The age of happily ever after, white picket fence monogamy is over. To be ordinary is to be invisible. 'We're going to get to a place where 10 or 20 per cent of dudes are fucking all the women,' he warns. To attract a woman in the twenty-first century, the students must first create the impression of an incredible life.

According to the marketing materials for the Men of Action programme, 'Being surrounded by attractive women is your *only* hope for having a dating life in the future.' Sartain calls this 'preselection': the idea that nothing attracts women like other women. The more beautiful women in your content, the more preselection you have and thus the higher your social status. 'The only point of your IG (Instagram) is to attract girls and show that other girls are attracted to you.'

Every time a new cohort of students arrives in Vegas, Sartain invites them to join him on the basketball court. It's part of forming a 'tribe' with the other students. 'One of the greatest gifts that you can give yourself is the ability to accomplish tasks with groups of other men,' he tells the students. 'So many of you just never really had a true locker room experience. So many of you just never had a community of guys that cared about you.'

Once the basketball is over, the students gather in a semi-circle so that Sartain can look at their social media content. He sees the same mistakes over and over: the bathroom selfies with flecks of toothpaste on the mirror; the bro shots of bawdy groups of men chugging beers in dive bars; and the gloomy headshots taken from inside of what looks to be a trash can. Sartain believes that social media has globalised the sexual marketplace, leaving a bourgeoning flotsam of involuntary celibate no-hopers in its wake. The majority of men are 'self-selecting' out of the dating pool because their social media 'looks like dogshit'. They are invisible to women; they are surplus men. 'Look around you in Walmart or wherever,' Sartain says. 'Who is fucking these guys?' *Silence.* 'No one. How do I get seventy Playboy models to come to my photo shoots?' *More Silence.* 'Your Instagram,' he says pointing to one of the students – 'you look like a child molester; you look like a human trafficker.'

The basketball court is on the ground floor of Panorama Towers, a high rise within walking distance of the electric sign gauntlet of the Las Vegas Strip. On the court, Sartain plays the pack leader, the alpha male who is not afraid to aggressively jostle the opposition and loudly berate teammates for failing to protect the basket. He barks orders during the game and roasts the students' Instagram profiles during timeout. 'Guys, what's step number one of the Men of Action programme? *Fix your fucking Instagram...* Every hot girl is on IG.'

The students are given a homework assignment to improve their free throws and their social media grids. They have been encouraged to ask themselves the same question about everything they post online: *Is this action making me more of a ten out of ten?* They need to look more like 'scumbags' – and less like the lost souls drifting around Walmart in billowy polo shirts and beige lawnmower pants.

I'm here to help them to do that. For the next seven days I will be one of their high-status social networking coaches.

My introduction to MOA was helpfully smoothed by Nick, a 24-year-old from West London whom I'd first met in Miami in 2019. I'd been doing research at the time, attending another workshop and soaking in as much as I could of what the masculinity demagogues were saying. MOA hadn't existed then (Sartain started it with his two business partners in 2020), but Nick seemed to know people in the Vegas scene. Through him, in the summer of 2019, I would meet some of the city's social networking coaches. For once I had a bit of money to my name – including part of the advance for this book – and I was entertaining visions of playing at being Hunter S. Thompson in the desert until it all ran out. Which I did if you factor in everything but the writing; and which it (the money) had by the time I returned to London three months later. Composing a terse email was about the extent of my literary capabilities by the time I got back to England.

But I'd done what I needed to do: I had my *in* with the city's status-maxxers. I had managed to finagle an introduction to Sartain and some of his flunkies. A couple of years later, once the worst of the pandemic had subsided and his MOA programme was up and running and open for business, I reached out to one of the coaches with a suggestion: I was going to be in Vegas again soon – might they need an extra volunteer to take the students out and show them the (velvet) ropes? I was 'offering value', just like I had been told. There was never any question of it not working.

A photoshoot has been arranged for the following day. One of the other coaches will pick up a rented Lamborghini from the dealership and we'll all drive out to the desert. The social media boot camp is designed to create a celebrity effect.

As well as attending seminars and photoshoots, students will be taken out on four occasions to some of the city's most exclusive nightclubs. Here, they will be shown how to start conversations with women, as well as how to network with 'high status' men. The latter involves identifying their motivations (which could be women or access to celebrity parties), 'offering value' (by suggesting introductions or having status in the local environment) and then closing the deal – i.e. exchanging contact details. The remainder of their days will be filled with post-nightclub debriefs and further seminars on how to use social media to build a life of material and sexual abundance.

While the logistics for the following day are being discussed, Sartain is busy showing a former sergeant in the US military how to use Facetune (an app popular among teenage girls) to make his upper body appear more muscular. 'Rule number four: social media is fake and I'm okay with that,'[1] Sartain says as he gives the man digitally enhanced trapezius muscles that bulge and flare.

*

Another Immersion coach, Austin, is picking up the Lamborghini Huracán and bringing it out to the Valley of Fire state park, located 15 miles west of Las Vegas. The late-afternoon sun casts a reddish hue across the arid landscape. Pink and purple mountains on the horizon. Clouds of sandstone dust swirling around trainers and dress shoes. The countdown to golden hour, when we will have thirty minutes of perfect light and twelve students to shoot. No time to mess about.

A smudge of sleek white paint streaks across the horizon as the $300,000 supercar travels along the serpentine freeway in the valley below. There is a noticeable buzz of excitement in our little section of the Nevada desert. The students discuss the technical specifications of the car as Austin accelerates down the deserted road, revving the devilish-sounding 601 horsepower V-10 engine violently before backing the car on to a patch of gravel by the roadside. 'This is super fucking dope,' a timorous and nasally voice trills from a cloud of sand. Phones are taken out and students rush forward to film the vehicle from every conceivable angle. Their appetite whetted by the session on the basketball court with Sartain, they are hungry for some high-status content.

Austin hangs an arm out of the wound-down driver's side window triumphantly. 'Pretty sweet, huh?' he says to a crowd of gaping men as he yanks himself out of the poky driver's cockpit, a camera swinging from a strap on his shoulder. Austin is twenty-nine and from Seattle. He is also MOA's designated photographer. 'All right. Who wants to go first?' he asks the students, who are busy opening backpacks and suitcases. An assortment of noisy shirts, pristinely ironed suit jackets, and jeans with large and obnoxious rips in them are disgorged onto the side of the road. Every student has brought along at least three changes of clothes. 'Can I get a shot in the jacket?' one of the men asks. I say sure, no problem, and surrender the leather jacket.

The first student hesitates as he approaches the vehicle. He licks a hand and smears down some obstinate hairs that are sticking up at the crown. 'How should I be?' he shouts at Austin. For some of the men, this isn't their first rodeo. For the less experienced – which from what I gather is most of them – it takes a moment to loosen up. Rigour sets in as soon as the camera is pointed in their direction. They stand stiffly, their arms tightly crossed, mean mugging at the shrubbery at the side of the road. As they grow in confidence, legs are draped nonchalantly across the bonnets of cars and assured and business-like stares are projected into the distance. One student pretends to be on his phone scoring a deal. Another, in his fifties and recently divorced, looks out from a pair of tinted Ray-Bans while nibbling on a Monte Cristo. He hitches up a sleeve when he sees the Rolex isn't showing.

The shoot is all about conveying the qualities of a high-status alpha male. It isn't something you can tell people. Telling people is low status, like bragging about your money. The MOA students are taught to show rather than tell, which means putting together what Sartain calls 'irrefutable visual evidence' at photoshoots like this. The students must demonstrate competency, relevancy and access to scarce resources.

When everyone has a photo with the sports car, Austin has the students climb one of the red sandstone outcrops that glower over the road. They take turns ascending the highest part on the rock, which isn't very high, before Austin shoots from an even steeper angle. The real magic is done in post-production, when a separate mountain peak will be photoshopped in. The results are impressive and show the students striking self-assured poses against a rugged Martian landscape – conveying adventurousness and travel. Sin City, Lambos, Monte Cristos – it is all supposed to add up to an incredible life.

Though MOA isn't teaching this, some men in the self-improvement space have gone even further, renting out green screens and chroma-keying themselves into infinity pools in Dubai or safaris in the Australian outback. The set-up involves a cabin that is kitted out inside to look like the interior of a private jet. Customers are urged to take their seats and recline in quality hand-stitched furnishings while a photographer buzzes about. Occasionally they will place a laptop on their lap and gaze pensively out of the window at the cotton-cloud earth (i.e. a suspended printout of the sky). The end product is uploaded to the internet with a suitably uplifting caption – ideally something that celebrates the capitalist ethos that has taken them to the top: *'Office for the day'; 'The higher the altitude, the higher the vision'; 'Put a few great men in a single room and watch as they redefine the world'.*

Some of the MOA students have been complaining that it all feels shallow and disingenuous. 'The world is shallow, the world is disingenuous,' Sartain snaps back. And besides, they don't need to change who they are outside of the digital realm. They just need to carefully choreograph what they are uploading to the world. It is important to be realistic. 'Unfortunately, the world reacts to shiny objects... The world is not a meritocracy, guys, you understand that? The world is full of fluffy, shiny objects.'

Most of the students are in their twenties, thirties and forties and discovered Sartain's MOA programme through Instagram. They watched his stories and saw him hanging out with all these beautiful women. He wasn't famous and he wasn't a male model. Their interest would have waned if he was. It was compelling because on some level he looked like them, even if his life didn't. Sartain's life resembled a movie. And so they threw down thousands of dollars and flew out to Vegas to follow their new mentor. The students didn't want to be surplus men. Being a man of action sounded better.

*

On a six-and-a-half-inch screen, the illusion of success is indistinguishable from the real thing. The poster boy of the art form was Sartain's hero, Dan 'Blitz' Bilzerian, the self-proclaimed 'king of Instagram' who became widely known in the 2010s for his ostentatious portrayal of bachelorhood. Bilzerian's 2011 autobiography, *The Setup,* is Sartain's bible. Sartain even rents an apartment in the same Vegas tower block where Bilzerian used to live.

Bilzerian became popular around the same time that the red pill and incel communities were beginning to grow. The two things were conceivably related. Bilzerian's persona had convinced at least some of the men on Sartain's MOA programme that dating was a winner-takes-all world where being average was no longer enough. Bilzerian had expanded the concept of the trophy wife into the trophy harem. The men who signed up to MOA were encouraged to build the same cartoonish lifestyle for themselves.

Social media was distorting what was normal and expected. For those pushing premium-priced lifestyle courses to lost young men, Bilzerian was a useful lodestone for the direction society was heading in. As Sartain told his students, soon '10 per cent of men' would be 'fucking all of the women'. The king of Instagram was pointed to as proof. Men of Action was a $10,000 programme designed for those who wanted to join 'the top 1 per cent of men with a lifestyle like Dan Bilzerian'.

While Sartain was full of libidinous awe for Bilzerian, the internet's most notorious playboy had taken inspiration from the more sedate world of freshwater fish. In *The Setup*, Bilzerian had written: 'There is a scientific study that showed when the female goldfish is trying to decide who to mate with, and since all male goldfish look alike, she goes with the male goldfish that has the most females around him.'

It made a certain sense. Social media was like a goldfish bowl, and so the former Navy Seal trainee would become a goldfish. Thereafter he was flanked by a harem of glamorous models wherever he went. They fed him grapes, fondled his beard and sat on his lap looking kittenish. Bilzerian made sure there was always a flunky on hand to capture these special moments. The 'aspirational' compositions were then knocked into shape in the editing suite before being uploaded (or unloaded) to social media for Bilzerian's rapidly growing audience. By April 2014, a little under two years after setting up his account, Bilzerian had amassed 1.34 million Instagram followers. By 2018 this had grown to 24 million. By 2024, 32.6 million. A representative shot of Bilzerian surrounded by five cinnamon-coloured women – not so much in swimwear as accompanied by it – was captioned: 'The mass of men lead lives of quiet desperation'.

Not Blitz though. Having decided in the early 2010s that he wanted to live a 'bucket-list sort of life' – a list that turned out to be remarkably short – Bilzerian had transformed himself into a lumpen Hugh Hefner. In place of a soft-core literary magazine he had guns, big cars and giant stacks of cash. Bilzerian didn't have time to read; his life was a hurricane of gambling, weed, partying and sex. Velvet smoking jackets were out too, replaced by budgie smugglers and anabolic steroids. The tanned and top-heavy Bilzerian recalled the late critic Clive James's description of the bodybuilder Arnold Schwarzenegger: he looked like a brown condom stuffed with walnuts.

But Bilzerian's fan base (made up of adolescent males of all ages) were not there to gape at their hero's chemically induced hypertrophy. They didn't care if his over-manicured beard made his head look like a hexagon. Or that there was something mule-like about his countenance when he shaved it off. They were enchanted by the lifestyle. Bilzerian's social currency was 'truckloads' of mute, pouting, sculpted, ornamental and methodically perfect female flesh. 'Ugly girls hurt my eyes, you're welcome,'[2] he wrote above a photo of himself at a nightclub buried under a heap of pneumatic blondes. Sex with beautiful women was synonymous with upward mobility, a barometer of one's place on the dominance hierarchy. Jordan Peterson would understand it even if he wouldn't approve. 'The dominant male, with his upright and confident posture, not only gets the prime real estate and the easiest access to the best hunting grounds. He also gets all the girls,' raptured Howdy Doody with the enthusiasm of Poindexter for the Jock. Women were one of the spoils, like the cars on Blitz's drive and his $300,000 watch.

'Celebrities need to stop being concerned with their image, be authentic,' Bilzerian tweeted in 2020.[3] Like many others whose lives are carefully choreographed illusions, Bilzerian liked to claim the mantle of authenticity. 'It irritates me when people say that I'm not authentic because I take great pride in being 100 per cent honest about everything,' he preened in his memoir. Bilzerian didn't like journalists much; perhaps because they tended to raise a sceptical eyebrow at such lofty self-assessments. 'Most journalists were never popular; they probably got bullied as kids, so when they're presented with the opportunity to take down celebrities while hiding safely behind a computer screen, they do so with glee because it makes them feel powerful.' Bilzerian preferred the podcast circuit, where sunny positivity seemed to foreclose any hard-nosed journalistic probing. 'You're living a life that doesn't seem real,' exclaimed Joe Rogan, the big silverback gorilla of the men's podcast circuit, in 2016.[4] Rogan's approach was to sit there vibing while occasionally emitting a mesmerised grunt ('Wow, man, that's crazy'): the ideal format for an image-conscious influencer.

In the end, it wasn't a journalist but one of Bilzerian's former employees who exposed the illusion. According to Curtis Heffernan, the former president of Bilzerian's cannabis company Ignite, Bilzerian was the human equivalent of a Ponzi scheme: his lifestyle a continuous cycle of self-perpetuating hype. Heffernan was an ex-executive at Procter & Gamble who joined Ignite in March 2020 and was made acting president eight months later. Later that year, he filed a lawsuit against Bilzerian for wrongful termination. Heffernan alleged that he was fired just two days after refusing to put through some extravagant outgoings as 'expenses' on the company tab. According to Heffernan, Bilzerian's lifestyle was mostly rented and usually charged to a credit card that someone else was paying off. Heffernan's lawyer claimed that even the women were hired and charged to Ignite's 'corporate tab'. Other expenses purportedly billed to Ignite, which posted $67 million in losses in 2019, included a $40,000 rock climbing wall, a $15,000 ping-pong table, $130,340 for a photoshoot in the Bahamas, and $26,000 to boost Bilzerian's Instagram followers.[5] The lawsuit alleged that Bilzerian didn't even own the house he lived in – a 31,000-square-foot L.A. mansion with twelve bedrooms and twenty-one bathrooms. This was rented out by Ignite for $200,000 a month. As soon as Heffernan went public, other Ignite employees spoke out. 'Ignite pays for everything,' one told *Forbes*. 'Models, events, yachts. Dan would just have it wrapped with the Ignite logo, and all of a sudden it was an Ignite expense and he would send them the bill.'

Daniel Brandon Bilzerian, born 7 December, 1980 in Tampa, Florida, was the oldest son of Paul Bilzerian, a moustachioed high-school dropout and Vietnam War veteran who was indicted by the US government in 1989 for securities fraud. Prosecutors said the ex-Wall Street corporate raider had illegally profited from hostile takeover bids by secretly accumulating stock in target companies, getting rejected by their boards and then making millions when friendlier companies (so-called white knights) came in with higher offers and the stock shot up.[6] Following a six-week trial, 39-year-old Paul Bilzerian was sentenced to four years in a federal prison and fined $1.5 million. Bilzerian's 'false testimony' to the court was an aggravating factor in the sentencing. 'In short, he lies,' said the presiding judge.[7] Bilzerian senior had profited handsomely from his crimes: financial statements seen by the court placed his net worth at $81.4 million.[8] However, the US government was only able to claw back a fraction of that. Paul Bilzerian was released from prison having served just thirteen months of his sentence, though in 1993 the SEC filed a civil lawsuit against him to the tune of $62 million – a sum made up of $33 million from unlawful gains and $29 million in prejudgement interest.[9] What followed was a cat and mouse game with the US government spanning nearly a quarter of a century. Initially, Bilzerian transferred the family home in Tampa – a 28,000-square-foot mansion – to his wife's name and filed for bankruptcy, prohibiting the government from seizing his assets. The rest of the money he concealed in a Byzantine network of partnerships, trusts and shell companies in lawsuit-proof tax havens.[10] As the *Wall Street Journal* reported,[11] Paul Bilzerian 'tied up regulators with dozens of lawsuits and motions – often acting as his own lawyer – and used offshore and domestic trusts, partnerships and charities to protect assets for his family. That included assets set aside for son Dan Bilzerian.'

With such a role model, it was perhaps not surprising that Dan Bilzerian liked to preach a secular prosperity gospel. 'Success is a matter of willpower,' he claimed, maybe thinking warmly of his father who had prevented such prodigious quantities of money being seized by the IRS. Dan Bilzerian admitted to having inherited a couple of million from his father when he turned thirty, but he claimed to have won the rest of his enormous fortune playing high stakes poker. Yet whenever Bilzerian played on camera he seemed to lose: he finished 180th[12] at the 2009 World Series of Poker (WSOP) and lasted just two hands[13] at the 2024 event in Las Vegas. Poker pros who watched him said he played like a conspicuously splashy 'whale' (a derogatory nickname given to rich guys who play badly).

Then again, you could afford to get a little sloppy when sitting on a seemingly inexhaustible pot of money. 2014 was a particularly good year for Dan, who claimed to have won $50 million in a private game of poker. ('Bilzerian's biggest wins always seemed to happen behind closed doors'.) It was a good year for Bilzerian senior too: the US Securities and

Exchange Commission finally conceded defeat in its pursuit of him. 'I would rather starve to death than earn a dollar to feed myself and pay the government a penny of it,' announced a triumphant Paul from his home on the Caribbean island of Saint Kitts and Nevis.[14] As for the money he had stashed away years earlier, nobody outside of the Bilzerian clan truly knew where it had gone, though in 2024 prosecutors would allege that Bilzerian senior had actually been running Ignite all along.[15]

The younger Bilzerian was right about one thing, though: you didn't need to possess any special talent to be famous. Sartain said he agreed with everything in Bilzerian's memoir; the main lesson being the importance of status, which on the internet was synonymous with 'clout' – i.e. the number of people who were paying tribute to you with 'follows' and 'likes' and 'shares'. Clout opened doors – and most of the time it didn't matter what you'd done to get it (which was how social media had destroyed the concept of shame). For Sartain, Bilzerian was 'one of the greatest geniuses of our generation', presumably up there with people like Stephen Hawking and Terence Tao.

*

Nick, as I mentioned earlier, was flying around Europe and North America when we first met. There were pickup and self-development workshops to attend. His life at this point was extraordinarily simple: he travelled the world searching for the elusive guru who had it all figured out.

Financially, Nick had done well for himself, creating a mobile phone app in his early twenties and selling it to a big company for a pretty penny. He'd put some of it down for a small flat in West London – not bad at all for someone in his mid-twenties with no family money. Speaking of which, Nick had helped his parents buy an apartment out in Spain on the Costa Blanca where the family holidayed twice a year, frequenting English bars and greasy spoons with all the other English people. The remainder of the money sat in his bank account, waiting to be wired to the next company with 'mindset' or 'wisdom' or 'actualisation' in the name. He bought a lot of designer clothes too (Armani, Gucci, Louis Vuitton, Stone Island, Off White, Hugo Boss). 'Important to have the basics sorted,' he'd say splashing Tom Ford on his neck before a trip to Mayfair.

Nick was over six feet tall and had nice white teeth, Labrador eyes and a healthy quotient of melanin courtesy of the sunbeds at the health club he frequented twice a week. When I first met him, it wasn't immediately obvious to me why Nick was paying so many pseudo-authority figures from the internet. He had looks, cash and some of the easy swagger of London done good. I was clearly missing something: in particular, any conception of what he thought he was missing. The outward trappings of success were visible; and yet internally there was a sense of inadequacy. Nick was not enough; or at least he thought he wasn't; and somewhere out there was a course that would fix him.

What the various dating and masculinity coaches were selling Nick was a fantasy of control. That if he performed a certain set of actions, he would get a reliable set of results. All of the unsettling variables would be extracted from the equation. All it would take was somebody with a bit of charisma going off on YouTube. Then the credit card would be out; another workshop booked in three weeks' time. He was a sucker for the promises of spectacular transformations and *'guaranteed results for a limited time only and there aren't many places left so register now while there's still time'*.

    I occasionally went out with Nick to the clubs and cocktail lounges of West London. Most of his mates from school were petty criminals, or wide boys from Fulham who were unreliable on a night out. They would drink too much and start talking about doing lines and it wasn't even midnight. Nick knew I was writing a book about the manosphere. He also knew that, as a freelancer, I had fewer excuses when it came to going out on a weeknight. I'd get a WhatsApp message in the afternoon asking if I was up for it. I'd reluctantly iron a shirt, put on uncomfortable shoes and tell myself that I might get some copy out of it.

    We usually ended up in a club in Mayfair. Nick might eventually approach a woman he was interested in. Occasionally the two of them would go home together at the end of the night. She'd notice him, glance over a few times coquettishly, and then after psyching himself up, Nick would glide over and introduce himself. From there it was usually smooth sailing: she'd like him from the off and he hadn't done anything to ruin the magic. Yet when I'd touch base with Nick the following day, his recollection of the night would usually differ from my own. For him it was all about the techniques he had used in the club: the power stances, the 'alpha' tonality and the dominant frame control.

Nick's emotional health would cycle through several different iterations on repeat. He would discover the latest influencer and seem contented for a while. Feelings of self-doubt would recede while the hidden code retained its novelty. He would like to proselytise about it too. We would meet at a bar or food court and he would wax enthusiastically about the latest stuff he was into. 'Women want a leader of men, but society put us inside these boxes and made us passive,' he said while making the shape of a cube with his hands. 'That way, we aren't a threat to the status quo.' Nick would radiate confidence and authority as he let me in on some newly acquired piece of forbidden knowledge. After a month or so of this, the disillusionment would steadily kick in. Nick was a poor disciple, for the same reason he was good with technology. He would always discover some flaw in their inelastic models of the world – some nugget that didn't quite sit right. Nick would take a few steps back and his search for answers would start over again, the zealous apostle metamorphosing back into the angst-ridden sceptic.

Nick reckoned he was fifteen when his dad tried to have a solemn talk with him about women. 'He acts like he knows a bit because the only woman he ever asked out said yes,' Nick, whose parents had been married for twenty-five years, told me through a smirk. 'In his mind he's got a 100 per cent success rate.' The Talk still made Nick cringe ten years later.

'He said if I liked a girl then I should buy her flowers, make a gesture and show her how I feel.' I asked Nick if he ever tried his dad's approach. 'Once,' he told me – when he was sixteen. 'Nothing really [happened]. She didn't take the piss, which was what I was most worried about. But it went nowhere. She ended up getting with another guy who wasn't doing any romantic stuff. He used to take the piss [out of her] in class. I thought he was being a dick. But there was another level I wasn't seeing.'

Nick had been looking for a girlfriend when I had first met him in Miami. He had a white board in his room with a 'vision' on it for where he wanted his life to be in six months' time. He was fully bought into the self-help dogma about building momentum and improving – always improving. He planned to drop down a few percentages of body fat, listen to more audiobooks (always on 1.5x speed), and find a quality girl to spend time with on weekends: someone to go out to restaurants with or watch films with on a rainy day. When Nick told me about the vision board, his goals sounded achievable and I was tentatively in favour of them. However, a few months later he scrubbed out the third goal and wrote a new one in its place. This one was more ambitious; it also seemed to have been implanted in Nick's head by someone else. Finding a girlfriend was no longer one of the objectives. Now he wanted a 'rotation': a micro-harem of women who would share him between themselves and never demand exclusivity. 'Women would rather share an alpha than get with a beta,' he told me, ventriloquising some red pill huckster.

LOST BOYS

*

London was getting Nick down. He'd recently attended another pickup boot camp – one of several over the preceding eighteen months. The instructor had got the students to do 'social pressure drills' in and around Leicester Square. First, he made them pair up and stand on opposite sides of the street in Piccadilly and yell at each other. Then he had them tap a stranger on the shoulder and attempt to start a conversation using gibberish – for example, 'Orange peels. I like orange peels.' The exercises were meant to desensitise the students to rejection so that, later on, when they were in the thick of the action in the nightclub, things would seem easy comparison.

It was the final drill that did it for Nick. The instructor told the men to attach themselves to lamp posts in one of the city's busiest thoroughfares. They were then to simulate having sex with it. Nick did what he was told because he was 'trusting the process' (another self-help dictum). As was often the case on these programmes, clients would spend a lot of money and then rationalise it by following orders.

Nick located a suitable piece of street furniture and took up the position. He began with a gentle motion of the hips. The instructor was bearing down on the students, ensuring they were pushing through the fear. 'Let's see some enthusiasm, guys,' he bellowed at the top of his voice. 'Imagine you've just pulled a hottie back to yours from the club. Visualise it.' Nick tried closing his eyes to shut out the passing crowds. He started pummelling away until he reached a steady rhythm. He felt himself letting go as the crowds began to dissolve; maybe it didn't matter what people thought of him.

It was at that moment that a tingling sensation began to radiate upwards from his loins. He snapped back to reality and looked down: his phone was vibrating inside his trouser pocket. The instructor was berating another student who had detached himself from a flange-plated lamp to swat away some track-suited teenagers. Nick slipped his phone out surreptitiously and saw the word 'Mum' flash on the screen. He had spoken with her already that day but took the call anyway; he assumed it must be important. She sounded choked up when he answered. It was his grandad. He hadn't been answering the phone all morning so one of his cousins had gone round. He'd had to go in through an upstairs window because he wasn't answering the door either. That's when he found her father – Nick's grandad – still lying in bed, propped up by a couple of pillows. He'd died during the night. 'It was a lot to take in,' Nick told me as he recounted the story for the first (though not for the last) time. The instructor wasn't letting up, though. 'Fight the fear,' he bellowed as Nick nestled the phone in-between his shoulder and ear and listlessly gyrated his hips. 'People [in the street] had completely faded out by that point,' Nick told me. 'I wasn't feeling fear because I wasn't feeling anything.' His mum was still on the line, fussing about her dad's affairs that would need sorting. Had his grandad wanted to be buried or cremated? How should he know? He was still half-heartedly going at the lamp post when the first salty tear ran down his cheek and into his mouth. '[At that point] it was like, what the fuck am I doing with my life?' Nick finally gave up when a drunken woman kicked him in-between the legs from behind with a bulky stiletto heel. The pain took a moment to radiate up into his stomach but when it did it brought some welcome clarity. Nick said goodbye to his mum, wiped his eyes on his sleeve and tottered in the direction of the nearest Underground station, hunching over to dull the pain.

*

Bilzerian's name came up a few times, as did Andrew Tate's. There were other influencers too whose names I hadn't heard before. I would look them up and invariably see the same loud and in-your-face wealth – enormous houses, luxury vehicles, yachts, private jets, money printing machines. But the most important prop of all was always the women, half-naked and willing – the more the better.

Nick regarded the Tate brothers, Andrew and Tristan, as high-status men. The brothers hadn't been arrested for sex trafficking at that point; I just knew Andrew as this obnoxious guy from the internet. For Nick, however, men like that were showing the world that it was OK to have muscles and a sports car and more than one girlfriend. And you weren't 'toxic' or 'problematic' for wanting those things too. A normal life seemed boring by comparison. Nick agreed with Tate when he said that not every man wanted beans on toast, television at night, a nine-to-five job and a homely wife. Some men had a fire inside of them; and Nick believed he was one of them.

There was also the question of expediency and not being

left behind. 'It does get rubbed in your face more nowadays,' he said one day out of the blue. 'You see some guys [on social media] getting all this attention.'

From this, Nick had concluded that women were no longer interested in 'average' men. Instead they wanted the best. Not just *some* women but *all* women. He was convinced he needed to lay the foundations of a high-status lifestyle. 'Social media has ruined it for average guys,' he told me one night while we were at a bar in East London. 'Girls see what they're missing out on. Polygyny is nature's equilibrium, and we're going back [there] because it's a better proposition for women than being with a beta.' Nick had been watching YouTube, listening to red pill podcasts. He'd also been reading up on evolutionary psychology, comparing the events that supposedly took place in our ancestral past with the things he was seeing on social media and out at the club. The reality was brutal and shouldn't be sugar-coated.

Nick liked to point out that 16 million men in the former Mongolian empire were direct descendants of the warrior-ruler Genghis Khan. 'This is what happens when hypergamy goes unchecked,' he told me one evening during a catch-up, blithely leaving out the raping and pillaging. 'Look around you,' Nick said to me wearily. 'High-status men have all the options.' We were getting food at BOXPARK in Shoreditch, East London, on a wet and windy January evening. We sat at a picnic table. Next to us were some mixed groups of twenty-somethings who, like us, were drinking beer out of plastic cups. 'You really believe that?' I asked Nick. 'On here I mean,' he said waving his phone in the air. He then laid it on the table and took in the flesh and blood world for a moment. 'They aren't fucking those dudes any more,' he added, pointing to a group of men sitting at an adjacent table. 'That girl, she's probably talking to a high-status guy behind his back, or at least hoping he'll slide into her DMs. That's what social media has done; it's changed expectations.'

I asked Nick if he thought his own sense of reality – and not just women's – had been distorted at all by social media. (He admitted to watching internet porn for 'at least ten minutes' on most days.) 'Maybe,' he replied before slamming the door firmly shut on that train of thought. 'But I reckon I would [still] want those things anyway,' he added. 'As men, we aren't programmed to be with one woman. Our proclivities weren't created by reason, but by natural selection.'

Nick was ventriloquising one of his favourite gurus again. This time it sounded like Michael Sartain.

11

ALPHA FUCKS, BETA BUCKS

Las Vegas (cont.)

'There's a bunch of girls that are going out tonight that are super fucking hot. And afterwards they're probably gonna go back to a hotel room with guys they've never met before. But you aren't invited. Not yet. Because you're surplus men.'

Twelve MOA students are gathered in the dimly lit karaoke room at the back of Sapphire, the world's largest gentlemen's club located a few blocks away from the Strip. Most of the MOA live training sessions take place here. There is a 90-inch television screen at the front of the room with a slide on it that says 'Women as Currency'. Sartain is at one end of the room, perched on a red-clothed pool table, his black Converse dangling in front of the ball window. The students, bleary-eyed from the night before, are listening attentively as Sartain expounds on the concept of surplus men. '[In the past] you always had this problem of surplus men. As we got into monogamous societies, what happened was low-status men got at least one girl that they could have sex with,' he says. 'Then after birth control and the sexual revolution we allowed people to choose more, and what women were all choosing was the high-status men, so these men at the bottom became surplus again. Which is why you guys are here.'

Sartain likens MOA to Noah's Ark, a life vessel designed to rescue men from sinking into the rising swamp of involuntary celibacy. He believes society is undergoing a fundamental transformation and ordinary men risk being left behind. The number of male virgins is growing. Men don't know what to do because the mainstream is lying to them. But Sartain is offering them a way out. 'This programme is not me standing on a pulpit... this is not Martin Luther King talking to the masses. This is Noah's Ark; this is the escape just for a few of you,' he says. 'You don't want to come that's fine; you can go watch ABC [and] listen to people explain to you that your heterosexuality is a social construct.'

But the men do want to come. They want to avoid a fate they believe awaits their friends back at home. It's a case of get in the life raft or be pulled under by the next wave.

'Your proclivities are created by natural selection, guys, not through reason. He died a virgin, guys, remember, he died a virgin.' Sartain is telling the apocryphal story of Sir Isaac Newton, the English philosopher who developed the theory of gravity after observing an apple fall from a tree. He wants the students to understand that they can't intellectualise their way to a successful dating life. 'The pretty girls don't care how smart you are,' he warns the class (at least one student lets out an audible sigh of relief). 'Super-rational people don't have social circles. You're not going to think your way through this.'

If Sartain is Noah then we, his Vegas Immersion high status social networking coaches, are tasked with showing Noah's disciples how to unhook life's velvet ropes. Students who sign up to MOA get weekly coaching calls with Sartain and access to an online video course designed to teach them how to build a social circle of 'heart-stopping women and elite men'. They are also offered (upsold for an additional fee to be precise) the chance to join a week-long course called Vegas Immersion. Whereas MOA can be done at home, Immersion is about putting the students in environments and around people they feel intimidated by.

The students want to become high-status males with 'elite' social networks. Yet they won't get very far if they can't hold eye contact. Some of this stuff is benign and – dare I say it – positive: showing socially awkward students how to have a conversation without using scripted lines or coming across like a pervert or a weirdo. The job of Vegas Immersion coaches is to take the men out to the city's most intimidating cocktail lounges, casinos and loud superclubs and get them feeling like they do in their own front rooms. The other coaches do it so they can mine Sartain for information without paying him (whereas I do it so that I can mine him for content and then write about it – we are not the same). The only requirement for the role is the ability to be a social butterfly on command. Which oddly enough I learned how to do at some point. The nervous wreck who staggered around Tiger Tiger pointing partygoers towards the bathrooms had been laid to rest, buried along with the blazer with the fuchsia pink interior.

Vegas Immersion is not a pickup programme. Trying to seduce women in bars and nightclubs is considered 'low status' by the generation coming through; now it's all about using social media to project status. Sartain wants the students to become high-status alpha males, not fedora-wearing dorks who do magic tricks in the club. According to Sartain, day-gaming at the mall is 'weird', 'toxic' and an 'exceptionally low-status activity'. Salespeople and the homeless walk up to strangers going about their day. High-status people have better things to do. The students should 'forget all that pickup artist bs [bullshit]'; 'being the best cold approach artist in the world is like being the tallest midget'. Instead, Sartain has appointed himself their 'military training instructor'. He is going to instil in them the 'boots on the ground knowledge' to build their own 'elite' social circle – 'the highest form of game'. The students assembled in the karaoke room look on, intoxicated with a vision of the glamorous lives they could soon be living.

*

The doorbell of the mansion is promptly answered by a fresh-faced MOA student in slippers and a Hefner robe. 'Heeeey, come in guys. Andreas is getting ready.' He apologises for the mess as the sole of my shoe clings momentarily to a coagulated blotch of tequila and cranberry on the tiled floor. Cushions and red plastic cups are strewn about the living room. As I zigzag through the clutter, another ebullient 'hey' rings out from the kitchen area where a young student is scooping mounds of powdered protein into a shaker. There's a young woman in the backyard, visible through the open blinds as she swishes a long telescopic pole across the surface of the pool.

Six MOA students are renting the house, a spacious mansion with giant glass chandeliers, a winding staircase, and a heated outdoor pool with a lanai and stacked-rock water slide. The property was built during the era of John F. Kennedy and the Rat Pack; the comedian Jerry Lewis lived a block away. The house is conveniently close to the Strip and a ten-minute walk from Trump Hotel, a 64-storey high rise wrapped in 24-carat-gold glass. The fifth highest building in the Vegas skyline, the word 'TRUMP' is emblazoned in capital letters across the top of the gleaming tower, ensuring the providential red pill favourite is always in the background. Some of the students seem to view Trump as one of them: as the supreme alpha, the Boss, the Don[ald]; the man sitting at the summit of the theoretical anthropomorphic wolf pack. Then again, perhaps it was hardly surprising that a politician like Trump – whose aura as a successful businessman was built on hot air – should be popular in a subculture of men who are trying to generate their own self-perpetuating hype. Trump was his own hype man, leasing his name out so that hoteliers could slap it on the front of their buildings. Everything was transactional for him too; relationships based on mutual exploitation. His nephew Fred Trump said he used people as pawns. If he could increase his status through someone then he took an interest. If not, they were worthless. Of course some of the students liked him.

I had stopped by at the house to pick up some students and head to the nightclub. A few months earlier, one of them had almost killed me in his car. I was riding shotgun and three students were in the back. We were on our way to the inaugural MOA Summit when we almost got T-boned by another vehicle on the freeway. When we arrived, around 100 men were sitting in the hall and the flaxen-haired crypt keeper of the red pill himself, Rollo Tomassi, was up on stage.

'I am the type of man that other men want to be and other women want to fuck,' he declared. For a millisecond I wondered if this was hell and I had died in the car a few moments ago. Then I remembered that Tomassi had been hanging out with Sartain a lot lately and the lifestyle seemed to be rubbing off. His hair, which had previously been a shade of light grey, had changed colour and grown 40 inches in just a few months. Some members of the ex-Red Pill subreddit were accusing him of wearing a wig, though it was impossible to tell because he always had on a bandana. His biceps had inflated too, thanks to the daily testosterone injections (just like Michael). On social media, he had started posting lots of photos of himself with women who weren't his wife.

Tomassi sometimes showed up at the karaoke room for MOA training at Sartain's behest; it was a chance to impart some boomer red pill wisdom to the students, some of whom were probably still operating under gynocentric social conditioning.

ALPHA FUCKS, BETA BUCKS

*

9.30 p.m. Sam – the young white South African who answered the door – is reclining on the brown leather couch while the others finish getting ready for the club. Martin Scorsese's *Wolf of Wall Street* is playing on a large television suspended midway up the living room wall. The film is a dark comedy based on the memoir of the same name by Jordan Belfort (played in the film by Leonardo DiCaprio), a former Wall Street trader and fast-talking hustler who served twenty-two months in prison for fraud and money laundering. The real-life Belfort is a convicted con artist who ripped off the people who invested in him. Yet the film airily depicts a merry-go-round of sex, drugs and debauchery. In this room at least, the film is not being interpreted as a cautionary tale.

Another student, twenty-five and from Boston, grins when I ask about the woman outside. She stayed over last night, though he doesn't know who brought her back. She is cleaning the pool because the roommates have agreed to ask any woman that comes over to help out with chores. This, the student says, is all part of 'training' them to be in touch with their 'feminine energy' – which I take to be a euphemism for treating women as helpers and servants. 'I appreciate a feminine woman who loves to cook and keep things tidy,' interjects Andreas, the student I've come to collect, who lurches from one of the bedrooms wearing a cobalt blazer over a crisp white cotton shirt with at least four buttons undone. 'How does zis look, guys?' he asks, spreading his long arms. '*Miami Vice!*' yells the student with the protein flask.

'Boom, looking sharp, bro,' says the South African. Andreas is forty-nine and has flown in from Germany to be part of MOA and Vegas Immersion. A single button on his blazer is done up over a well-upholstered paunch and he sports a pair of sunglasses even though the sun went down two hours ago. 'Did you smash last night?' the roommate sitting on the couch asks him. Apparently, it was Andreas who brought the young woman back to the house. He looks uncomfortable and tries to laugh it off. 'Two minutes, guys,' he pleads as he darts back to his room to change into a pair of ripped jeans he purchased especially for Vegas.

*

Sunday is the first night of Vegas Immersion and Marquee is the club of choice. I have plans to meet my three students at 10.15 p.m. inside the Cosmopolitan Hotel and Casino. Andreas and Sam are with me already; we're just waiting for the final student to arrive. Then I will run through the drills for the night and we will make our way to the line. The MOA students are expected to undertake several challenges when we get inside the club. One involves introducing themselves to the VIP hosts and getting some business cards. The hosts are the gatekeepers for things like bottle service tables, which usually cost around $4,000 in a club like Marquee. That's how much the tourists are paying – very often groups of men away on business, eager to flaunt their wealth at the masses in the GA (General Admission). But once you know how to play the game you don't pay anything.

You get to know the VIP host and then you build a social circle with at least a few women in it. You message your host on the day you want to go to the club and you show up flanked by at least five women, and as long as you have followed the process correctly they will give you the VIP table for nothing. The students are being sent out to try and exchange social media contact details with women so they can invite them out to their VIP table on another night. '[The real] currency of the club is girls,' Sartain tells the students. And it's more or less true. If you are lucky enough to show up to the club flanked by half a dozen women, they will often treat you like a VIP. You show up to the table with a bunch of women and document everything for social media. Once you get to one of these expensive tables, people will often assume you must be *somebody*, which is the end goal for a lot of the men who sign up to the programme. It's about leveraging access to VIP events and inner sanctums. Over time, this would (in theory at least) allow them to build a social circle filled with models, celebrities and 'elite' men. Michael Sartain started with nightclub tables too. Now he hosts Maxim parties and gets to hang out with Dan Bilzerian and O. J. Simpson.

Despite paying for a course dedicated to meeting more women, not all of the students seem to enjoy their real-life company. They want to be admired by other men, and women are indispensable to that. Social media is the medium through which they can broadcast their 'high status lifestyle' to a bigger audience. This is the celebrity effect in action; and so long as they follow the tenets of the programme, they may yet avoid the fate that befell Isaac Newton. *'He died a virgin, guys, remember that.'*

*

Some of the other students are at the Cosmopolitan already, waiting for the others to arrive. There are four coaches in total on the programme; each is in charge of three students. We stand and wait amid the rows of slot machines that make the sound of a cash register each time someone pulls the handle. The conversation among the men is slow and desultory at first but picks up as more students arrive. The men share a common Esperanto: part red pill, part entrepreneurial patter, part conspiracy. I catch fragments of it as the men talk among themselves.

'The most expensive woman I ever paid for was my ex-wife.'

...

'Women nowadays only want attention from the most valuable men in the world.'

...

'I'm not going out to meet the person I'm going to meet tonight, I'm going out to meet the person I'm going to meet in ninety days.'

...

'Hard times create strong men, strong men create good times, et cetera – have you heard that one?'

...

ALPHA FUCKS, BETA BUCKS

'I escaped nine-to-five slavery a few years ago. Never going back, bro.'

Once we get inside the nightclub, I take two of my students, Andreas and Sam the South African, over to a bottle service table on the rooftop terrace. My third student, an Indian American software engineer from California, is hiding downstairs in a different section of the club. He's scared I'll make him talk to a woman and he's loading up on drinks. This cat and mouse game will go on for most of the evening.

Sitting at the VIP table next to us are six strict-faced Playboy Playmates whose heads are an explosion of platinum and neon yellow. One of the women I know, and she's been nice enough to let me bring two of the students over. These women are what the students call 'Vegas 10s': thoroughbreds who are filled out in the appropriate places and skinny everywhere else.

Sartain's MOA and Immersion courses are an improvement on the old pickup scene in at least one respect: the students are explicitly told *not* to hit on women in the nightclub or use pickup lines. Instead, Sartain wants them to make friends with women.

In the club, it's my job to bridge the gap between the high-status havers and the high-status seekers. The problem with courses like this one is that men are essentially being taught to view women as prettifying props: ornamentation for their high-status content. Everything must be documented for 'The Gram'. As a case in point, we've been at the table no more than five minutes when Sam starts belligerently asking the women for a photo. 'Hey, girls. Can I get a photo?' he says as he pushes an iPhone into my hands and slides in between two of the women; they promptly squirm out from under the two unsolicited arms he wraps around their lower backs. Some of the students have an unpleasant effect on women, though it has little to do with their physical appearance. It's downstream from the sense of obnoxious entitlement. Once I've taken the photo, Sam begins to complain. 'You've taken a landscape photo, bro,' he says. 'This isn't a regulation MOA photo. Every photo should be 4x5 resolution. This isn't what Michael teaches.' He's paid a lot of money and feels entitled to be treated a certain way. Fortunately he stops calling me bro and I manage not to lose my cool. Maybe this is what happens when you design a course that encourages men to treat people as commodities.

I try to stay on the periphery of it all. I'm here to observe and document, not to be some kind of low-rent dating coach. My role in all of this is not a million miles away from that of a nightclub promoter. I've been asked to take the students to the club and give them a few pointers on how to start a conversation. That's it; though while I've got them under my wing I figure I should try to steer the students in a certain direction. I try to convey the full spectrum of options before them. They can try to improve their social interactions by going down the pickup and red pill route, adopting a phalanx of phoney behaviours to make themselves look 'alpha'. Or they can start viewing the people they are interacting with as human beings. They've been flailing up to now because they've been taught to view people – and women in particular – as means to an end.

They're creepy because they want something; and no amount of masking will stop it from leaking into their interactions.

*

It was time for me to leave Vegas. I hadn't gone out there to save anybody; but I didn't want to participate (inadvertently or otherwise) in making anybody worse either. I was exhausted by the merry-go-round of electric pastel clubs, narcoleptic bedtimes and pay-as-you-go sincerity. They could keep their Lambos, ripped jeans, velvet ropes, red-carpet events, bikini competitions, Playboy playmates, high-status social networks, Facetuned deltoids and Dan Bilzerian. I just wanted to get home and have a nice cup of tea, even if it wouldn't generate a lot of heat on the 'gram.

*

Influential figures in the manosphere complained a lot about the contemporary dating landscape and women's supposedly unrealistic standards. '[The] ugly truth is that *most* women simply don't like *most men* that much and never really did,' wrote Myron Gaines (real name Amrou Fudl), co-host of the *Fresh&Fit* podcast, in his 2023 book *Why Women Deserve Less*. 'Of course, women still like men, just the top-tier ones,' he added.

For Gaines and others in the manosphere, feminism and the sexual revolution were responsible for 'burning' the old social contract that pressured women into getting with 'ordinary' men (and made it nearly impossible to leave them).

Gaines's version of the past is idyllic, a time when 'men and women needed each other, and as a consequence would team up to form families'. Nowadays, by contrast, young women are only interested in pursuing high-status men. Tomassi is of the same opinion. 'Prior to the Sexual Revolution and the millennia leading up to it, social and religious controls were instituted to keep rampant hypergamy in check,' he moaned. Social media apps such as Instagram, TikTok and Snapchat were said to have made women 'delusional' about their dating prospects. 'Gone are the days of boy meets girl, eyes fixed across a crowded high school gym Homecoming dance floor. Gone are the days of meeting your "bride" at church camp. Those are old-order romanticism and ones that we still want to force-fit our new-order reality,' wrote Tomassi.[1]

Social media was accused of 'grossly inflating [women's] egos'.[2] Smartphones had globalised the sexual marketplace and furnished women with a limitless pool of options. As a result, too many women were chasing too few men. Whereas previously men had only had to compete with local rivals – other inhabitants of, say, the same town or village – thanks to social media, women could now hold out for the 'elite' men. According to Tomassi, 'Given the current state of the Global Sexual Marketplace, 80 per cent of men are the *Undesirables*, 20 per cent of men are the *Qualifiers*, and roughly 4.5 per cent [of that 20 per cent] are *High-Value Men*'.[3]

Blue-pilled men were also at fault. The average 'thirsty' guy was accused of stoking women's 'hubristic entitlements' (Tomassi)[4] by liking all of her pictures, dropping heart-eye and fire emojis in the comments below, and sliding into her DMs promising the princess treatment. With validation on tap from these 'simps', 'orbiters' and 'nice guys', was it any wonder that social media had made women – in Gaines's words – 'delusional'?

Of course, the most delusional thing here was the idea that social media was boosting women's self-esteem. Or that the so-called Nice Guys™ of the internet were truly nice. In fact, Instagram has made body image issues worse for one in three girls[5] according to internal Meta research leaked to the *Wall Street Journal*. In one study of teenagers in the UK and the US, more than 40 per cent of Instagram users who felt 'unattractive' said they started to feel that way after using the app.

Meanwhile, a 2022 study of fifty-one countries found that 38 per cent of women had experienced online harassment.[6] Nearly nine in ten of the women had chosen to limit their online activity as a result. Around a third of women (33 per cent) said they had been sexually harassed online, with 33 per cent of women under thirty-five experiencing it (compared to 11 per cent of men under thirty-five).[7] As for dating apps, roughly six in ten women aged between eighteen and thirty-four who used them had been harassed.[8] In Britain, 39 per cent of British women had felt the need to block or report someone.[9] Were the content creators of the manosphere to spend more time listening to women as opposed to riling up an audience of angry and frustrated men, perhaps they would be less inclined to throw around baseless accusations of 'hubristic entitlement'. I doubt it though.

The late black American content creator Kevin Samuels was arguably the pioneer of the dunking on women economy (podcasts and YouTube channels in which women are invited on and publicly humiliated). Samuels, an image consultant and twice-divorced proponent of 'traditional values', was the most recognisable influencer in the black manosphere until his death aged fifty-three in 2022. His go-to knee slapper involved asking women who phoned into his YouTube show (1.4 million subscribers) to rate themselves on a scale of one to ten. He would then put them 'on blast' for having 'unrealistic' standards. Samuels shared many of the red pill's resentments and antipathies. He described unmarried women over the age of thirty-five as 'leftover', and modern women as a 'party of one'.[10] It was Samuels who first popularised the term 'high value man'.

Fresh&Fit hosts Myron Gaines and Walter Weekes have since taken up the late image consultant's mantle. Models and e-girls are regularly invited on to the podcast (the presence of women boosts audience numbers) only to be roasted for everything from their professional credentials ('men don't want a woman who is too educated') to their sexual histories ('promiscuous' women 'belong to the streets'). Female guests are encouraged to input their dating preferences into an online tool called the 'Female Delusion Calculator', a rage-bait gimmick designed to placate an audience of men who feel unfairly overlooked. The waft of desperation is palpable. The purpose of the 'calculator' is to reinforce the idea that women are 'delusional' for having any standards at all.

That a male might feel a pang of insecurity about a woman's previous lovers is at least an intelligible if pointless source of rumination. Yet in the manosphere even domestic pets induce similar feelings of inadequacy. If a woman is considered too selective when inputting her preferences into the Female Delusion Calculator, the website calls her an 'aspiring cat lady' or 'cat enthusiast', expressions of a wider sense of paranoia directed at women's feline companions.

*

Red pill content mills churned out an endless barrage of content that was designed to make women look dumb and convince a male audience that society was turning into a polygynous hellscape. Average men were becoming surplus men, and therefore they needed to buy the expensive courses and programmes that these same masculinity hucksters were usually offering. Sartain was even worried about domestic suicide bombers. 'The problem happens when guys in the US start strapping bombs on their backs like in Iraq,' he told MOA students. 'We aren't there yet – does anybody want to take a guess why that isn't happening? Porn.' It was Sartain's contention that this was 'holding the floor' and preventing the surplus men from blowing things (and themselves) up.

And yet other, ostensibly more serious figures, were repeating a similar message. 'If a polygynous society develops, a small minority of men get all the women,' Jordan Peterson warned on Joe Rogan in 2018.[11]

It added up to a relentless diet of fear porn – designed either to sell courses or make the case for a return to a more traditional society (i.e. a society where constraints were reimposed on women's behaviour).

In the early days of the manosphere, men often stumbled across the pickup forums while looking for tips on what cologne to wear or how to ask someone out. Two decades later, masculinity influencers were warning that even men in ostensibly loving relationships were at risk. 'Women pick a monogamous marriage and they cheat with high-status guys,' Peterson told Rogan in 2018. Justin Waller, a business partner of Andrew Tate and popular masculinity influencer in his own right (and a sometime guest at Donald Trump's Mar-a-Lago resort), told his 1.1 million followers that a woman would only love them until she found a better option. 'You think she won't leave you for that guy who makes a little bit more money? Promise you she will.'

Men are around twice as likely to cheat on a partner as women.[12] Yet rhetoric like this helped to fuel the preoccupation in the manosphere with paternity fraud – i.e. when a man is told (falsely) that a child is biologically his by the child's mother. There was a widespread perception that huge numbers of men were unwittingly raising children that were not their own. Multiple speakers at the 21 Convention claimed that married men were seen as potential 'targets' of paternity fraud by duplicitous women. Meanwhile on social media, Tomassi was calling for the 'Federally mandated DNA paternity testing of all births'.[13] A heightened sense of paranoia about the paternity of one's children was downstream from the red pill trope that women were biologically programmed to seek out 'alpha sperm' behind the back of her 'beta provider' husband. In 2018, Jordan Peterson claimed that paternity fraud was 'more common than anybody suspected'.[14] It was not unusual in the manosphere to hear the claim that between 10 and 30 per cent of children were being raised by men who were unaware they were not the biological father.

Yet despite the ubiquity of such eye-catching figures, cases of misattributed paternity are exceedingly rare. A 1999 study found the extent of paternity discrepancy in the UK to be just 1.6 per cent.[15] Meanwhile the most reliable study for North America has put the non-paternity rate at between 1 and 3 per cent.

The 30 per cent figure appears to have originated from a transcript of a small symposium on the ethics of artificial insemination that was carried out in a town in south-east England in 1972. The results from the study were never published so the method of testing and population sample were not independently verified, though one participant in the symposium is reported to have described the sample as 'highly biased'.[16] Moreover, DNA techniques in the early 1970s were unsophisticated compared to DNA profiling as we know it today, which wasn't developed until the 1980s. A 2016 review of the scientific literature found a much lower incidence of misattributed paternity than the figures commonly cited in the manosphere. The authors of the review were dismissive of the idea that women cheat to secure the best genes for their offspring. 'The observed low EPP [extra-pair paternity] rates challenge the idea that women routinely "shop around" for good genes by engaging in extra-pair copulations... Human EPP rates have stayed near constant at around 1 per cent across several human societies over the past several hundred years.'[17]

Not that this has prevented the exaggerated figure from taking on a life of its own. 'Talkback radio gave [the 30 per cent figure] a new lease of life, and so has the internet,'[18] concluded the Australian professor Michael Gilding in a 2011 article which looked at the issue.

Zombie statistics like this one are useful to the manosphere for the patina of scientific credibility they bestow on their theories about female behaviour.[19] If large numbers of men are being 'cuckolded'[20] by duplicitous women, then is it not 'proof' that women are biologically programmed to seek out alpha males? Does it not show just how disastrous women's unrestrained 'hypergamy' has been for western society? After all, it's 'just science, bro'.

Tomassi calls it 'Alpha Fucks, Beta Bucks' (AF/BB) – the idea that a woman locks down a 'beta' provider for his American Express Gold Card and then has an affair with a dominant alpha during the most fertile phase of her menstrual cycle. She wants to fuck the 'hot guy at the foam party in Cancun', as Tomassi puts it, and then find a safe and reliable beta to help bring up the child. The sidebar on the Red

Pill subreddit lays out AF/BB in characteristically crude and misogynistic language:

> We all know that bitches have a dualistic mating strategy: they want the Jerkboy Alpha Sperm Donor to squirt a strong baby inside them, and they want a Dependable Beta Money Dispenser to foot the bill for their IKEA nesting instincts.

AF/BB is parasitic on a theory from evolutionary psychology called the dual mating hypothesis. It posits that, whereas men are 'hard-wired' to seek out as many sexual partners as possible, women want to be inseminated with superior genes. The dual mating hypothesis has largely been abandoned by mainstream evolutionary psychology: recent research has failed to replicate effects supporting the theory.[21] Professor David Buss, a highly respected figure in the field, notes in a 2019 paper that 'empirical support for the hypothesized dual mating function of women's short-term mating is weak or mixed'.[22]

Not that this has stopped masculinist influencers from presenting AF/BB as settled science. Jordan Peterson has said that it is a 'factual biological claim' that women 'gerrymander' monogamy by having affairs.[23] Tomassi acknowledges the growing scientific scepticism of the mainstream towards the dual mating hypothesis; however, he blames this on a conspiracy among scientists and academics. 'Most evolutionary psychologists' are, he says, 'try[ing] not to upset the Gynocentric academia that looms over their tenure'.[24] In other words, the dual mating hypothesis is failing to replicate not because it jars with reality, but because researchers are afraid to reveal the 'unflattering truth about female nature'.[25]

It was par for the course. Unsettling new evidence was ignored in favour of theories that were powered by little more than anecdotes, cherry-picked data and 'just so' stories. The same men liked to self-servingly contrast their own rationality with the purported whimsy and emotion of women. They prided themselves on possessing an absolute fealty to the facts – and then built theories about women based on their subjective feelings.

12

SURPLUS MEN

Rage was simmering away below the surface. Rage at feminists for supposedly emasculating men. Rage at society for being insufficiently deferential to alphas. Rage at women for the careers they were prioritising instead of being kept little wives, subservient and agreeable. Rage at social media for giving women an expanded suite of romantic options – and rage at women for choosing the wrong men.

A small portion of this fury was directed at men who inhabited the same masculinist ecosystem, though women ultimately bore the brunt of that too. Despite a preponderance of slick marketing materials promising earth-shattering results, the pickup industry had failed to deliver for most of those who invested time and money in it. Men were dropping thousands of dollars on workshops and were still no closer to having a girlfriend than when they started. The industry was overrun with opportunists charging eye-watering sums for minimal effort boot camps and other pointless add-on products. It didn't take any special skill to take men out to a nightclub and point women out for them to approach. The instructors portrayed themselves as living the playboy lifestyle and yet the footage they uploaded to YouTube (showing their audacious attempts at getting women's phone numbers in nightclubs, malls and coffee shops) was occasionally faked and always selectively edited. Some pickup companies were even caught using £200 escorts in their videos. On the programmes themselves, clients who demonstrated any sort of critical thinking or failed to behave with sufficient deference towards instructors were treated derisively and accused of having 'limiting beliefs' and a 'victim mindset'. Those who challenged the prevailing dogmas at live events were berated in front of an unctuous audience that refused to see its own source of hope taken away. The biggest pickup companies resembled cults.

What the multi-million-dollar pickup industry did possess within its ranks was a preponderance of men who were highly skilled at sales and marketing and restrained by few ethical considerations. Sex was a game and women were interchangeable commodities: fleshy objects for exploitation and domination. The seduction gurus had learned that charisma and authority were forms of social jiu-jitsu that nearly always triumphed over logic or reason. They became adept at toying with people's emotions. Perhaps unsurprisingly, the techniques they used on women were soon turned on the men who were asking for help. They cheated their clients like they cheated on women, sometimes using the same techniques. They negged the men (lowering their self-esteem) before aggressively segueing into their high-pressure sales pitch. ('Look at you, you're not doing anything with your life; women don't respect you; you need this product more than anyone – though you'd better hurry because it's available for a limited time.') As Minnie Lane had put it, 'Anything that convinces you that you've got a problem, and then positions itself as the solution to your problem, is going to be attractive.'

The clients themselves desperately wanted to believe. That they could find the woman of their dreams; that the products they were spending huge amounts of money on would 'fix' them; that they could acquire any woman with the correct set of moves or by demonstrating enough 'value'.

Popular culture had become less accommodating of the industry over time. But anti-pickup artist sentiment was also growing among a demographic of men who had initially been warm to the idea of manipulating women into bed. Men had taken 'programme after programme and read book after book, and watched YouTube video after YouTube video, and they found it doesn't really work and they still don't have a supermodel,' said Zan Perrion, one of the original pickup artists who featured in *The Game*. Perrion believed that disillusionment with the seduction industry helped to birth some of the more strident forms of male resentment we hear about today. 'You see how the conversation [has] become more aggressive, which is kind of the red pill,' he told me when we chatted in the summer of 2023.

Several *anti*-pickup artist websites appeared on the internet in the late 2000s and early 2010s. The most prominent of these, PUAHate.com, was created in 2009 by a disillusioned former student of Real Social Dynamics. The website claimed to be at 'the forefront of the anti-pickup-artist movement'; it dedicated an entire page to 'exposing' the tips and tricks that pickup artists were using to 'deceive men and profit from them'. Users frequented a sub-forum of the site – entitled 'Bash the Scene' – to vent and complain about being 'scammed' and 'ripped off' by the pickup companies. They would regularly make fun of well-known PUAs and their lucrative hustles. Anybody who claimed to have had any kind of success with pickup was treated with derision. The tone of the website was bitter and abrasive and various bigotries were on display. But so was humour – and the pickup artists, with their preposterous clothing and stilted behaviours, were worthy targets.

Users would sometimes show up on the forum with 'genuine questions' as to how they might improve their fortunes with women. Pickup hadn't worked and it was good to vent about it; but they were still in the dark about how to become more attractive to women. That led to the creation of a sub-forum called 'Shitty Advice'. It was designated as a place where users could share dating advice – advice that should under no circumstances be derived from seduction industry hustlers. Yet it didn't take long for the forum to be subsumed under a misanthropic ooze of trolling and bullying and self-pitying complaints by users about how grotesque and unfuckable they were. Drawing on their negative experiences with pickup, most posters rejected the notion that personality or game were factors when it came to attracting a sexual or romantic partner. Instead, everything about the process of courtship and intimate relations was viewed as more or less genetically pre-determined.

Initially, pickup artists had been the main targets of opprobrium on PUAhate.com; however, blame soon shifted on to women. Forum users marinated in rigid, pseudo-scientific theories that purported to explain female sexuality, many of them parasitic on the red pill. 'Hypergamy is rampant in my social circle,' wrote one PUAhate.com user. 'What's the consensus? Are men under 6'2" considered genetic trash?' asked another. One user wondered: 'Will I ever beat being a sub-8 male?'

Users would sometimes discuss 'looksmaxxing', a synonym for a male attempting to boost his SMV through changes to his physical appearance. There were radically different degrees to which a person could looksmaxx, from the relatively benign to the risky and expensive. Though the word isn't typically used, women are essentially expected to looksmaxx for much of their lives – to wear make-up, maintain their 'figure', and be appropriately feminine. However the terrain was relatively new for a lot of men. Basic forms of looksmaxxing could include lifting weights, growing facial hair or simply getting better clothes and a more relevant haircut. 'Any experts on teeth whitening here?' asked one PUAhate.com user on Christmas Day 2013. Others sought recommendations for affordable plastic surgeons, or uploaded photos of their anatomy and discussed radical interventions like leg lengthening, jaw surgery or going under the knife for a comprehensive physical revamp known as the 'male model package'.

Some misogynist incels were afflicted with a deep sense of self-loathing that nothing in their lives had been able to alleviate. Resigned to the idea that it was 'over' for them as far as dating was concerned, they were uninterested in looksmaxxing. By contrast, those who hoped to 'ascend' out of the community were frequently wedded to a singular aesthetic vision: they hoped, via surgeries, to one day become the perfect physical specimen – or at least a convincing replica of the imagined genetic ideal. They had convinced themselves that this was what women wanted; and they longed to be wanted, even by the people they hated.

*

Conversations within the manosphere frequently slipped into the language of social Darwinism and market economics. The so-called sexual marketplace was a winner-takes-all world whose distribution curve was said to follow the 80/20 rule (the so-called Pareto principle). A majority (80 per cent) of women were purportedly hooking up with a minority (20 per cent, sometimes 10 per cent, at other times less) of high-status alpha males. This left the remaining 80 per cent of betas competing for just 20 per cent of women. These were the surplus men that Michael Sartain had talked about, the sexual no-hopers left on the shelf by women's fickle desire for the best genetic material for their offspring. Unlike the alpha, who was still valued for his superior genes, according to manosphere logic the beta was surplus to requirements. The modern career woman had her own money; she didn't need a 'provider' to support her. A modern man had to bring something else to the table — a frightening prospect for a lot of the men in the manosphere and beyond.

Followers of the red pill typically subscribed to a theory called 'LMS'. This was the idea that looks, money and status (a variation of this is *money, muscles and game*) were the things women looked for in a partner. The red pill treated a man's SMV as malleable: i.e. he could boost it by making more money, pumping iron at the gym, mimicking the alpha (learning game), or elevating his social status. Social media was said to have made status more important relative to the other attributes: men who signed up for MOA were encouraged to believe that they could join the 'sexual elite' if they created a 'celebrity aura' on social media.

Despite their similarities, there were important differences between the black pill and the red pill. Followers of the black pill tended to be fatalistic about their chances of boosting their SMV (which was determined by genetics). Pickup artistry was little more than a 'cope' — a futile coping strategy. Women primarily cared about a man's height (over six foot tall), his body type (wide shoulders, V-shaped torso) and his ethnicity (the acronym 'JBW', or Just Be White, was a common reference to the supposed sexual advantages enjoyed by white men). Most important was a man's face. Bodybuilding wouldn't help you if your bone structure was too feminine or your carnal tilt too long. A 'sub-5' face meant that it was 'over' for you as far as sex and relationships were concerned.

Followers of the black pill referred to good-looking men as 'Chads' (their version of the alpha male). Discussions on incel forums frequently revolved around the facial aesthetics of celebrities and male models. The archetypal Chad was said to be a genetic superior who lived life on easy mode. In college, Chad was usually the 'jock' or quarterback – the popular guy who was good at sports and got all the girls. He had learned at an early age that he could 'elicit near-universal positive female sexual attention at will'.[1] High SMV women meanwhile were referred to as 'Stacies'; less desirable women as 'Beckies'. Women in general were referred to as 'femoids' or 'foids' (abbreviations for 'female humanoid'). Followers of the black pill mostly refer to themselves as 'incels', shorthand for involuntary celibates. Although the topic of sex comes up a lot on misogynistic incel forums, it is often a proxy for love and affection: many incels reject the idea of using sex workers because they say they want to be loved and admired by a woman.

The black pill was a term that was coined in the early 2010s by the author of a blog called 'Omega Virgin Revolt'. He wanted to distinguish his own anti-feminist beliefs from the red pill. He didn't object to the red pill's lowly estimation of women. But he was opposed to the concept of 'game' because he didn't believe it worked. Instead, the author encouraged men to abstain from women altogether (presumably there wasn't always much choice in the matter). If the blue pill was synonymous with ignorance and the red pill about understanding the matrix to manipulate it, the black pill was the decision to relinquish hope altogether. Self-improvement was replaced by nihilism, self-loathing and virulent misogyny. Men often discovered the red pill via pickup or YouTube. Sometimes they did what I had done back in 2005: they typed 'How to find a girlfriend?' into a search engine and stumbled across a bewildering array of forums. Maybe they wanted a few pointers – advice other than 'just be yourself'. But what followed was a form of radicalisation. The world slowly began to change as they consumed more red pill content. They 'learned' that relations between the sexes were dictated by a rigid sexual hierarchy; that women were emotional creatures with the mental capacity of children; and that the alpha was the only man that women truly wanted. Each new revelation was accompanied by some sciencey-sounding theory.

The final capsule – the black pill – was usually swallowed later, when the red pill had thrown up more questions than it answered; when the pickup lines, attempts at 'frame control' and being 'alpha' had repelled women even more. Some men walked away from the manosphere at this point, acknowledging that the theories had withered on contact with reality. Some persevered, the few successes they did have reinforcing in their minds the essential soundness of the ideas. Others, indoctrinated in social-Darwinian thinking about relations between the sexes via 'game', succumbed to the black pill. It wasn't that red pill theories about women were necessarily wrong. It was that there must be something wrong with *them*. They were condemned to reside at the bottom of the male dominance hierarchy because they were too ugly and unfuckable. Yet they had no intention of transcending or subverting the system of domination. They still wanted to believe much of what the red pill had taught them. After all, women were still beneath them. They wore the chains in the hope that someday they might bequeath them to others.

*

Data from some of the world's biggest online dating apps seemed initially to lend weight to the idea, ubiquitous in the manosphere, that women were sexually interested in a small cohort of men. On the dating app Tinder, where potential romantic prospects are mostly judged on how well they present themselves in a photo, one study found that a man of average attractiveness can expect to be liked by less than 1 per cent of women.[2] The study found that men 'liked' more than 60 per cent of the female profiles they viewed, whereas women 'liked' only 4.5 per cent of male profiles.[3]

It was a statistic that quickly travelled around the internet, boosted by those eager to fling themselves on any piece of evidence which cast doubt on the prudence of granting women the same sexual freedoms as men. The data was quickly transposed to the offline world and cited as 'proof' that trouble was brewing.

Predictably enough, a closer inspection of the data revealed that much of the politically motivated doom-mongering was misplaced. According to the study of user activity on Tinder, while women on the app did tend to rate men more poorly in terms of their looks, they were also more likely to message the poorly rated men. By contrast, men tended to rate women better in terms of looks, but a majority were only messaging the top third of women. This was a reversal of the much-trumpeted 80/20 rule, whereby 80 per cent of men were supposedly messaging 20 per cent of women.

Parallel to the apocalyptic data that was being touted, there was growing chatter about a sex 'crisis' supposedly afflicting young men. Research published by the national General Social Survey (GSS) in 2019 found that 28 per cent of American men under thirty hadn't had sex in the previous twelve months. It attributed the increase to screen time, job insecurity and more people living with their parents.[4] The manosphere ignored this disclaimer (of course) and blamed the figures on Chads and alpha males monopolising all the women. American men were said to be in a 'sex recession'. Another apparent decline in the number of Americans having sex in 2021 led commentators to ask whether the sex recession was turning into a sex depression.[5] Similarly, a 2022 Pew Research study found[6] that, among American men under thirty, 63 per cent described themselves as single, more than double that of women in the same age bracket; though women appeared to be catching up with men: in the 2021 data, young women reported the highest level of celibacy since 1989. Meanwhile, a 2019 study of 34,000 Britons aged between sixteen and forty-four found that couples were having less sex than in the previous two decades. Professor Kaye Wellings, the study's lead author, told me that gender equality might be one of the factors behind the apparent drop.

'There was a time when women were taught to lie back and think of England. And so they satisfied male urges to please their partner, even if they didn't feel like sex themselves,' Wellings told me when we talked over the phone. 'In general, men have a desire for more sex than women. If it's up to just the men, there would be a greater frequency. And if it's up to the women, there might be less frequency but higher quality [sex].' The study's gender split appeared to support Wellings' point, with half of British women compared to almost two-thirds of men saying they wanted more sex.

Every age cohort experienced a drop in sexual activity during the Covid-19 pandemic, which is hardly surprising. On average, young women were more inclined to stay at home during 2020–21 than young men, perhaps because men tend on average to be bigger risk takers than women.[7] Yet the GSS data for 2023, which revealed that levels of sexual activity among young Americans – both men and women – reached *highs* not seen in a quarter of a century, was widely ignored in the manosphere. They were powerfully incentivised to perpetuate the idea that unrestrained 'hypergamy' was leading society over the abyss. Some wanted to portray women's sexual freedoms as the problem: as a force which needed to be reined in to prevent a backlash by angry and frustrated young men. Others wanted to sell their self-improvement courses: *'pay me and you too can be an alpha male',* etc. If high-status men were not shagging all the women, then it became harder to capitalise on the sexual anxieties of the surplus men. So the gurus continued to beat a familiar drum, warning their impressionable male audiences that it was effectively over for them, romantically speaking, unless they took decisive action to become an alpha male. And there happened to be a programme or course designed for a guy just like them. All they had to do was punch in their credit card details and be prepared to do whatever their instructor told them. It was a crazy world out there and as a man you could easily be left behind. Fortunately, your favourite masculinity influencer had a life raft with some space left on it – just for a few of you.

*

The dehumanising rhetoric of the incel forums had a tendency to spill offline. 'I treat girls at my work with utter disrespect,' wrote one poster on PUAhate.com. Another forum user boasted of physically harassing people who made him feel jealous and resentful. He trailed several couples from his local Starbucks in the college town of Isla Vista in Santa Barbara County, California, splashing them with coffee. In his diary he fantasised about how 'sweet and just it would be to kill every single young couple at my college or in Isla Vista'. While at a house party, the 22-year-old made a failed attempt to push a group of women off a ledge because they refused to talk to him. 'The girls don't flock to the gentlemen. They flock to the alpha male,' he complained bitterly.

Elliot Rodger didn't identify as an incel but he considered PUAHate.com to be a community of like-minded men. He was also making tentative plans to go on the offensive. 'If we can't solve our problems we must DESTROY our problems,' he wrote on PUAhate.com in November 2013. Rodger egged on other users, urging them to 'overthrow this oppressive feminist system' and 'start envisioning a world where WOMEN FEAR YOU'. He planned his 'day of retribution' for at least a year, purchasing handguns and booking sessions at a local shooting range. 'After I picked up the handgun, I brought it back to my room and felt a new sense of power,' he wrote. 'I was now armed. *Who's the alpha male now, bitches?* I thought to myself, regarding all of the girls who've looked down on me in the past.'

The spoiled English American son of a Hollywood filmmaker, Rodger believed himself to be the 'supreme gentleman', cruelly overlooked by women in favour of 'obnoxious brutes'. As a young boy, Rodger had attended a fee-paying all boys school in West Sussex, England. Aged five, the family had relocated to an upscale neighbourhood in Los Angeles. He was given a $40,000 BMW and used his social media accounts to show off a luxurious lifestyle of first-class travel, limousines and red-carpet events. Yet it wasn't enough for Rodger: he harboured dreams of becoming even wealthier, seeing money as a way to elevate himself above over people. He obsessively played the lottery, on one occasion spending $700 on tickets. He believed that if he became a 'young multi-millionaire' then women would 'finally see me as the supreme man that I'm meant to be'. When his numbers failed to come up, he 'sank into one of the worst depressions of my life... because I failed to win the lottery jackpot that would enable me to rise above them ALL'.

For Rodger, a superior man was a sexually successful man. Material wealth had conferred on him certain status objects – and adulation from women was supposed to follow. 'These sunglasses here are $300, Giorgio Armani,' Rodger boasted in one video. 'I have a nice car, a BMW. Well, nicer than 90 per cent of the people in my college,' he cooed. 'And yet you girls, you never give me a chance.'

Women were the most important status symbol of all. Yet at twenty-two years old, Elliot Rodger was still a virgin – he hadn't even kissed a girl.

When he was seven, his parents divorced. A year later, his father married a Moroccan-born French actress. Though he would ultimately make plans to murder his stepmother, Rodger had initially approved of his father's 'acquisition' of a new girlfriend so soon after the divorce. 'I subconsciously held him in higher regard,' he wrote. 'It is very interesting how this phenomenon works... that males who can easily find female mates garner more respect from their fellow men.'

Whiteness and blondness were especially strong markers of status and prestige for Rodger, the biracial son of a British father and a Malaysian Chinese mother. 'I always envied and admired blonde-haired people,' he wrote in his 141-page manifesto. White girls, he said, are the 'only girls I'm attracted to, especially the blondes'. And yet not only were they denying Rodger – the self-proclaimed 'supreme gentleman' – what he believed he was entitled to, but they were having sex with 'unworthy' men instead. When his roommates invited over a young black friend of theirs – a friend who bragged about losing his virginity to a white girl – Rodger was consumed with racial anxiety. 'How could an inferior, ugly black boy be able to get a white girl and not me?' he seethed. 'I am beautiful, and I am half white myself. I am descended from British aristocracy. He is descended from slaves.' For Rodger, the episode was proof of 'how ridiculous the female gender is'.

*

'To all those girls I've desired so much, you will finally see that I am the superior one, the true alpha male.'[8]

Rodger was recording the explanatory video from behind the wheel of his black BMW coupé, his face bathed in the late afternoon California sunshine. In the video, which he would title 'Elliot Rodger's Retribution' and upload to his YouTube channel the following day, 23 May 2014, Rodger recounted his isolation and sexual frustration and alluded to plans for revenge. 'I don't know why you girls aren't attracted to me, but I will punish you for it,' he said. By the time the video appeared online, Rodger had stabbed to death his two roommates, Weihan Wang and Cheng Hong, and a friend, George Chen, ambushing them separately as they entered the shared apartment building. He'd changed into a clean set of clothes, gone to Starbucks and calmly ordered a triple-vanilla latte. He then emailed a 107,000-word autobiographical manifesto, 'My Twisted World: The Story of Elliot Rodger', to thirty-four people including family members, acquaintances, professors and mental health providers. In the document, which Rodger posted to PUAhate.com, he accused the world of failing to provide 'the beautiful girlfriend I know I deserve'. The manifesto also betrayed Rodger's terroristic intent. He declared a 'war on women' and wrote that 'I cannot kill every single female on earth, but I can deliver a devastating blow that will shake all of them to the core of their wicked hearts.'

Rodger arrived at the Alpha Phi sorority house near the UCSB campus just minutes after sending out the mass email. He chose the location because it contained the 'stuck-up blonde sluts' that Rodger had 'always desired but was never able to have'. They represented everything he hated about women, and his thwarted sense of entitlement had curdled into murderous rage. 'If I can't have you girls, I will destroy you,' he had said in the video.[9]

Rodger pounded on the front door of the sorority house when he arrived. He banged for several minutes but nobody came. He then went back to his vehicle before spotting three female students. Rodger edged his car towards them. Assuming it was someone who wanted directions, the three women turned around, only for Rodger to pull out a pistol and start firing. Veronica Weiss, nineteen, and Katherine Cooper, twenty-two, would both die from multiple gunshot wounds. Another young woman, Bianca de Kock, was severely wounded but would survive.

Rodger then made his way eastbound and through a popular night spot. He fired a single round into an unoccupied coffee shop and six shots into a Deli, one of which struck Christopher Michaels-Martinez, puncturing his liver and the right ventricle of his heart. The twenty-year-old was the last person Rodger was able to kill, though he would inflict further injuries on pedestrians, cyclists and skateboarders with the gun and by ramming them with his car. Witnesses who saw Rodger that evening described him as having a 'creepy laugh' or 'a little grin'.[10] Following a brief gun battle with the police, Rodger struck a male cyclist before shooting himself in the head, his black BMW careening into another vehicle and coming to a stop. During the eight-minute rampage, Elliot Rodger had murdered six people and injured fourteen others. The victims were all students at UCSB. When they searched his vehicle, law enforcement officers found the two hunting knives used in the apartment murders, three 9mm semi-automatic pistols, six empty ten-round magazines and 548 live rounds of ammunition. The firearms had all been legally purchased at commercial gun shops.

*

The Santa Barbara killings of May 2014 brought widespread media attention to the misogynist incel community. The community's most popular websites were sluthate.com, lookism.net, Looksmax.org, incels.co, incels.me, love-shy.com, as well as the subreddits r/braincels and r/ForeverAlone. Misogynist incels also posted on unmoderated boards such as 4chan and 8chan. Reddit shut down[11] its biggest incel forum (r/Incels, which had 41,000 members) in November 2017 after it had become a repository for misogynistic abuse, rape threats and the glorification of violence against women and sexually active people. Several years later, a disturbing overlap was uncovered between misogynist incel communities and a website linked with at least 100 suicides. The website was run by two self-identified incels who also moderated several misogynistic incel forums, where suicidal ideation was not uncommon. Users of the forums who uploaded photos of themselves were often encouraged to 'rope' (i.e. commit suicide by hanging) – sometimes flippantly, sometimes not. A 2019 survey of the website incels.co – one of the forums linked with the notorious suicide website – found that 67.5 per cent of users had at some point considered suicide.[12]

Following the Isla Vista killings, some users of PUAHate.com posted tributes to the killer, hailing 'Saint Elliot Rodger'. When it was reported in the media that Rodger had been an active user of the website, it was swiftly shut down for 'maintenance', never to be seen again. However new incel forums, ostensibly set up as support groups for men, usually sprang up soon after a popular site had been banned or taken down. Websites such as sluthate.com, which replaced PUAHate.com, no longer bothered to conceal their misogyny behind anti-pickup artist rhetoric.

Since 2014, multiple perpetrators of mass violence have referenced the Santa Barbara killer.[13] In April 2018, a 25-year-old misogynist incel named Alek Minassian murdered ten people (eight of whom were women) by driving a van down a crowded street in Toronto, Canada. Prior to carrying out the attacks, Minassian had posted a grandiose mission statement to Facebook announcing the start of the 'incel rebellion' and paying homage to the 'supreme gentleman Elliot Rodger'. The Toronto van killer also posted to 4chan calling for a 'beta uprising' that would overthrow the 'Chads and Stacies'.

The Toronto van attacks were the second deadliest mass killings in Canada's recent history. The deadliest, which occurred in 1989, was similarly motivated by frenzied misogyny. On 6 December of that year, fourteen female engineering students were murdered at Montreal's École Polytechnique by a rifle-wielding killer who wrote in the page-long suicide note that he was 'fighting feminism'. 25-year-old Marc Lépine had targeted the engineering school deliberately because he didn't believe that women should be allowed to become engineers. 'Feminists have always enraged me,' wrote Lépine. 'I have decided to send the feminists, who have always ruined my life, to their Maker.'

Since 2009, there have been more than ten mass killings committed by individuals who identify as part of the incel community or sympathise with it. In 2021, a 22-year-old man killed his mother and fatally shot four others, including a three-year-old girl, in the UK town of Plymouth.[14] Jake Davison had previously used misogynist incel forums to rant about single mothers, his own mother, and his inability to find a girlfriend, though he claimed not to be an incel himself.

Post Isla Vista, incel killers have frequently mentioned Elliot Rodger in material they have left behind. On 1 October 2015, a 26-year-old college student named Chris Harper-Mercer killed nine people, himself, and injured eight others at the Umpqua Community College in Oregon. He modelled his manifesto on Rodger's and mentioned him four times in it, praising him as a 'god'. Five days prior to murdering seventeen students and staffers and injuring seventeen others in Parkland, Florida, on Valentine's Day 2018, nineteen-year-old Nikolas Cruz had posted that 'Elliot Rodger will not be forgotten.' (Cruz had also searched 'how to get a girlfriend'.) In September 2018, Scott Beierle, a forty-year-old army veteran, walked into a hot yoga studio in Tallahassee, Florida, and shot and killed two women and then himself. Beierle, who had previously been arrested for grabbing and harassing women, had uploaded a video to YouTube entitled 'The Rebirth of My Misogynism' in which he praised Elliot Rodger and claimed to have hated women since eighth grade.

Some misogynist incels have a term of reverence for this type of killing spree. They call it 'Going ER', a play on Rodger's initials. Prior to Isla Vista, however, 'Going Sodini' was the preferred shorthand for community-approved mass murder. George Sodini, a 48-year-old IT professional, had murdered three women in Collier Township, Pennsylvania, in 2009. At 8 p.m. on Tuesday 4 August, Sodini, dressed in all black, had walked into a women's aerobics class, turned off the lights, pulled out two handguns from a duffel bag and opened fire, spraying fifty-two bullets in the darkened room as screams filled the gymnasium. Twelve women were hit. Three women – Elizabeth Gannon, forty-nine, Heidi Overmier, forty-six, and Jody Billingsley, thirty-seven – were killed and nine others were left seriously injured.[15] Sodini put the fifty-third bullet in his own head.

Reclusive, socially isolated and resentful at women for turning down his romantic and sexual overtures, Sodini had plotted his revenge for at least a year, deliberately targeting the Latin Impact aerobics class at the LA Fitness gym because he held all women responsible for his romantic failures. 'Girls and women don't even give me a second look ANYWHERE,' he complained in an online journal alongside other furious and self-pitying rants. 'There is something BLATANTLY wrong with me that NO goddam person will tell me what it is,' Sodini wrote. His view of relationships was transactional and formulaic. He believed that he had done everything 'right' but to no avail: he hadn't had a girlfriend since 1984 and had not had sex since 1990, when he was twenty-nine. 'I dress good, am clean-shaven, bathe, touch of cologne, yet 30 million women rejected me over an 18- or 25-year period. That is how I see it. Thirty million is my rough guesstimate of how many desirable single women there are.'

A year prior to the killings, Sodini had turned to the pickup industry for help. He attended a three-day workshop by self-proclaimed dating expert R. Don Steele (real name John J. White), the author of a 1987 book entitled *How to Date Young Women: For Men Over 35*. Steele, sixty-nine years old and married to a woman thirty-four years his junior, had described women over thirty as 'bitter' and[16] claimed that 'women need men to take charge'. Sodini, a fan of Steele's book, also liked them young: he had researched age of consent laws and wrote that he was looking for a woman at least ten or twenty years younger than himself. He described the 'young girls' who frequented his local gym as looking 'so beautiful as to not be human, very edible'.

Videos of the workshop show Sodini wearing a smart shirt and sitting near the back of the seminar room as the white-haired dating guru holds court. At one point, Steele can be seen writing 'NICE GUY MUST DIE' on a white board and telling the men that their real 'problem' is they are 'too nice' to women, and that women don't respect it. The most chilling moment in the clip occurs when Sodini comes into shot again as Steele encourages the men to make themselves memorable to women. 'Make her remember your name,' he tells them as Sodini looks on, listening intently.

There is no evidence that Steele promoted any form of violence during the seminar. Nor, as far as we know, did he have any direct contact with Sodini outside of the three-day event. By the time he attended the workshop, Sodini was already buying guns and ammunition and scoping out the fitness centre for what he described in his diary as an 'exit plan'. The 'nice guy' had already died (if he ever existed) without the help of any wince-inducing dating coach who wore a red tie as a 'phallic symbol'. Sodini knew there was something 'blatantly wrong' with him. Which was probably why women kept on telling him what a 'nice guy' he was (which he complained bitterly about in his journal). For any woman who had the misfortune to cross Sodini's path, a few kindly words of reassurance were probably a way of tiptoeing around the lights of volatility that were flickering away behind the eyeballs. Better to let him down gently. Safer to stroke the ego of a man like that while quickly working out one's own exit strategy.

*

Elliot Rodger had done an internet search for George Sodini in the months leading up to his own attack. Like Sodini, Rodger had taken a brief interest in the seduction community. When the police searched Rodger's disordered apartment following the murders, they discovered a copy of *The Art of Seduction,* a book by the self-help author Robert Greene. There is nothing in the book that encourages violence against women; it is merely a compendium of 'seductive' male archetypes. Yet the book was on the recommended reading lists of a number of pickup artist websites. This, as well as the fact that Rodger was an active member of an *anti*-pickup artist forum, suggests at least some familiarity with the subculture. Sodini and Rodger were also reciting sentiments that were common in red pill and pickup artist spaces. Rodger couched his misogyny in pseudo-scientific rationalisations about female nature. He scolded women for being 'incapable of having morals or thinking rationally'. He said that women having the right to choose their own partners could 'hinder the advancement of humanity', asserting that 'civilized men of intelligence' should decide whom women could mate with. For Sodini, women were status objects, commodities that reaffirmed a man's sense of his own masculinity. 'A man needs a woman for confidence,' Sodini wrote. He also expressed racist anxieties about black men dating young white 'hoes'.

Some in the pickup artist community and the wider culturally conservative ecosystem responded to incel violence by suggesting that the killers had acted the way they did because women wouldn't give them sex. Responding to the Isla Vista murders, Roosh V suggested that such mass killings were 'inevitable' unless men were able to secure access to women's bodies through manipulation or the exploitation of economic disparities. 'Until you give men like Rodger a way to have sex, either by encouraging them to learn game, seek out a Thai wife, or engage in legalised prostitution... it's inevitable for another massacre to occur,' he wrote. Following the Toronto van attack, Robin Hanson, a conservative economist and professor at George Mason University, floated the idea that sex could be 'directly redistributed' to involuntary celibates on the basis that they 'suffer to a similar degree as those with low income'.[17]

Meanwhile, in a column for the *New York Times*, the conservative commentator Ross Douthat mulled whether such homicidal impulses would disappear if men's libidinal urges were satiated with easy access to prostitutes and sex robots.[18] The Toronto attack prompted Jordan Peterson to pontificate about 'enforced monogamy' as a potential solution to keeping lonely and disgruntled men from unleashing carnage. 'He was angry at God because women were rejecting him,' Peterson said of Minassian. 'The cure for that is enforced monogamy. That's actually why monogamy emerges.' Following a public backlash, Peterson wrote a rejoinder to his 'motivated critics',[19] clarifying that he did not believe in the 'arbitrary dealing out of damsels to incels'. Instead, quoting from a comment on Reddit by one of his fans, he said that he had merely been suggesting a 'socially-promoted, culturally-inculcated' monogamy. In his own words, Peterson added that the 'dangerousness of frustrated young men (even if that frustration stems from their own incompetence) has to be regulated socially' and that 'tilting most societies towards monogamy' was the best way to do it.

Despite Peterson's attempts at clarification, he was guilty of what the late journalist Christopher Hitchens once called the moral offence of euphemism. Peterson was notably vague about what 'culturally inculcated' monogamy would entail. Nor were readers any the wiser about how society might be 'tilted' in that direction. Judging by Peterson's various public statements, it didn't seem unreasonable to assume that he was hinting at certain 'enforced' restrictions on women's behaviour. Peterson has said it isn't 'obvious to him' that the liberalisation of divorce laws had been in everyone's best interest;[20] that the advent of the contraceptive pill has led to the 'pornographication of society';[21] and that it was too early to tell if men and women could share the same workspace. He also described abortion as 'morally wrong', 'profoundly undesirable' and a procedure undertaken by women who had 'made a lot of very serious moral errors'.[22]

The idea that a more tightly enforced culture of monogamy would have prevented any of the recent incel killings should be treated with scepticism. It overlooks the fact that huge numbers of women are killed every year by their intimate partners. Analysis by the Centers for Disease Control and Prevention (CDC) in 2015 found that, in the United States between the years 2003 and 2014, more than half (55 per cent) of the killings of American women were 'intimate partner violence-related' (meaning they occurred at the hands of current or former partners or the partner's family or friends).[23] Men who kill their wives, girlfriends or other family members also tend to get lighter sentences.[24] The author of the CDC paper called this the 'intimacy discount' and said it may derive from the fact that women are sometimes seen by judges as the 'property' of male partners.

Men do not decide to murder women because they are unable to find an intimate partner. Self-development might be worth pursuing for its own sake, but emphasising it as a route out of inceldom erroneously assumes that misogyny is a by-product of low social status. In fact, research suggests that high-status men are more likely to use sexual coercion than isolated loners.[25] Men who use sexual coercion tend, on average, to view themselves as sexually successful and to have had an extensive history of uncommitted sexual relationships.[26] It is therefore a mistake to assume that ameliorating feelings of low self-esteem will inevitably foster a healthier attitude towards women. Pickup artists are a cautionary tale in this regard. The industry was filled with men who had upgraded their interpersonal skills – and who had become more socially effective misogynists in the process.

*

The trajectory of the former incel Jack Peterson (no relation to Jordan) was further evidence that ideological change was not necessarily a byproduct of social ascension. Following the 2018 Toronto attack, Peterson began to appear on some of the world's major news channels. The media portrayed the then nineteen-year-old as an incel insider who, unlike some fellow members of his community, was speaking out against violence. Anointed by the media as an unofficial spokesperson for the incel community, Peterson did the rounds on the BBC and ABC News and featured in *Vice*, the *Guardian*, the *Huffington Post* and the *Daily Beast*. Following a backlash by misogynistic incels – who rejected Peterson's overtures to the mainstream and said, effectively, that yes, they really were as misogynistic as their critics claimed – Peterson uploaded a video to YouTube entitled 'Why I'm leaving Incels'. There followed a sympathetic interview with the *Guardian* in which Peterson renounced the incel community and denied being a misogynist. 'Listen, I'm not a bad guy, I'm not a sexist person, I'm not a violent person, and I don't think most incels are,' he told the paper.[27]

I spoke to Peterson over Zoom during the first Covid lockdown in March 2020. During our conversation he disavowed much of what he had told the media following the Minassian killings, which he said had been 'disingenuous'. Peterson, who was twenty-one when we talked, told me he was 'probably more misogynistic' than he made himself out to be during his various media appearances. 'In a cynical way, while all those eyes were on me at the time, I was trying to take advantage of it in any way I could,' he admitted.

Peterson hails from Chicago and was born 'Kalerthon Demetro', though he adopted his mother's last name after his violent father walked out when he was two years old. He had few friends growing up and was bullied for the way he looked (he told me he was 'chubby' and 'goofy' and had severe acne). 'It gets in your head,' he said of the bullying.

Peterson was eleven when he first discovered the nihilistic 4chan message boards. He began to fall into what he called its 'loser culture' – 'a culture of self-loathing and cynicism about women that permeates throughout the entire website... parts of 4chan are just as much incel as the incel websites'. Perhaps unusually for somebody who would go on to identify as an incel, Peterson had two girlfriends in middle school – something other incels would use against him following his media appearances to claim he wasn't one of them. But the bullying left its mark. 'That's the fucking crime of bullying; it really can destroy many years of your life because of self-esteem issues... You don't know how to judge yourself. Even if you are having some positive interactions with women, the bullying kind of drowns it out.'

Peterson had been talking to a woman online for several years and they finally met when he was sixteen. She lived on the other side of the country and was four years older than him. He ended up losing his virginity to her. They even went on a few holidays together. But then things went 'off the rails' as Peterson put it. She cheated on him. She also tried to run him over in a car. Peterson retaliated by sending nude photos of her to her parents and college professors. 'In my mind she's supposed to make it all better. But she just tears my confidence apart,' he told me. He got drawn deeper into the world of the incels. 'This is the real truth about incels,' he said. 'I wouldn't say a lot of these things [in the media] because I didn't want to look bad. But the truth is [that] when something like that happens to you, suddenly the concept of people on incel forums writing [things] like, "man, I just want to fucking kill all women", that's how you get to that point – when you have all these horrible experiences… that's how you get to that extreme point.'

There were moments during our conversation when Peterson displayed a degree of self-awareness – about the incel community and his own behaviour. 'A lot of the time you'll talk to incels and they'll say, "I've actually never used a dating app," or "I've never gone to bars or really done anything." So it's like, are you really an incel or are you just sitting inside not doing anything? You could put a male model in a room by himself for years and he's not going to get any pussy.' He also admitted that he had acted like 'an asshole' in his previous relationship. 'I did a lot of fucked up shit to her. It's not like I'm innocent in that story, but I never tried to hurt her or anything.'

Peterson was dating again when we spoke and said he had little difficulty meeting women through dating apps. He also acknowledged that some of what he and others in the incel and red pill communities disparagingly refer to as 'typical blue pill' dating advice was not without merit. While he made sure to tell me that he was 'not saying this in some sort of feminist or pro-women way', he had noticed that 'the more I just act natural with women, not suck up to them, but act nice, like polite, I seem to have more luck'.

Yet there was little evidence to suggest that Peterson had disavowed his misogynistic views, despite becoming more socially successful. 'I don't really think they [women] have control of their behaviour,' he said at one point during our conversation, before adding, by way of a 'scientific' explanation, that there was 'all this very deep biological stuff going on'. He also bemoaned technology for 'ruining' dating by giving women too many options. 'Women are not supposed to have access to an infinity of men... they're not supposed to have a phone where they can contact any man in the world and have all those options.'

In September 2021, Jack Peterson was featured in the media again, this time on the popular North American talk show *Dr. Phil*.[28] I had almost forgotten about him by this point but some of the things he was saying caught my attention. Peterson told the show that he had 'gone gay' and had a boyfriend because he 'couldn't put up with women any more'. I was surprised because Peterson had been exclusively dating women when we had spoken in 2020. However, some of the other things he said during the programme seemed to confirm something he had told me during our conversation: that he was 'probably more misogynistic' than he had made himself out to be when he was being hotfooted around television studios and given glowing newspaper write-ups as the former incel who had rejected misogyny. In a pre-recorded voiceover for the show, Peterson called women 'bitches' and described them as 'evil and manipulative' and 'lying fucking whores'.[29] He also said men needed to 'regain control of women again, the way it used to be in the 1950s'. A little over a year later, Peterson would upload a video to his YouTube channel in which he would perform another about-turn. In it, he said that he regretted going gay and called his previous behaviour 'sinful'.[30] Having apparently undergone some kind of religious conversion, he said he was ready to 'repent' thanks to his newfound 'faith in Jesus Christ'.

As was often the case with young men steeped in the murky subcultures of the internet, it was hard to be sure whether Jack Peterson's erratic public statements were genuine or a series of puerile attempts at getting a rise out of the media. Either way, while Peterson clearly felt it important to publicly repudiate the idea that he was living a 'gay lifestyle', he felt no similar compunction to apologise for the misogynistic things he had said about women. Having officially left the incel community behind, it wasn't obvious that being more sexually successful had done anything to purge Jack Peterson of his toxic beliefs.

13

TOP G

The nineteenth-century German philosopher Friedrich Nietzsche once said that 'when one has not had a good father, one must create one'. If Jordan Peterson was a surrogate father for some young men, then Andrew Tate, a former kickboxer, was the rebellious older brother, a bad boy with enough blunt charisma to cut through the internet's wall of noise. Some of the MOA students were members of Tate's War Room, a members only network of 'elite' men relentlessly pursuing financial success. It cost $8,000 (£6,200) to join the War Room and by doing so men were hoping to gain access to Tate's inner circle. These were the 'Top Gs' – the 'high-status' men with a penchant for tight-fitting suits and expensive cigars who appeared in Tate's social media content, usually boarding super-yachts and private jets.

Those who joined Tate's courses could earn affiliate income by signing up new members. Setting up copycat accounts and posting controversial clips of the influencer was one way of doing that – hence why videos of Tate were regularly going viral on TikTok and Instagram during the summer of 2022. A lot of Tate's money came from the eleven online courses he had created. A subscription to Hustlers University[1] (HU), a video series released by Tate in 2021 which promises to teach men how to 'escape the Matrix' by building wealth on the internet, cost $49.99 per month. By October 2022, HU reportedly had over 221,000 subscribers,[2] netting Tate around $8 million a month.[3] Men who signed up to HU were given access to video lessons on practical skills including website building, copywriting, email marketing, affiliate marketing, drop shipping and crypto currency. Tate's other courses featured advice on things like fitness, how to date women using Instagram, and how to start a webcam business employing the women you form relationships with. Tate's Pimpin' Hoes Degree (PHD), a $450 video course released on his website in 2018 but deleted in 2022, features him sitting behind a desk and dishing out advice on how to be a high value man. I watched the course on the streaming platform Rumble, where Tate had relaunched himself in 2022 (having been banned from most other platforms) while boasting that he was 'immune to cancel culture'. The course restates several manosphere talking points. Tate refers to a 'sexual marketplace' in which women are 'biologically programmed to share an alpha male'. He talks about how difficult dating is for men due to the 'unlimited attention' women receive on the internet. He says women are driven by their emotions; that a woman's 'value' is directly proportional to her beauty; and that feminism has destroyed women's understanding of 'their natural roles and desires'; he claims that women are inherently disloyal. Tate's advice on how men should use social media sounded familiar. Tate told men to 'fix their fucking Instagram' by uploading photos of themselves in exotic locations or with luxury cars. 'I don't care what lie you have to tell,' Tate said. 'We live in a world where you cannot play fair any more.'

At one point in the course, Tate tells viewers to 'get rid of any hate or resentment' they have towards women. He then proceeds to refer to women as 'bitches', 'hoes' and 'selfish cunts' who are 'barely sentient'. The harsh and dehumanising tone of Tate's PHD course is striking. The ideal woman is depicted as 'submissive' and 'in touch with her feminine energy'. Tate's rules for relationships are pathologically controlling. It is a woman's job to make her man 'feel important and look important'. A female partner is not really a partner at all and must be 'kept in line' and 'put in her fucking place' because 'women are not evolutionarily designed for power and they don't want power'. According to Tate, if you allow a girlfriend to have any male friends she will eventually cheat. Not that cheating is wrong in Andrew Tate's world. He tells his male audience to cheat if they want to and to gaslight their partner when they eventually get caught. 'Hide it the best you can until she finds out and [then]... completely trivialise her feelings.' For Tate, who says he doesn't date women over twenty-five and prefers being intimate with eighteen- and nineteen-year-olds because 'they've been through less dick', the ideal relationship is one of absolute subjugation. 'If

I died she would commit suicide,' he says of his girlfriend. 'I am her everything... It's like trying to take God away from a Christian... What's the point of being alive without God? That's how your woman has to think of you. When you get to that point you can do whatever the fuck you want. I can fuck who I want because she ain't gonna leave. She doesn't even cry about it any more.'

*

In other videos, mainly cut from podcast appearances recorded before he was famous, Tate openly describes himself as a 'pimp' and says that most of his money comes not from kickboxing but from 'pimp game'.

'Having sex with girls is all good, but how do you get them to do as you say, make you money, obey you, allow you to cheat on them in front of their face, and still love you? That's the game,' he says in one video. Elsewhere he openly admits to using 'sex as a tool to make women love me so they would obey me and live in my house and make me money'. While many of Tate's young fans see him as the personification of a virile and ultra-masculine heterosexuality, Tate himself doesn't appear to enjoy having sex with women. Instead, sex is merely a way of gaining power over another person. As Tate says in a video of him sitting behind the wheel of a luxury car: 'I have to fuck her so she obeys me. I don't give a shit about having sex with beautiful women. I fuck them so they listen to me, so I can get what I *actually* want, which is not them – it's a means to an end.'

In his PHD course, Tate suggests that men start their own webcam porn business as soon as they have 'a couple of girls' that are in love with them. He likens this type of business to 'free money'. In the early 2010s, Andrew and his brother Tristan started a webcam business with seventy-five female models. The models would take calls from men who were paying $4 a minute. The women would receive 40 per cent of this while the studio pocketed the rest. 'My MO was find girls, make them love me and make them work for me. And that's how I got rich,' Andrew says in another video clip. In 2015, Hertfordshire Police would open an investigation into Andrew and his brother Tristan after three women made allegations of sexual and physical abuse while working for the webcam business.[4] It would be another four years before the police would refer the case to the Crown Prosecution Service, which then decided that there was no realistic prospect of a conviction. Seven years passed again before the law eventually caught up with the brothers.

In December 2022, Andrew and Tristan Tate were arrested in Romania on charges of rape, human trafficking and forming an organised crime group to sexually exploit women. Several others were arrested along with them, including Georgiana Naghel, believed to be in a romantic relationship with Andrew. Romanian anti-organised crime agency DIICOT said it had identified six victims who were subjected to 'acts of physical violence and mental coercion'. Some of the victims were allegedly sexually exploited by group members with one said to have been violently sexually assaulted in

March 2022. The brothers were accused by prosecutors of using the 'loverboy method' – a tactic that involves getting a woman to fall in love with you – to ensnare the women they were accused of trafficking. Andrew Tate was formally charged on 20 June 2023 by Romanian authorities with rape, human trafficking and forming an organised crime group to sexually exploit women. His brother Tristan and two associates also faced charges. The indictment deposited with the Bucharest court alleged that the four defendants had formed an organised criminal group in 2021 to commit human trafficking in Romania and other countries including the US and the UK. Romanian authorities said that seven alleged victims were recruited to produce pornographic content by the Tate brothers through false promises of love and marriage. Andrew Tate was also facing a rape charge.[5] All of the accused deny the allegations[6] and are currently awaiting trial. In March 2024, Bedfordshire Police obtained a European arrest warrant for Andrew and Tristan Tate on charges of 'sexual aggression' dating back to between 2012 and 2015.[7]

Andrew and Tristan Tate had moved to Romania in 2017. It was a decision that was partly motivated by Andrew's desire to avoid further allegations of rape. He said that '40 per cent' of the reason he moved to Romania was because Romanian police were less likely to pursue sexual assault allegations. 'I'm not a fucking rapist, but I like the idea of just being able to do what I want. I like being free,' Tate said.[8]

The belief that there is an epidemic of women making false rape allegations (usually because they regret having sex) is widely held in the manosphere. In reality, the number of rapes and sexual assaults that are never reported hugely outweigh the number of men convicted of rape having been falsely accused. The vast majority of victims of rape are denied justice. US Bureau of Justice Statistics suggest that only 35 per cent of all sexual assaults are reported to the police. On the other hand, estimates of false reports in the US tend to converge between 2 and 8 per cent.[9] In the UK, an analysis of 2,643 sexual assault cases reported to the police found that just 2 per cent of allegations were found to be false under official criteria. Research from the Home Office suggests that only 4 per cent of cases of sexual violence reported to the police are found or suspected to be false.[10] Even these figures are likely to be inflated. Police may state 'no crime' or 'unfounded' on a police record if an accuser drops charges; however, this does not mean that the allegations are necessarily false – not being convicted of a crime is not the same as being found innocent. In Britain, a man is more likely to be raped by another man than be falsely accused of rape by a woman.[11] False accusations of sexual assault can clearly be devastating but according to the UK's Crown Prosecution Service (CPS) they are 'serious but rare'. They also very rarely lead to convictions or jail time. The CPS estimates that there is one prosecution for a false rape claim out of every 161 rape cases prosecuted.[12] In the United States, a man is more likely to be falsely *convicted* of murder than he is to be falsely *accused* of rape,[13] though one never heard anybody in the manosphere worrying about that.

Following his arrest in Romania, Andrew Tate tried to tap into the same hyperbole around false rape allegations that he had alluded to previously. In a statement to Romanian police in April 2023, Tate claimed (without evidence) that the accusations against him were made by 'jealous women' who know how to use the judicial system to 'punish men'.[14] If self-exculpatory claims of this sort were highly implausible in the UK, they were virtually impossible to take seriously in Romania, a country that has repeatedly found itself at the bottom of the European Union's gender equality index.[15] According to the Romanian General Prosecutor's Office, just 3.3 per cent of cases of domestic violence cases recorded by Romanian police in 2020 were heard in court. Nor were public attitudes in the country especially conducive to the reporting of sexual violence. Nearly a third (30 per cent) of respondents to a 2016 survey said that rape could be justified if a woman was in a group that was using drugs and alcohol, while 25 per cent said that dressing 'provocatively' could be a reasonable ground for sexual abuse.[16] Half of the survey's respondents considered non-consensual contact to be justifiable in certain situations.

'THE WAR ROOM Network has my life completely in order while I'm unjustly detained,' Tate reassured his followers on X in January 2023. 'I have brothers on the outside who have taken on my responsibilities.' One of these 'brothers' was a man named Miles Sonkin, a self-proclaimed wizard who went under the alias of Iggy Semmelweis. Sonkin, who has previously described women as 'nothing more than tools to be utilised',[17] was revealed to be the War Room's intellectual driving force[18] by a 2023 BBC investigation. The BBC also uncovered leaked Telegram messages sent by Sonkin encouraging War Room members to isolate women from their family and friends. Also revealed in the chat logs was evidence that some War Room members were grooming women into sex work. The BBC identified forty-five potential victims between March 2019 and April 2020, though it estimated that the total number was likely to be higher. A whistleblower named Eli, who told the BBC that he was 'brainwashed' by the Tate group, said: 'The War Room is all about you getting women that serve you in your life.'

Another prominent War Room member was arrested by Romanian police in June 2023 along with two other suspects. The men were accused of sexually exploiting at least seven women. Vlad Obuzic, a diminutive Romanian citizen whose social media accounts showed pictures of him with the two Tate brothers, was accused of using violence to force women to make porn. Obuzic, who had previously been arrested in 2021 for throwing liquor bottles off a balcony at female pedestrians, was also accused of making women get tattoos of his name or face or the words 'toy' or 'dog' as 'proof he owned them'.[19] In October 2023, Obuzic and three others were charged with human trafficking, forming an organised criminal group and public incitement.

*

In April 2023, while the Tate brothers were under house arrest in Romania (they would be released in August 2023 under the proviso that they remain in the country while they await trial),[20] I first met Andreas, a student on Michael Sartain's Men of Action programme who was also a member of Tate's War Room. I asked him what it was about Tate that appealed to him. 'Everybody wants to be a victim nowadays,' he told me. 'I like that Tate talks about self-discipline because so much of the culture now is about taking the easy option.'

The seriousness of the allegations levelled against the Tate brothers by Romanian prosecutors did not seem to be having much of an impact on some of the men I was spending time with. They had a seemingly endless list of excuses. Tate was said to be 'playing a character' or he 'doesn't really mean it' or he is 'baiting people' to game the algorithm. Sartain was still referring to Andrew Tate as a 'friend' and describing the case against him as a 'farce'. He was also using imagery of Andrew Tate in his social media content to promote MOA. When Tate was finally charged by the Romanian authorities in June 2023, Sartain said that if Tate was found guilty he would accept it – though he said the 'probability shows me he's not'.[21] Sartain was usually more critical of the Romanian government than of Tate, who he 'really hoped' would be acquitted.[22]

While Tate was still under house arrest – but before he was formally charged – I asked Andreas if it bothered him that a man he was giving money to in exchange for life advice was accused of terrible crimes. Initially, Andreas tried to play down the accusations against Tate. 'It was *suspicion* of trafficking,' he told me, emphasising that they were still allegations at this point. 'They [the police] raided [Tate's house] and they didn't find anything [and] they let him go and then they fucking hit him again.' Andreas thought the alleged victims might have tried to 'frame' the Tate brothers after being caught spending time at their compound on the outskirts of Bucharest. 'They [the women] were probably having a good time and then the boyfriends found out so they had to think up excuses,' he told me. 'Girls do stuff like that sometimes.' Another MOA student, who had been listening to my conversation with Andreas, then chimed in to make a joke. 'That's why you gotta make them [women] sign [consent] forms, bro,' he said laughing. On another occasion, in February 2023, I overheard one of the MOA coaches say that he didn't know 'if [he] could live in Romania any more after Andrew Tate'.

Andreas conceded that Tate could sometimes make extreme and controversial statements – though he believed these were 'provocations' designed to cut through the noise of social media and reach 'the men who need his guidance'. He also hinted at some kind of conspiracy. 'It's because he [Tate] is disrupting a lot of things,' Andreas told me. 'He's saying a lot of shit against governments that strengthens the minds of the youth. The youth is what coordinates revolutions. The things he [Tate] says go against the Matrix, as we call it. Governments don't want the youth being strong and powerful.'

Nearly identical rhetoric was coming from Andrew Tate himself. Following his initial arrest in December 2022, Tate blamed 'the Matrix' for his incarceration. 'The Matrix sent their agents,'[23] read a tweet to his six million followers. After he was sentenced to a further thirty days in jail, another tweet from Tate's account read: 'The Matrix will only tell you what the Matrix needs you to believe.'[24] It was a nod to QAnon-adjacent[25] conspiracy theories about a 'deep state' that was intent on silencing anybody who challenged so-called liberal elites. In his various public statements, Tate presented his imprisonment as an act of martyrdom against political forces that resented his popularity and influence among young men. Sartain seemed to agree. 'The reason they cancelled him [Andrew Tate] is because he was starting to make sense for a lot of people, and that was troublesome for so many people,' he said in a reel posted to his Instagram page on 17 August 2024. Five days later, on 22 August, Andrew Tate was placed under house arrest and Tristan Tate was placed under 'judiciary control'[26] by a Romanian judge as prosecutors investigated new allegations. These involved thirty-five alleged victims, including a woman who was fifteen at the time.[27] According to DIICOT, six people were detained in total for crimes including forming an organised criminal group, human trafficking, trafficking of minors, sexual intercourse with a minor and money laundering.

*

Andrew Tate's young followers are taught to view life solely through the lens of getting rich – to define themselves by their consumption habits and robotically pursue the gauche trappings of a 'G' lifestyle. A favourite insult among his fans is to dismiss his detractors on the basis that they are not as rich as their hero – they are 'broke'. Andrew Tate frequently expresses an absolute faith in the power of capitalism to reward those who work hard. The son of an American chess master and an English mother who worked as a catering assistant, Tate and his brother Tristan talk frequently of their experiences growing up on a council estate in Luton, Bedfordshire. They had been so poor that as children they claimed to have scavenged for leftover chicken at their local KFC. They were poor guys who had got rich. From such inauspicious beginnings they had accumulated a fleet of thirty-two super-cars – a collection that included a Bugatti, a Rolls-Royce and a Lamborghini. According to Andrew Tate, getting rich was easy – you just had to stop feeling sorry for yourself. If the Tates could rise like that, then what was your excuse?

Tate was adjacent to 'hustle' culture, a wider cultural phenomenon that told young people they should derive a sense of self-worth from their degree of productivity. If you weren't a six-figure entrepreneur you had supposedly failed at life. Tate warned his fans that they needed to be 'outcompeting all the other people on the planet who are hyper-competitive'.[28] If you were poor then according to Tate it was because you were either lazy, arrogant or stupid.[29] He also said that depression wasn't real and anyway it could be cured by lifting weights. 'If I'm awake then I'm working,' Tate claimed. 'I don't relax, I don't rest, I don't stop, I don't chill. I'm either asleep or at work.'[30] Although the self-styled king of toxic masculinity told fans this, two journalists who spent time at his compound in Romania observed that Tate spent much of his time 'lounging around the pool with a cigar and chatting shit with his brother'.[31]

Self-help gurus have long promoted the idea that all a person needs for success is grit and determination (and whatever book or course they are selling). During the pre-internet days, these 'business personalities' usually appeared in the back pages of magazines where they promised to reveal the foolproof secrets of how to get rich. Purchasing the product in question was usually about as useful as buying a handful of magic beans. In the modern age, social media had made it easier for entrepreneurial hucksters to captivate audiences with lifestyle and personality. 'You'll see people online saying, "This is how I earned a billion dollars in cryptocurrency." But then if you look into it [it turns out] their dad owns a gold mine,' says Alex. 'Or you see Andrew Tate. He wasn't some sort of magic businessman who can grow money on trees. Elon Musk as well. His family is very wealthy, and all these people were all born to generational wealth or have got lucky through certain circumstances. But of course [their fans] don't see that. They just see the money and the massive houses.'

The more extreme somebody is in the internet influencer game, the more cult-like their following tends to be. Andrew Tate used social media to create an aura around himself. He exuded gangster charisma and an outlaw image. His bombastic persona was gradually refined over time and became part of a larger business model designed to extract money from those who bought into its pied-piper-like appeal.

Tate was also selling his followers a lifestyle. He continually flashed the trappings of wealth on social media – financial independence, luxury travel, exotic locations, big houses, nice cars, fine cigars, diamond watches, good food, beautiful women – while telling his fans that they too could live like this – that they could 'escape the Matrix and get rich'.[32] In common with other 'business entrepreneurs' that have proliferated on social media in recent years, Tate left out the most important piece of information: that this financial 'success' largely depended on the willingness of a cult-like following to pay him.

Tate claimed to be helping his fans to beat the system. In reality he was turning them into the slaves of a rigid code of masculinity and a puerile cult of narcissistic greed. Far from standing for something rebellious or subversive, Tate represented the suffusion of capitalist logic into all social relations. His overt misogyny was frequently of the old-fashioned kind: he described women as men's 'property' and said they belonged in the kitchen.[33] But his hatred of women also seemed to stem from his view of them as status symbols and commodities. 'I only have so many [girls] because there's a whole bunch of dudes out there with none,' he boasted. 'That's the way the world works.'

Men were instrumentalised too, albeit as clients and stakeholders or as 'paypigs' and 'marks'. In the Tates' world, money was the *sine qua non* of friendship and fans were encouraged to cut unproductive 'losers' out of their lives. As War Room 'lieutenant' and close friend of the brothers Justin Waller put it, 'I don't want to be friends with you unless we can make money together.'

The Tates would openly admit that their earlier webcam business was 'a total scam' designed to 'lure men in'.[34] Tristan boasted that clients of the business – some of whom had been fooled into believing they were in relationships with the models – racked up huge debts, including one man who parted with a £20,000 inheritance. Sometimes the clients were not even having real conversations with the women they were sending money to. The other women – or even Andrew Tate himself – would type out the messages to clients while the model sat in front of the camera holding a keyboard that wasn't plugged in.[35] The models, some of whom would level their own allegations against the Tate brothers in subsequent years, were, according to Tristan, tasked with 'getting men hooked, finding out their interests, the name of their dog... It's an operation of professionals who lure these men in.' Two lines had been inserted into the terms and conditions which meant the models were free to lie to clients. 'One is broadcasting "for entertainment purposes only",' Tristan admitted. 'That means if a model says she has a sick dog or a sick grandma it doesn't have to be true.' The second line stipulated that all cash given to the models was 'a voluntary sign of gratitude for their time broadcasting'.

Eli, a whistleblower who spent two years as the Tate organisation's head of sales and marketing, told the BBC that the War Room was a 'cult' and that some men were spending more than $250,000 on the various courses[36] offered by the Tate brothers. War Room members and ex-members could regularly be found online complaining that, far from fraternising with an inner circle of 'high value' men, they have effectively paid $8,000 to join a glorified Telegram group. They had expected to be hanging out with 'elite' men – only to find themselves in a chat room with other beginners. According to one former member of the War Room, though Andrew Tate might appear in the Telegram group once or twice a week, when he did, he would 'say something with no value'.[37] If War Room members were unhappy with the experience they were encouraged to purchase more expensive add-on products. Members of the War Room had to purchase five courses and attend a live event (costing around $5,000) in order to gain access to the 'Elite Room', which offered the tantalising prospect of going deeper into Tate's inner sanctum. 'Unless you have 100k, don't join... You need to attend events, which cost around 40k,' complained one ex-War Room member.

*

Alex is from Leeds, West Yorkshire. He grew up with a 'very abusive' mother who had a lot of boyfriends, some of whom were misogynistic and abusive. '[My mum] was married to [one man] for about ten years. He thought that if you don't know how to fight you're not a real man. Or if you don't have fifty women on your arm at all times you're a soy boy, that kind of thing.' Alex struggled to make friends at school – he says he was part of the 'nerdy gang' – and was bullied by girls about his height. He tells me he is 'very short'. He thinks this made him look up to his stepfather more, despite his misogynistic views. 'I didn't have my real dad around, and I have all sisters, so you kind of cling to whatever male figure that you have when you feel like you need guidance.'

Alex initially discovered the MGTOW community on Reddit when he was just twelve. He remembers reading negative posts about women on the forum and finding them 'enticing' because of his own experiences. 'Growing up around domestic violence and having a lot of toxic masculinity hanging over me, I feel like I was the perfect target for that kind of thing,' he tells me. As well as frequenting forums, Alex would sometimes watch YouTube. 'Awful content [where] they would pick up on a tiny thing and be like, "Wow, this is why all women suck." And they kind of play it off as a joke, so you don't realise that you're being radicalised. You think, oh we're all just having a laugh.'

Alex's biological father, whom he didn't meet until he was twelve or thirteen, was gay, which led Alex to question whether he might be gay too. 'I've figured out now that I'm not [gay], but I wondered if I was, and that kind of phobia [of being gay] probably influenced [my interest in the manosphere] too.'

Alex was a child when he was first exposed to red pill content on YouTube. 'You're probably not going to have very good media literacy [at that age],' he says looking back. 'And if some guy you look up to is telling you this stuff, you're probably going to take his word for it.'

Alex first encountered Andrew Tate when he was looking for videos about kickboxing, which he was interested in at the time. 'I watched videos about [the sport] on YouTube and because he has a background in MMA (mixed martial arts), YouTube would push me Andrew Tate videos. It would start off with quite innocent stuff. And he seemed like a really personable, smart guy. Then all of a sudden these [misogynistic] videos started creeping in.'

Alex didn't sign up for any of Andrew Tate's courses – he says he already had one foot out of the door of the manosphere just as Tate was starting to become popular – but he did think about paying for other 'alpha male' courses. 'I did consider it at one point. Because if you grow up in an abusive household, you're probably going to be walked all over [by people] because that's what you're used to. So I thought I needed to sign up for a course to find out how to be more assertive and "alpha".'

Not feeling sufficiently masculine can also lead to negative body issues. A 2025 study published in the *Psychology of Men & Masculinities* journal found that adolescent boys were increasingly using anabolic steroids in order to achieve the muscular physiques idealised on social media (and embodied by influencers like Tate).[38]

Alex tells me that a lot of people in his sixth form did sign up for Tate's Hustlers University. 'They think it's a golden bullet. They think this guy [Andrew Tate] is really confident; I'm going to pay him money so that I can be rich and famous like he is. And I feel like a lot of men run to it because they don't have that much of an input from their dad or from society in general... So the only place they feel they can get some information is from these people who give them what they want but radicalise them at the same time.'

There's an element of what Alex terms 'manosphere charisma' with certain red pill YouTubers. 'They demean you for being small and pathetic and ugly and [say that] all women find you repulsive and you're a beta male,' Alex says. 'Then they will say, "This is how you stop being a beta soy boy, now buy my course or you're useless." It's kind of like a drill sergeant bullying you into submission.'

As to how he managed to leave the manosphere, Alex says that as he got older he began to realise 'you can't just generalise [about women] from a few per cent of the population'. He also started spending more time around women and reading a lot. 'Seeing more of the news and more of the world in general, [I realised] that they [the manosphere] were lying and massively blowing things out of proportion.' Alex cites something called the 'Freedom Programme', designed for victims of domestic violence, as something that helped him come to terms with his abusive childhood. 'I would read it and say, "I recognise that behaviour. I recognise that sentiment." And it would remind me of male figures I had grown up with. And I would think, "Wow, that was abusive. They weren't alpha. They were narcissists."'

Learning more about the effect of domestic violence on women was also the 'last straw' in encouraging Alex to leave the manosphere. 'It's very shocking, seeing the way that some of these terrible behaviours are so normalised within society. Like, this is so much more than all the stuff the MRAs (men's rights activists) are whingeing about. For me that was the last straw. I'm done with it.'

Alex, who is now eighteen, has come a long way since his MGTOW days. Nowadays he calls himself a feminist. 'I'd say that I went from being an anti-feminist thinking they [feminists] were anti-men and hated us all, to becoming one over time without noticing. I would say I'm quite a strong feminist [now] and always want to look at my own privilege, because I think sometimes you don't realise it.'

EPILOGUE

Since I started writing this book, the internet's algorithms have tried to foist 'controversial' content on me. It started out with self-improvement videos where influencers would talk about how tough it was nowadays to be a man. From there I might be directed to a video that blamed feminism and the political left. Before long, my timeline had been infiltrated by a seemingly bottomless well of influencers who seemed to spend all their time berating women. Inscrutable algorithms were trying to shape what I was watching and listening to. The tech platforms wanted to keep me glued to my screen seething to rage-bait. The incentive structure was broken for creators too. Content that caused anger or indignation was more likely to go viral and so being radical was a way to stand out. Julia Ebner called it the 'monetisation of polarisation'. A 2024 experiment in Australia found that a teenage boy showing an interest in Jordan Peterson on Instagram would encounter Andrew Tate within an hour. If that teenage boy then watched or liked more Tate content by the two-hour mark, the platform would almost exclusively feed him that content.[1]

It wasn't just the manosphere that was all about status and social proof. We had all seemingly come to live in a world where 'confidence men' were bamboozling people with little more than charisma and clout. Status and social proof had become the deciding factor in whom we were choosing to listen to online. In sifting fact from fiction, people were turning to their online mentors for guidance. The more clout an influencer had, the more likely we were to treat that person as a reputable source of information. Michael Sartain was right about one thing: status was status was status. Oftentimes it didn't matter what somebody was famous for; we felt compelled to pay attention.

Expertise in one area was also frequently treated as expertise in another. Research from the Reuters Institute[2] found that politicians, celebrities and public figures generated 69 per cent of social media engagement around coronavirus misinformation, despite only posting 20 per cent of misleading posts. 'Trust in the social media age is very person associated,' says Ebner. 'The institutional trust that we had previously in established media outlets or in democratic institutions has to some extent been replaced by individuals, essentially influencers, who might have credentials in some area but not in others.'

Some of this has to do with algorithms. But certain influencers can themselves open the door to more radical beliefs. When we met up, I had asked Ebner if she believed someone like Jordan Peterson could radicalise men. Or might his content prevent people from going down a more extreme path – perhaps by teaching them qualities such as discipline and structure? 'I'm sure there is some valuable stuff [in Peterson's work] that can help young men,' she told me. 'But he also feeds into a hyper-conservative view of women and this very essentialist idea of gender, which is very much based on nature not on nurture. I think that can open up other radical perspectives of misogyny.'

Peterson has undergone something of a radicalisation of his own in recent years, his folksy self-help advice giving way to hysterical warnings about 'woke totalitarianism'[3] and vaccine conspiracies.[4] Abortion is another issue on which Peterson has become shriller and more extreme. In 2018, as he was becoming a recognisable public figure, Peterson described abortion as 'morally wrong'. And yet he tended to equivocate on whether it should be outlawed. Nowadays, however, Peterson can be found on social media equating abortion with the mass murder of children.[5] His political pronouncements are no less hysterical. In 2024, Peterson was warning that Britain was about to become a communist dictatorship under mild-mannered leader of the Labour Party Keir Starmer. A year earlier, Peterson had launched into a deranged social media diatribe against a paper towel dispenser that asked people to be less wasteful. It was, he said, 'woke tyranny'.

Peterson would not be the only public figure to radicalise in recent years – something covered in the second part of this book. The reasons are complex. But social media is certainly playing a role. As Sean Illing has put it with reference to the Washington insurrectionists of 6 January 2021, one of whom I met at the 21 Summit before he was sent to jail: 'We reached this precipice because millions of Americans have had a firehose of falsehoods blasted into their brains for months on end.'

In a profit-driven media landscape that prioritises clicks and likes and virality, there are powerful incentives for content creators to grow their audiences by becoming more extreme or branching out from one conspiracy to another. They may even radicalise themselves in the process. 'You might be very sceptical in other aspects of life and then go online and not care about it any more because it's social media,' says Ebner. 'But if you're exposed to it regularly you can still get radicalised without even noticing.' While writing this book I have seen various masculinity influencers fall deeper into the world of conspiracy theories. There was evidence that people who believed in one form of pseudoscience were more likely to believe in multiple forms – all a product of the same sloppy thinking. Known as crank magnetism, it is the tendency of conspiratorial beliefs to attract each other and be magnetic. What a person thinks is in some ways less important than how he or she thinks.

The red pill is a conspiracy theory that women run the world. It is perhaps unsurprising that people who subscribe to it are prone to other implausible beliefs. What makes the manosphere especially toxic is the contradiction at its heart. Women (feminists in particular) are depicted as powerful manipulators of the political system. Yet they are also cast as submissive and hysterical and incapable of thinking logically. It is difficult to see how one can hold on to both beliefs. Which perhaps explains the growing tendency in the manosphere to

EPILOGUE

view women as helpless marionettes, controlled by dark forces lurking in the shadows.'

Through his manipulation of online algorithms, Andrew Tate became a distinctly twenty-first-century phenomenon. Yet his rhetoric frequently evoked the paranoid movements of the past. He blamed 'the Matrix' for his legal problems; he said it was 'the perfect word to describe the current world which is controlled by the powerful entities behind it'.[6] This rhetoric slotted Tate firmly into what the late American historian Richard Hofstadter called 'the paranoid style'.[7] The central image of the paranoid style was that of a 'vast and sinister conspiracy... a gigantic and yet subtle machinery of influence set in motion to undermine and destroy a way of life'. Following his arrest in August 2024, Tate took to social media to rubbish the latest allegations against him. 'All they try to do is damage my name with complete bullshit,'[8] he wrote. He didn't immediately elaborate on who 'they' were, yet he appeared to be gravitating towards a familiar historical scapegoat. A few days prior to his arrest, in a livestream with his brother, Tristan, Andrew Tate had said that 'They [Israel] control the Matrix. They control narratives. The problem is the narrative is breaking to the point where they're trying to get TikTok banned because they can't lie any more.'

It wasn't the first time that Tate had dabbled in anti-semitism. In January 2024, he urged his followers to question whether 'they' had lied about the Second World War – and consequently whether the Nazis were really the 'bad guys'.[9] For somebody who boasted about not reading books because he 'already knows everything about everything',[10] Tate's historical ignorance was hardly surprising. But it did represent a growing convergence between the manosphere and the far right. Following his August 2024 arrest, Tate retweeted a post by the American white supremacist Nick Fuentes. 'Just 2 days after Andrew Tate said that "the Matrix" is really just the Jewish mafia – his house was raided and he was arrested again,'[11] said Fuentes in the tweet shared by Tate. Fuentes,[12] who describes himself as a 'proud incel',[13] is a Holocaust[14] denier who has made various racist and antisemitic statements.[15] He has also said rape is 'so not a big deal'[16] and claimed that women are too emotional to make political decisions. Following Donald Trump's victory in the 2024 presidential election, a tweet by Fuentes which said, 'Your body, my choice' – a reference to women's reproductive rights thought to be under further threat from another Trump administration – received more than 52,000 likes.

Fuentes has appeared as a guest on the *Fresh&Fit* podcast, which bills itself as 'the #1 men's podcast in the world'. Perhaps influenced by his guest, co-host of the show Myron Gaines has been making his own bizarre claims about Jews. 'Stop calling "them" Globalists, Elitists, Frankists, Sabbateanists, Communists, Deep State, Zionists, Oligarchists, Rothschild Bankers JUST SAY JEWS...', Gaines tweeted on 24 August 2024. Sneako, another Tate wannabe with 200,000 subscribers on Rumble and another frequent guest on *Fresh&Fit*, tweeted 'Welcome home' at the Tates following their release from Romanian custody in August 2024. 'Tell the truth, whatever the cost,' he added. 'The Matrix is Israel,' he wrote in another tweet later that day.[17]

In Orlando, a speaker named Ian Smith had talked ominously of a 'game' being played in the shadows. 'You can call them globalist interests, you can call them bankers, you can call them whatever,' he warned. 'These people control things behind the scenes and have been around for a very long time.'

It didn't take long to work out who Smith might be alluding to, not least because he was saying it out loud on the internet. In 2023, Smith appeared on an episode of a far-right podcast where he claimed that Jewish people were behind the 'things that are used to control us'.[18] He was also speculating that the 'good guys' might not have won World War II, a conflict he described as an 'engineered White genocide facilitated by international usurers'.[19] To his followers he recommended a revisionist film that portrayed Germany as the victim and shared a meme[20] that described 'all this woke stuff' as 'coming from the Jews'.

Trust fund playboy Dan Bilzerian also had Jews on the brain. During an appearance on a talk show in August 2024, Bilzerian claimed that 'the Jews killed JFK' and 'knew about 9/11'. He also described Israel as a 'fucking parasite' and accused Jewish people of playing the 'victim card' over the Holocaust. 'Ever since I was a little kid, I knew that Nazis were not bad people,' Bilzerian said.[21] The influencer also shared a meme on X which made the bogus claim that the Talmud, a foundational Jewish religious text, permitted the rape and murder of non-Jews. Bilzerian topped all that in January 2025 with straight up Holocaust minimisation. '6 million jews did not die during WW2, they lied to you,' he wrote on X.

Meanwhile, Jordan Peterson was frequently accusing the 'radical left' of wanting to impose 'Cultural Marxism' on the West – a phrase that has long been a dog whistle for the far right. The concept of Cultural Marxism originated out of a conspiracy theory directed at the – predominantly Jewish – postwar Frankfurt School. It recycled a much older antisemitic trope which said that a shadowy cabal of Jews were conniving to overthrow society and impose Marxism. Anders Breivik, the Norwegian neo-Nazi who murdered seventy-seven people in 2011, invoked 'Cultural Marxism' repeatedly in his 1,500-page manifesto.

*

When Andrew Tate blew up the internet during the summer of 2022, there was a great deal of hand-wringing in the media. The search for answers began in earnest. Many commentators blamed the internet or an entrenched culture of patriarchy. Others claimed that Tate was an indictment of society's failure to provide enough suitable role models for men. Richard V. Reeves, the author of an influential book, *Of Boys and Men*, described Tate's rise to prominence as 'our fault'. 'The failure to address the real problems of boys and men creates a dangerous vacuum in our culture and politics,' wrote Reeves.

There is something to this. One way that influencers in the manosphere can effectively recruit is by pointing to genuine issues that affect men. Places where there were large numbers

EPILOGUE

of men without jobs have been fertile ground for Trump's MAGA movement (Trump's electoral success was partly built on his telling this section of his base that the remaining fragments of status they clung onto were under mortal threat).

As Reeves, writing about the United States, noted in his book:

> The gender gap in college degrees awarded is wider today than it was in the early 1970s, but in the opposite direction. The wages of most men are lower today than they were in 1979, while women's wages have risen across the board. One in five fathers are not living with their children. Men account for almost three out of four 'deaths of despair', either from a suicide or an overdose.

Conservatives and manosphere influencers will often jump on statistics like this to make a case for turning the clock back on women's rights. However, that doesn't mean there is no truth mixed in with the falsehoods. A lot of men are struggling and it doesn't undermine the causes that women are fighting for by acknowledging it. As Susan Faludi noted in her 1991 book *Backlash*, a book which assessed how progress towards equality was usually followed by an apoplectic reaction: pushback against efforts by women to improve their status have often come from men who are themselves grappling with 'real threats to their economic and social well-being'.[22] This is part of the populist coding of the manosphere. The cult of patriarchy that prevails can make men who have little economic capital feel powerful – without disrupting any of the power of genuine elites. As Julia Ebner had observed, the manosphere would single out feminism as the point at which things began to go south for men. From there it said that in order for men to feel powerful again, they should seek to dominate in their relationships. 'If you don't feel like a king in your house, how are you to feel like a king anywhere else?' Tate asked his legions of young fans. This was just one of the ways that women could end up carrying the can for the lowly role allotted to some men by the capitalist system. 'On the one hand there have been all these rapid [economic] changes and a perceived loss of [men's] status or privileges,' Ebner pointed out, 'and on the other hand there has been little work at the societal or psychological level to allow men to cope with that or to give them a new role.'

Some of the men I spent time with felt that they were being pulled in opposing directions. Progressive institutions were constantly telling them to embrace tolerance and equality. Meanwhile, in their day-to-day lives, they had to compete in an economic system that rewarded ruthless accumulation and 'coming out on top'. They were caught between the cultural progressivism of the administrative state and the behaviours required of an ideal neoliberal subject. One way to resolve these competing narratives was to retreat back to the certainties of traditional gender roles. This brought things into a sort of uneasy alignment.

The same forces were acting on women too of course; however, the pressure was applied at different points. Men inhabited a world in which their own masculinity was (still) tightly bound up with their identity as a 'provider'. The manosphere may have tried to indoctrinate men into believing that being a 'high-status' wage earner was a prerequisite to having a successful relationship. However, it was simply amplifying a message the mainstream was already telling them.

Though overwhelmingly made up of men, anti-feminist movements also sometimes contain women. For her previous book *Going Dark,* Ebner infiltrated the 'trad wives' (short for Traditional Wives) movement and Red Pill Women, a group whose members say they are not interested in being 'saved' by feminism. Both movements promote traditional gender roles and there is a significant crossover with the manosphere in terms of rhetoric. A recent study found that the biggest viewers of online #tradwife content are right-leaning men.[23] Red Pill Women discuss each other's 'SMV' and couch their pseudo-scientific theories about the 'gender polarity' in a taxonomy which draws heavily on evolutionary psychology. I encountered some 'trad' women during my own research journey. At one of the talks I attended in Orlando, a female panellist claimed that there were no feminist reforms to society that she would keep. 'I think the [contraceptive] pill was absolutely detrimental to our society... I don't think women should have access to education, not as it is now,' she told the audience.

'Similar to the men joining the manosphere, the search for love is what radicalises most trad wives,' Ebner writes in her book. On this point she told me: 'A lot of the questions [Red Pill Women] were dealing with were about double burdens of feeling rejected by men or feeling like hook-up culture didn't work for them. Or they were afraid of being played by men or being on dating apps and not finding someone who was serious.'

A person can be more prone to radicalisation into extremist communities when they are going through personal or psychological challenges. Some kind of vulnerability or an insecurity often precipitates the initial journey into the manosphere. I know this from personal experience. Back in 2005, I had discovered an online world where gurus claimed to have all the answers. This was before social media and streaming video platforms existed. Today it is much easier to discover these communities. Ebner believes that we are all potentially vulnerable to radicalisation if the material finds us in the right moment. During the research for her own book, Ebner felt at one point as if she too might be susceptible to radicalisation. 'I was in a personally difficult situation and I felt like I could be radicalised towards the red pill movement,' she told me. 'My own grievances or my own vulnerability matched the narratives that were dealt with in that community.' For those who are feeling confused and insecure, the certainties of radical ideology can restore a sense of control and serenity.

Yet one must be wary of blaming everything on algorithms or the power of radicalisation. Victimhood has long been a talking point of those who resent having to cede any of their privileges. 'A struggle for women's rights gained force in the mid-nineteenth century, the early 1900s, the early 1940s and the early 1970s,' noted Faludi. 'In each case, the struggle yielded to backlash.' The growth of the manosphere is part of a wider rejection of women's rights that is taking place across the world. Between 2019 and 2022, nearly 40 per cent of countries stagnated or declined on gender equality.[24] In 2022, Roe v. Wade, the American Supreme Court decision of 1973 to make access to abortion a federal right, was overturned by a conservative-stacked Supreme Court. In 2021, the UN released a report showing that violence against women had increased to unprecedented levels during the pandemic.[25] A 2024 investigation by UK police chiefs estimates that at least one in every twelve women will be a victim of violence every year: around two million women. Nearly 3,000 crimes of violence against women are recorded each day in Britain, a number police are calling the 'tip of the iceberg' because the figures do not include unreported crimes. In this sense, the manosphere is part of what the charity Hope not Hate describes as 'an organised, conscious political effort by some to turn back the clock on gender equality'.[26] This can be evidenced by the pushback in the United States against laws that legalise abortion.

The problem with wanting to be dominant and powerful is that it requires others, particularly women, to play a subservient role – to play valet to the male ego. And if they refuse to submit to your new identity as an alpha male? Well, that's when the online can spill over into the offline world.

*

During his successful presidential campaign of 2024, Donald Trump raised the testosterone quotient of the Republican ticket. Hulk Hogan and Kid Rock were wheeled out at the Republican National Convention, as was the Ultimate Fighting Championship (UFC) chief executive Dana White. Trump even attended a UFC match in New York City's Madison Square Garden. The President-elect cast himself as the 'protector' of women... 'whether they like it or not'. His running mate, Senator J. D. Vance, described himself as 'red pilled' and talked disparagingly about 'childless cat ladies'. During the campaign, Trump had called radio host Howard Stern a 'beta male' and his spokesperson ridiculed Kamala Harris's campaign as 'cucked'. Trump took to the stage at the Republican National Convention with 'It's A Man's Man's Man's World' by James Brown playing in the background. Later on, during his confirmation hearing, his new defence secretary Pete Hegseth was asked how many push-ups he could do.[27]

Donald Trump was helped in his victory over Kamala Harris by a transformed media landscape. In 2023, the then presidential candidate Robert F. Kennedy Jr. had predicted that the following year's election would be 'decided by podcasts'. It was a rare moment of insight from the man whom Trump had once appositely called 'the dumbest Kennedy' (and whom he would subsequently appoint as his health secretary). By 2024, cable news was no longer the mainstay of American households. Instead, roughly 20 per cent of Americans – Republicans and Democrats alike – got their news primarily from podcasts and social media. The figure for under-30s was 37 per cent.[28]

Trump thrived on the podcast and YouTube circuit, where charisma and one-liners were valued more highly than careful elucidations of policy. Reportedly on the advice of his eighteen-year-old son Barron, Trump worked hard to woo various manosphere adjacent influencers. His outreach campaign culminated in a three-hour interview on *The Joe Rogan Experience*, a podcast with an audience of more than 11 million listeners that skews around 81 per cent male.

Though Trump was already popular on the male influencer circuit, his outreach to new media's big players helped bring swathes of the male demographic decisively into the Republican camp. In 2020,[29] Joe Biden had beaten Trump with male voters under forty-five. In 2024, however,[30] Trump captured 54 per cent of the male vote compared with 45 per cent of the female vote. He also won 57 per cent of young male voters (ages eighteen to twenty-nine).[31] Trump has always enjoyed a high level of support from white men, but in 2024 he also won 43 per cent of male Latino voters and 25 per cent of Black male voters. Young Latino men's views of the Democratic Party were much more negative than in 2020,[32] while young Black men's views of the party stayed broadly the same.[33]

The progressive YouTuber David Pakman[34] has observed that a lot of the ostensibly non-political online media that has emerged in recent years – encompassing a range of topics including dating, weightlifting, combat sports, cryptocurrency and gambling – is 'right-wing coded'. Values like self-reliance are revered and contrasted favourably with 'wokeness' and depending on the government. Audiences are encouraged to look up to 'high-status' men such as Trump and Elon Musk.[35] For a lot of the men who inhabit these communities, voting for Trump was a cultural statement as much as a rational economic calculation.

Towards the end of 2024, Anthony Johnson resigned as president of the manosphere. It had, he said, devolved into 'micro cults of personality' to the point where 'most influencers and most podcasters are just complete garbage'. Johnson's wife had also recently had her first child; he was a family man now with bigger responsibilities.

And yet I wondered if there was any point in being the president of a subculture that was blending so seamlessly into the mainstream. Just as Anthony Johnson was stepping down from his role in the manosphere, Donald Trump was returning to the White House. In February 2025, Andrew and Tristan Tate flew to Florida after a travel ban imposed by a Romanian judge was lifted. Trump claimed he knew 'nothing about it'; however the Romanian foreign minister Emil Hurezeanu told the media that Trump's special envoy Richard Grenell had mentioned the Tates at a security conference that took place in Munich earlier that month.[36] Guests at Trump's inauguration included the boxer and influencer Jake Paul and his brother Logan, a wrestler and influencer; the mixed martial arts fighter Conor McGregor; as well as the new feudal lords of the internet, Mark Zuckerberg, Jeff

EPILOGUE

Bezos and Elon Musk. Bezos had bulked up at the gym and left his wife of 25 years for a glamorous socialite. Musk, who would soon have his very own government department, was promoting a theory on social media that democracy should be replaced by a Republic of 'high [testosterone] alpha males'. And in January 2025, Zuckerberg sat down with Joe Rogan and said that American business culture needed to rediscover its manhood. 'The corporate world is pretty culturally neutered,' said the Meta chief executive. 'A culture that celebrates aggression a bit more has its own merits.' 'Masculine energy, I think, is good,' he added.

Like Anthony Johnson, I too was ready to leave the manosphere – this time for good. What I hadn't reckoned on was the possibility that the manosphere might not be done with me. By the time I finished writing, things were coming full circle. Wherever I looked, a type of media con man I recognised was seemingly everywhere, discrediting the mainstream and claiming to have all the answers (answers kept from populations by 'corporate interests' and the like). Populist demagogues were making inroads through inflammatory appeals to the brittle resentments of the mob. Meanwhile, the world's richest oligarchs were pushing the idea that success meant embodying the opposite of anything feminine. At the head of it all was the leader of the so-called free world – a politician who was permanently high on his own supply; whose entire career was built on demagogic charisma and the illusion of success; who was obsessed with dominating, overwhelming and conquering those around him.

I couldn't fully extract myself from the manosphere because, though I had reached the end of my journey, I seemed to be living in a world that increasingly reflected many of the subculture's hang-ups and obsessions.

ACKNOWLEDGMENTS

Books like this are a collective endeavour so I would like to thank Leticia for the love and support; Andrew Gordon at David Higham Associates for steering me in the right direction; Shoaib Rokadiya for being an engaged and conscientious editor; Atlantic Books for being patient; Mike Harpley for initially pushing me to write the book; Pedro for being a dependable if insubordinate feline companion; and Julia Ebner, Alexander Reid Ross, Minnie Lane, Aaron Clarey, Jack Peterson, Toby Theo, Zan Perrion, Alexander Beaumont, Anthony Johnson, Rashad Ali, Simon Rawles, Itamar Klasmer, Adam Barnett, Nick, Luis, Patrick, and everyone else who was generous with their time these past few years.

ENDNOTES

1. https://www.dictionary.com/browse/manosphere

1: Body Count

1. Adult women are frequently given this child-like designation by members of the pickup community.
2. Alt_seduction_fast
3. By 2018, the industry would be estimated to be worth more than $100 million.
4. Known among pickup artists as 'daygame'.
5. https://www.theatlantic.com/entertainment/archive/2015/10/neil-strauss-the-game/409789/
6. *The Mystery Method: How to Get Beautiful Women into Bed*, 2007.
7. Based on the theory that a male peacock will display his feathers to attract a female – peacocking in the pickup artist community involves wearing flashy clothing and accessories to attract women.

2: Return of the Brute

1. https://www.thedailybeast.com/pickup-artists-preyed-on-drunk-women-brought-them-home-and-raped-them
2. *The Pickup Game*, 2019.
3. *The Pickup Game*, 2019.
4. https://www.latimes.com/archives/la-xpm-1991-07-19-vw-2498-story.html

5. Susan Faludi, *Backlash*, 1991.
6. {$NOTE_LABEL}. https://eprints.whiterose.ac.uk/117025/1/O_Neill_SRO_accepted_manuscript.pdf
7. In 2021, the model Emily Ratajkowski, who appeared in the music video for 'Blurred Lines', accused Thicke of sexually harassing her while they were filming the video.
8. https://www.thedailybeast.com/blurred-lines-robin-thickes-summer-anthem-is-kind-of-rapey
9. https://www.change.org/p/liquid-web-inc-take-down-julien-blanc-and-rsd-s-seminars-and-web-content-takedownjulienblanc
10. https://www.dailymail.co.uk/news/article-2839028/Boss-vile-American-Pick-Artist-Julien-Blanc-facing-UK-ban-bragged-raping-stripper-totally-not-mood.html
11. https://www.theguardian.com/commentisfree/2016/jan/22/jeff-allen-and-other-pickup-artists-advocate-its-right-he-had-his-visa-cancelled
12. https://www.theguardian.com/news/2014/dec/30/-sp-rebecca-solnit-listen-up-women-are-telling-their-story-now
13. https://slate.com/human-interest/2014/12/2014-was-a-good-year-for-feminism-what-s-going-to-happen-in-2015.html
14. https://www.mirror.co.uk/news/uk-news/roosh-v-make-rape-legal-5193802
15. https://www.comedy.co.uk/tv/news/1651/itv_end_dapper_laughs_show_sexist_claims/
16. https://deadspin.com/the-future-of-the-culture-wars-is-here-and-its-gamerga-1646145844/
17. https://www.researchgate.net/publication/380537001_Patriarchal_pacts_in_the_neo-archaic_manosphere_warband_brotherhoods_as_fascist_masculinity
18. https://www.bostonmagazine.com/news/2015/04/28/gamergate/
19. https://www.breitbart.com/europe/2014/11/12/the-authoritarian-left-was-on-course-to-win-the-culture-wars-then-along-came-gamergate/
20. https://eu.usatoday.com/story/tech/talkingtech/2017/07/18/steve-bannon-learned-harness-troll-army-world-warcraft/489713001/

ENDNOTES

3: Angry Men on the Internet

1. https://www.facebook.com/TheAgenda/videos/free-speech-vs-social-justice/10153825632530047/
2. https://www.telegraph.co.uk/men/thinking-man/did-controversial-psychologist-jordan-peterson-become-right/
3. https://www.youtube.com/watch?v=aMcjxSThD54
4. By late 2023 the video had amassed almost 47 million views.
5. https://www.nytimes.com/2018/01/25/opinion/jordan-peterson-moment.html
6. https://www.newyorker.com/magazine/2018/03/05/jordan-petersons-gospel-of-masculinity
7. https://www.theguardian.com/society/2018/jan/19/channel-4-calls-in-security-experts-after-cathy-newman-suffers-online-abuse
8. https://hopenothate.org.uk/wp-content/uploads/2020/08/youth-fear-and-hope-2020-07-v2final.pdf
9. https://www.youtube.com/watch?v=KlL7JhL-q30
10. https://www.youtube.com/watch?v=V-7ZlqTDaSQ&t=1s
11. https://www.youtube.com/watch?v=qOJ0lUSBI14
12. https://x.com/jordanbpeterson/status/1373498658352726017?lang=en

4: The 10 Commandments of Game

1. Moneyberg would later release a business course titled 'The 10 Commandments of Business'.
2. 1 Thou Shall Accept No False Gods Before You – you are in charge of your life, not anyone else.
   2 Thou Shall Answer the Three Sacred Questions – What kind of man am I?, What kind of life do I want to live?, Who would be a good companion for that life?
   3 Thou Shall Open Like You Mean It – go direct.
   4 Thou Shall Discern the Logistics and Social Dynamic of The Interaction.

    5   Thou Shall Convey Your Identity.
    6   Thou Shall Remember to Have Sincere Fun.
    7   Thou Shall Invite Her to Join Your Adventure – build a life that she would want to be part of.
    8   Thou Shall Make the Sex Happen.
    9   Thou Shall help others accomplish their goals – build a quality social circle.
    10 Thou Shall always be building your value.
3. A euphemism used by pickup artists.
4. https://www.bbc.co.uk/news/uk-scotland-49957059
5. Todd Valentine, Alex Treasure and Max Tornow had all left the company by this point. Julien Blanc meanwhile had rebranded himself as a trauma coach.
6. *The Evolution of the Manosphere across the Web*, Ribeiro, 2021.

5: Origins of the Red Pill

1. *Not All Dead White Men: Classics and Misogyny in the Digital Age* (2018), Donna Zuckerberg.
2. https://www.washingtonpost.com/wellness/2022/12/06/liver-king-steroids-apology-ancestral-diet/
3. https://www.thetimes.co.uk/article/review-we-are-the-nerds-the-birth-and-tumultuous-life-of-reddit-the-internets-culture-laboratory-by-christine-lagorio-chafkin-where-trolls-love-to-hate-s3jwcfv6s
4. https://www.abc.net.au/triplej/programs/hack/reddit-stop-spread-hateful-material-did-not-work/12874066
5. https://archive.is/20150610190226/www.reddit.com/r/TheRedPill/comments/12v1hf/almost_a_hundred_subscribers_welcome_newcomers/
6. https://www.ncbi.nlm.nih.gov/pmc/articles/PMC8336807/
7. https://x.com/RationalMale/status/1549764123503763456?lang=en-GB
8. https://therationalmale.com/2019/10/31/an-essay-for-women/

ENDNOTES

9. https://therationalmale.com/2018/01/02/dangerous-times-part-2/
10. https://therationalmale.com/tag/notch-count/
11. https://x.com/RationalMale/status/1850915620919079154
12. https://therationalmale.com/2011/11/22/youve-been-with-how-many-girls/
13. https://x.com/RationalMale/status/1854281316759740566
14. https://therationalmale.com/2019/10/31/an-essay-for-women/
15. https://therationalmale.com/tag/alpha-widows/
16. Similarly, the middle-aged red pill YouTuber Donovan Sharpe has described women over twenty-three as 'leftovers'.
17. https://therationalmale.com/2012/07/18/the-wall/
18. https://therationalmale.com/2012/06/04/final-exam-navigating-the-smp/
19. https://therationalmale.com/2011/10/12/frame/
20. https://bpb-us-e2.wpmucdn.com/sites.middlebury.edu/dist/7/1905/files/2019/07/RedPill.pdf
21. https://www.thetimes.com/article/hillarys-playing-the-womans-card-get-me-one-of-those-3xk76569g
22. https://fivethirtyeight.com/features/dissecting-trumps-most-rabid-online-following/
23. https://www.thedailybeast.com/red-pill-boss-all-feminists-want-to-be-raped

6: Make Men Great Again

1. James Bond from the *007* movies, Tyler Durden from *Fight Club*, and Tom Cruise's character from *Top Gun*.
2. https://21studios.com/dream/
3. The event took place between 1 and 3 May 2020.
4. https://journal.media-culture.org.au/index.php/mcjournal/article/view/1655/0
5. https://www.bbc.co.uk/news/newsbeat-36524693
6. https://www.mirror.co.uk/tv/tv-news/andrew-tates-ex-sets-record-8213969

7. The Dangerous Rise of Andrew Tate, *Vice Special Report*, 12 January 2023.
8. Andrew Tate's kickboxing ring name was King Cobra.
9. https://www.theguardian.com/technology/2022/aug/06/andrew-tate-violent-misogynistic-world-of-tiktok-new-star
10. https://www.theguardian.com/technology/2022/nov/06/tiktok-still-hosting-toxic-posts-of-banned-influencer-andrew-tate#:~:text=Two%20weeks%20later%2C%20it%20announced,action%20by%20Instagram%20and%20Facebook
11. https://www.theguardian.com/technology/2022/nov/06/tiktok-still-hosting-toxic-posts-of-banned-influencer-andrew-tate#:~:text=Two%20weeks%20later%2C%20it%20announced,action%20by%20Instagram%20and%20Facebook
12. https://www.cbsnews.com/news/twitter-accounts-reinstated-elon-musk-donald-trump-kanye-ye-jordan-peterson-kathy-griffin-andrew-tate/
13. https://www.washingtonpost.com/technology/2022/08/21/andrew-tate-tiktok-instagram/
14. https://m.facebook.com/story.php?story_fbid=10159117682767405&id=325059967404&m_entstream_source=permalink
15. The photo was taken following a podcast interview Johnson did with Tate in Warsaw, Poland in 2019.
16. https://www.youtube.com/watch?v=9aOdk1pK5xA
17. https://lithub.com/on-the-misogyny-paradox-and-the-crisis-of-heterosexual-coupledom/
18. https://www.jack-donovan.com/sowilo/2024/07/06/living-the-dream-with-anthony-dream-johnson/
19. https://law.justia.com/cases/texas/fifth-court-of-appeals/2018/05-16-01412-cv.html
20. He was also engaged in a lengthy court battle with his ex-wife over custody of their child, who identifies as transgender.
21. https://ballotpedia.org/Jeff_Younger

ENDNOTES

7: 'War is Coming': The Story of Lyndon McLeod

1. https://www.forbes.com/sites/conormurray/2023/08/31/what-we-know-about-andrew-tates-war-room-as-report-alleges-global-network-to-exploit-women/
2. https://ojs.aaai.org/index.php/ICWSM/article/view/18053/17856
3. https://21studios.com/statement-president-anthony-dream-johnson-on-robert-teesdale-ivan-throne/
4. https://www.adl.org/resources/backgrounder/patriot-front
5. https://x.com/punch_sideiron/status/1237092847926607873
6. https://www.reddit.com/r/gammasecretkings/comments/v6en0i/a_couple_of_bizarre_offerings_from_ivan_throne_2/
7. *The Code of the Woosters*, P. G. Wodehouse.
8. https://www.dailymail.co.uk/news/article-10351893/The-weak-better-buckle-Denver-gunman-espoused-alt-right-masculine-supremacy-theories.html
9. https://x.com/roman_mcclay/status/1222957591036227584
10. https://www.splcenter.org/fighting-hate/extremist-files/individual/mike-cernovich
11. https://x.com/ZubyMusic/status/1311050385939890185
12. https://x.com/kattenbarge/status/1628821622965633024
13. https://snowdon.substack.com/p/basic-statistics-for-anti-vaxxers
14. https://x.com/Johnnthelefty/status/1476308750310916096?s=20
15. https://www.denverpost.com/2021/12/28/denver-lakewood-shooting-spree-suspect-locations-victims/
16. https://www.vice.com/en/article/3ab5gy/denver-shooter-lyndon-mcleod-movie
17. https://www.cbsnews.com/colorado/news/jeremy-costilow-mcleod-denver-shooting-spree/
18. https://x.com/ZubyMusic/status/1476660655746920456
19. https://gist.github.com/travisbrown/9886193d039a48deda9b533329c7c623
20. https://21studios.com/manosphere-statement-jack-murphy-roman-mcclay/

21. https://www.vice.com/en/article/3ab5gy/denver-shooter-lyndon-mcleod-movie
22. https://www.denverpost.com/2022/01/04/denver-shootings-police-warning/
23. https://www.denverpost.com/2022/01/04/denver-shootings-police-warning/
24. https://www.denverpost.com/2022/01/28/denver-shooting-lyndon-mcleod-felony-menacing/
25. https://www.vice.com/en/article/3ab5gy/denver-shooter-lyndon-mcleod-movie
26. https://politicalresearch.org/2015/06/19/terror-network-or-lone-wolf
27. https://icct.nl/sites/default/files/2023-01/Special-Edition-1-3.pdf
28. https://x.com/roman_mcclay/status/1255668816526356480
29. https://x.com/RVAwonk/status/1476385938624454656/photo/3
30. https://denvergazette.com/news/accused-denver-metro-killer-was-a-member-of-a-polygamous-cult-friend-says/article_2b0bd740-691e-11ec-9a32-c34c197cc1da.html
31. https://www.vice.com/en/article/3ab5gy/denver-shooter-lyndon-mcleod-movie
32. https://coloradotimesrecorder.com/2022/01/a-portrait-of-a-mass-murderer/42178/
33. https://www.vice.com/en/article/3ab5gy/denver-shooter-lyndon-mcleod-movie
34. https://x.com/roman_mcclay/status/1253778031249850370
35. https://x.com/roman_mcclay/status/1255538472875634697?s=20
36. https://www.vice.com/en/article/3ab5gy/denver-shooter-lyndon-mcleod-movie

8: Waiting for Caesar

1. https://www.thetimes.com/world/russia-ukraine-war/article/unlike-in-2017-russia-is-under-no-illusion-trump-will-rebuild-ties-nb6wjxj8d

ENDNOTES

2. https://www.thedailybeast.com/gonzalo-lira-red-pill-dating-coach-who-is-accused-of-shilling-for-putin-is-arrested-in-ukraine/
3. https://www.thedailybeast.com/gonzalo-lira-is-a-pro-putin-shill-in-ukraine-and-a-sleazy-manosphere-dating-coach/
4. https://www.youtube.com/watch?v=eV4iXfjonqI
5. https://www.bellingcat.com/news/americas/2022/01/06/how-the-denver-shooters-digital-trail-exposes-the-violent-fantasies-of-the-manosphere/
6. https://gnet-research.org/2022/01/03/examining-the-denver-shooters-ideological-views/
7. https://x.com/Johnnthelefty/status/1476080195341668352
8. https://www.jack-donovan.com/sowilo/2010/09/11/violence-is-golden/
9. https://starttheworld.com/products/og-violence-is-golden-t-shirt
10. https://search.worldcat.org/title/androphilia-a-manifesto-rejecting-the-gay-identity-reclaiming-masculinity/oclc/838124219
11. In 2018, the *Fight Club* author Chuck Palahniuk cited Donovan as an influence on his writing. Palahniuk has also been interviewed by Donovan on the latter's podcast.
12. https://rosecityantifa.org/articles/the-wolves-of-vinland-a-fascist-countercultural-tribe-in-the-pacific-northwest/
13. *CTRL – ALT – DELETE: The origins and ideology of the Alternative Right*, Matthew N. Lyons. https://politicalresearch.org/sites/default/files/2019-05/Lyons_CtrlAltDelete_PRINT.pdf
14. https://rw-ktf.univie.ac.at/fileadmin/user_upload/i_religionswiss/Operation_Werewolf__Radical_Traditionalism_and_Julius_Evola_s_Doctrine_Put_into_Practice__Alice_Y._Yahyaie_2021_.pdf
15. https://gnet-research.org/2022/01/03/examining-the-denver-shooters-ideological-views/
16. https://bristowbeat.com/stories/arsonist-pleads-guilty-to-starting-mt-pleasant-baptist-church-fire,1151
17. https://www.buzzfeednews.com/article/rosiegray/katie-mchugh
18. The idea that progress is an illusion, and that history proceeds in cycles, is a common trope in reactionary circles. *Generation Zero*, a

2015 documentary by Steve Bannon, draws heavily on *The Fourth Turning* by William Strauss and Neil Howe, which presents history as unfolding in eighty- to a hundred-year cycles or 'turnings'.
19. https://politicalresearch.org/2020/11/09/total-life-reform
20. https://www.techagainstterrorism.org/hubfs/CTEC__TAT-Accelerationism-Report-.pdf
21. https://www.accresearch.org/shortanalysis/an-introduction-to-militant-accelerationism
22. https://www.fairobserver.com/region/north_america/matthew-feldman-bethan-johnson-james-mason-siege-culture-neo-nazi-groups-radical-right-news-12512/
23. https://www.splcenter.org/fighting-hate/extremist-files/individual/james-mason
24. https://www.accresearch.org/shortanalysis/an-introduction-to-militant-accelerationism
25. https://ctc.westpoint.edu/uniting-for-total-collapse-the-january-6-boost-to-accelerationism/
26. https://gnet-research.org/2022/05/30/understanding-accelerationist-narratives-the-great-replacement-theory/
27. https://www.nytimes.com/2019/08/03/us/patrick-crusius-el-paso-shooter-manifesto.html
28. https://gnet-research.org/2022/05/30/understanding-accelerationist-narratives-the-great-replacement-theory/
29. https://www.theguardian.com/uk-news/2018/jun/12/man-pleads-guilty-to-plot-to-labour-mp-rosie-cooper
30. https://www.middlebury.edu/institute/academics/centers-initiatives/ctec/ctec-publications/dangerous-organizations-and-bad-actors-5
31. *Terrorist Situation and Trend Report 2022*: https://www.europol.europa.eu/publication-events/main-reports/european-union-terrorism-situation-and-trend-report-2022-te-sat
32. https://www.europol.europa.eu/cms/sites/default/files/documents/Tesat_Report_2022_0.pdf
33. https://www.jaccusepaper.co.uk/p/communittar-fools
34. https://www.theguardian.com/us-news/2023/jul/26/desantis-campaign-video-nazi-symbol-fired-aide

ENDNOTES

35. https://www.nytimes.com/2022/08/03/magazine/claremont-institute-conservative.html
36. https://x.com/Luke_Turner/status/1476088759221374976/photo/1
37. https://x.com/roman_mcclay/status/1232060523539136512
38. https://x.com/Luke_Turner/status/1476088764627881985/photo/1
39. https://x.com/sebjenseb/status/1811397998745924031
40. https://x.com/Luke_Turner/status/1452643082655182856
41. Anton was the author of a notorious essay entitled 'The Flight 93 Election'.
42. https://claremontreviewofbooks.com/are-the-kids-altright/
43. https://x.com/elonmusk/status/1587498907336118274?lang=en
44. https://www.theguardian.com/commentisfree/2018/jul/16/tommy-robinson-cheerleaders-hypocrites-far-right
45. https://x.com/roman_mcclay/status/1256189013402308608
46. https://edition.cnn.com/world/live-news/coronavirus-pandemic-05-18-20-intl/h_07bf06f9ea92b33ff358352abbb54c6c
47. https://www.nj.com/coronavirus/2020/03/coronavirus-in-new-jersey-a-timeline-of-the-outbreak.html
48. https://www.fox29.com/news/atilis-gym-facing-over-1-2m-in-fines-for-defying-njs-coronavirus-lockdown-orders-owner-says
49. I wasn't entirely convinced that Grannon, who plugged expensive courses on his website with titles including 'Unplug from the Matrix of Narcissistic Abuse' (£246) and 'Break Narcissistic Possession' (£49.98), was subscribing to the same ascetic lifestyle he preached. On his Instagram page were photos of him in exotic locations wearing expensive designer sunglasses and smoking cigars.

10: Men of Action

1. Not all social media platforms are equal according to Michael. Instagram is the world's biggest dating app, whereas X is for people who don't have a social life. Meanwhile, Facebook is for Boomers and Snapchat is for 'prostitutes'.

2. https://x.com/DanBilzerian/status/529020255558176768
3. https://x.com/DanBilzerian/status/1253069960634499072
4. https://www.youtube.com/watch?v=RX5Iw-XsWu4
5. https://www.einnews.com/pr_news/521215817/lawsuit-dan-bilzerian-used-cbd-company-to-fund-lavish-lifestyle-fired-company-president-who-questioned-expenses
6. https://www.tampabay.com/archive/2001/06/22/fbi-agents-raid-bilzerian-home/
7. https://www.upi.com/Archives/1989/09/27/Corporate-raider-Bilzerian-gets-prison-term-fine/4070622872000/
8. https://www.upi.com/Archives/1989/09/27/Corporate-raider-Bilzerian-gets-prison-term-fine/4070622872000/
9. https://www.sec.gov/files/litigation/litreleases/lr15146.txt
10. https://www.wsj.com/articles/for-decades-ex-corporate-raider-holds-off-sec-effort-to-collect-62-million-judgment-1410892550
11. https://www.wsj.com/articles/for-decades-ex-corporate-raider-holds-off-sec-effort-to-collect-62-million-judgment-1410892550
12. https://www.wsop.com/players/profile/?playerid=64978
13. https://www.pokernews.com/news/2024/07/dan-bilzerian-busts-wsop-main-event-46462.htm
14. https://www.wsj.com/articles/for-decades-ex-corporate-raider-holds-off-sec-effort-to-collect-62-million-judgment-1410892550
15. https://www.latimes.com/california/story/2024-09-27/paul-bilzerian-cannabis-company

11: Alpha Fucks, Beta Bucks

1. https://rationalmale.substack.com/p/a-new-age-of-enlightenment
2. https://x.com/RationalMale/status/965975778239291392
3. https://rationalmale.substack.com/p/marriage-is-settling
4. https://x.com/RationalMale/status/1503474941236195329
5. https://www.wsj.com/articles/facebook-knows-instagram-is-toxic-for-teen-girls-company-documents-show-11631620739
6. https://www.unwomen.org/sites/default/files/2022-09/Progress-

ENDNOTES

on-the-sustainable-development-goals-the-gender-snapshot-2022-en_0.pdf

7. https://www.pewresearch.org/internet/2021/01/13/the-state-of-online-harassment/#:~:text=Women%2C%20on%20the%20other%20hand,have%20experienced%20sexual%20harassment%20online.
8. https://www.pewresearch.org/internet/2020/02/06/the-virtues-and-downsides-of-online-dating/
9. https://www.bbc.com/mediacentre/proginfo/2022/08/datings-dangerous-secrets
10. https://www.instagram.com/kevinrsamuels/reel/CdKdJIQIQ8A/
11. https://www.youtube.com/watch?v=rf3Eub1Hvhs
12. https://x.com/datepsych/status/1635560720292098049
13. https://x.com/rationalmale/status/1394093414023454721
14. https://www.youtube.com/watch?v=xbLvAbjJ2E4
15. https://www.ncbi.nlm.nih.gov/pmc/articles/PMC1733152/pdf/v059p00749.pdf
16. https://insidestory.org.au/the-fatherhood-myth/
17. https://pubmed.ncbi.nlm.nih.gov/27107336/
18. https://insidestory.org.au/the-fatherhood-myth/
19. The inflated statistics also proved useful when it came to rationalising away damaging male behaviours. It is claimed in red pill spaces that men are 'hard-wired' to be jealous and controlling because they are (understandably) worried about paternity.
20. The noun 'cuck' is used to describe a husband whose wife is unfaithful. The word derives from cuckoo birds (the female cuckoo lays her eggs in another bird's nest to save herself the effort of having to raise her own young). Though the word 'cuckold' has been in use since the thirteenth century, the growing influence of the manosphere on right-wing politics has seen 'cuck' become a popular insult. Men considered weak or ineffectual, or conservative politicians deemed insufficiently radical or supportive of Donald Trump, are labelled as 'cuckservatives' or 'beta cucks'. Cuckoldry discourse often comes marinated in (I was going to say *pregnant with*) racial anxiety. In pornography, the cuckolded

husband is usually white whereas the wife's affair partner is typically black. The sexual kick for the viewer is delivered in the form of an erotically charged racial anxiety as the white husband is emasculated by his perceived social inferior.

21. https://datepsychology.com/why-dual-mating-hypothesis-research-has-failed-to-replicate/
22. https://labs.la.utexas.edu/buss/files/2019/03/mate-preferences-and-their-behavioral-manifestations-FINAL-PUBLISHED-2019.pdf
23. https://www.youtube.com/watch?v=9Xc7DN-noAc
24. https://rationalmale.substack.com/p/cuckoldry-is-a-beta-male-mating-strategy
25. https://thepowermoves.com/rollo-tomassi-analysis/

12: Surplus Men

1. https://incels.wiki/w/Chad
2. https://medium.com/@worstonlinedater/tinder-experiments-ii-guys-unless-you-are-really-hot-you-are-probably-better-off-not-wasting-your-2ddf370a6e9a
3. https://www.sciencedirect.com/science/article/pii/S0272775719301104?ref=quillette.com
4. https://www.washingtonpost.com/business/2019/03/29/share-americans-not-having-sex-has-reached-record-high/
5. https://ifstudies.org/blog/is-the-sex-recession-turning-into-a-great-sex-depression
6. {$NOTE_LABEL}. https://www.pewresearch.org/fact-tank/2023/02/08/for-valentines-day-5-facts-about-single-americans
7. https://ifstudies.org/blog/is-the-sex-recession-over
8. https://www.nytimes.com/video/opinion/100000009438727/contractions.html?playlistId=video/video
9. https://schoolshooters.info/sites/default/files/rodger_video_1.0.pdf
10. https://www.wtsglobal.com/public_html/wp-content/uploads/2018/04/Isla-Vista-JTAM-SGWhite-2017.pdf
11. https://www.bbc.co.uk/news/blogs-trending-41926687

ENDNOTES

12. https://www.qualitativecriminology.com/pub/z1961qto/release/1
13. file:///Users/jamesbloodworth/Downloads/850267.pdf
14. https://www.theguardian.com/uk-news/2021/aug/13/plymouth-shooting-suspect-what-we-know-jake-davison
15. https://www.nytimes.com/2009/08/06/us/06shoot.html
16. https://www.nbcnews.com/id/wbna32335641
17. https://www.overcomingbias.com/p/two-types-of-envyhtml
18. https://www.nytimes.com/2018/05/02/opinion/incels-sex-robots-redistribution.html
19. https://www.jordanbpeterson.com/media/on-the-new-york-times-and-enforced-monogamy/
20. https://www.youtube.com/watch?v=YSIPtB3LMcM
21. https://www.youtube.com/watch?v=d3fvs3bRPng
22. https://weneedalaw.ca/2018/06/dr-peterson-abortion-laws/
23. https://www.theatlantic.com/health/archive/2017/07/homicides-women/534306/
24. https://www.cbc.ca/news/canada/men-femicide-kill-female-partners-sentencing-1.3330171
25. *Bad Men: The Hidden Roots of Sexual Deception, Harassment and Assault*, Professor David Buss: 'men with money, status, popularity, and power are more likely to be sexual predators'.
26. https://www.sciencedirect.com/science/article/abs/pii/0191886996000591?ref=quillette.com
27. https://www.theguardian.com/world/2018/jun/19/incels-why-jack-peterson-left-elliot-rodger
28. https://www.youtube.com/watch?v=lO0A2eSZiOs
29. https://www.youtube.com/watch?v=lO0A2eSZiOs
30. https://www.youtube.com/watch?v=Ed-lBdbsVGQ

13: Top G

1. Tate has since renamed the course 'The Real World'.
2. https://www.buzzfeednews.com/article/ikrd/andrew-tate-hustlers-university

3. https://www.buzzfeednews.com/article/ikrd/andrew-tate-hustlers-university?bfsource=relatedmanual
4. https://www.vice.com/en/article/bvm43q/andrew-tate-arrest
5. https://www.nytimes.com/2023/06/20/world/europe/andrew-tate-romania.html
6. https://www.bbc.co.uk/news/world-europe-65959097
7. https://www.theguardian.com/uk-news/2024/mar/12/andrew-tate-brother-tristan-arrested-romania-uk-warrant
8. https://www.reddit.com/r/gammasecretkings/comments/u3ih83/andrew_tate_explains_the_primary_reason_he_moved/
9. https://evawintl.org/best_practice_faqs/false-reports-percentage/
10. https://research.open.ac.uk/news/false-accusations-sexual-violence#:~:text=While%20the%20statistics%20on%20false,or%20suspected%20to%20be%20false
11. https://www.channel4.com/news/factcheck/factcheck-men-are-more-likely-to-be-raped-than-be-falsely-accused-of-rape
12. https://www.channel4.com/news/factcheck/factcheck-men-are-more-likely-to-be-raped-than-be-falsely-accused-of-rape
13. https://www.law.umich.edu/special/exoneration/Pages/Basic-Patterns.aspx
14. https://www.dailymail.co.uk/news/article-11930057/Andrew-Tate-blames-jealous-women-know-arrest.html
15. https://eige.europa.eu/gender-equality-index/2023/country/RO#:~:text=Progress%20in%20gender%20equality,the%20EU%20as%20a%20whole
16. https://europa.eu/eurobarometer/surveys/detail/2115
17. https://x.com/Therealsuzywyn1/status/1680780875846369280
18. https://www.bbc.co.uk/news/world-europe-66604827
19. https://www.theguardian.com/news/2023/jun/13/andrew-tate-romanian-authorities-change-human-trafficking-charge
20. https://www.nytimes.com/2023/08/04/world/europe/andrew-tate-romania-house-arrest.html
21. https://www.youtube.com/watch?v=xKpOV62oooQ
22. https://www.youtube.com/watch?v=xKpOV62oooQ
23. https://x.com/Cobratate/status/1608772573692854272?lang=en

ENDNOTES

24. https://x.com/Cobratate/status/1608982819879137282
25. An American far-right conspiracy theory which believed a cabal of satanic cannibalistic child molesters are operating a global sex trafficking ring that conspired against Donald Trump.
26. https://www.nytimes.com/article/andrew-tate-arrests-explained. html#:~:text=Andrew%20Tate%2C%20an%20online%20 influencer,prosecutors%20that%20include%20human%20 trafficking
27. https://www.bbc.co.uk/news/articles/clyglgy8j3eo.amp
28. https://www.youtube.com/watch?v=56_mT91sinc
29. https://rumble.com/v1efqbf-andrew-tate-reasons-your-poor.html
30. https://www.youtube.com/watch?v=Mi83nwTMgDg&t=142s
31. *Clown World*, Matt Shea and Jamie Tahsin, 2024.
32. https://escapethematrix.money/
33. In a subsequent interview with Piers Morgan for Talk TV, Tate defended his belief that, once married, a woman was a man's 'property': https://www.youtube.com/watch?v=VGWGcESPltM&t=933s
34. https://www.mirror.co.uk/news/uk-news/brothers-make-millions-using-webcam-26508739
35. https://www.mirror.co.uk/news/uk-news/brothers-make-millions-using-webcam-26508739
36. https://www.thenewsmovement.com/articles/andrew-tates-dollar8000-members-club-the-war-room-exposed-by-insider-elixanpa
37. https://www.reddit.com/r/gammasecretkings/comments/rltxux/exwar_room_member_warns_others_not_to_join_andrew/#lightbox
38. https://psycnet.apa.org/doiLanding?doi=10.1037%2Fmen0000487

Epilogue

1. https://www.abc.net.au/news/2024-08-19/raygun-imane-khelif-social-media-regulation/104239836

2. https://reutersinstitute.politics.ox.ac.uk/types-sources-and-claims-covid-19-misinformation
3. By 2022, Peterson was warning that a 'woke totalitarian social credit system is highly probable'.
4. He questioned the safety of the Covid-19 vaccine and falsely claimed that a new Covid variant was announced whenever pharmaceutical share prices dipped.
5. https://x.com/jordanbpeterson/status/1673078885062176769
6. https://escapethematrix.money/
7. *The Paranoid Style in American Politics*, Richard Hofstadter, 1964.
8. https://x.com/Cobratate/status/1826563186931237178
9. https://x.com/Cobratate/status/1750020111178576219?t=fnQAyPQlCVXDWTL3GxTrLw&s=08
10. https://www.youtube.com/watch?v=56_mT91sinc
11. https://x.com/NickJFuentes/status/1826257880653443112
12. In 2022, Donald Trump hosted Fuentes, along with Kanye West and several others, for dinner at his Mar-a-Lago resort in Palm Beach, Florida. Trump later claimed not to know who Fuentes was. https://www.politico.com/news/2022/11/25/trump-white-nationalist-nick-fuentes-kanye-00070825
13. https://x.com/RightWingWatch/status/1484204621388210178?s=20&t=gWUZOburSlS7i3O3lehoxQ
14. https://x.com/CalebJHull/status/1189594371030695937
15. https://www.adl.org/resources/blog/nicholas-j-fuentes-five-things-know
16. https://x.com/bennyjohnson/status/1196605327124451328?s=46&t=mth2WpQ0iT0nJ5yYk3ZOaw
17. https://x.com/sneako/status/1826689418767597954
18. https://rumble.com/v31fvbq-episode-926-asking-forbidden-questions-w-ian-smith.html
19. https://x.com/iansmithfitness/status/1684193350365085696?s=46&t=PN52ydwTvFusTeuJ-h77RA
20. https://www.mediamatters.org/eric-trump/trump-doral-event-eric-trump-will-feature-ian-smith-hitler-promoting-antisemite-who
21. https://www.jpost.com/diaspora/article-815144

ENDNOTES

22. Susan Faldo, *Backlash*, p.13, 1992.
23. https://www.mediamatters.org/tiktok/study-tradwife-influencers-are-quietly-spreading-far-right-conspiracy-theories
24. https://www.theguardian.com/global-development/article/2024/sep/04/gender-equality-stalling-or-going-backwards-for-1bn-women-and-girls
25. https://news.harvard.edu/gazette/story/2022/06/shadow-pandemic-of-domestic-violence/
26. https://hopenothate.org.uk/wp-content/uploads/2019/02/state-of-hate-2019-final-1.pdf
27. https://www.youtube.com/watch?v=Q_6ctbzAVBY
28. https://www.cdpinstitute.org/news/twenty-percent-of-americans-get-news-from-influencers-pew/#:~:text=Twenty%20percent%20of%20Americans%20are,%25%20search%20and%205%25%20podcasts
29. https://ropercenter.cornell.edu/how-groups-voted-2020
30. https://apnews.com/article/election-harris-trump-women-latinos-black-voters-0f3fbda3362f3dcfe41aa6b858f22d12
31. https://navigatorresearch.org/2024-post-election-survey-gender-and-age-analysis-of-2024-election-results/
32. https://2024electionpoll.us/wp-content/uploads/2024/11/7.-Latino-crosstab.pdf
33. https://apnews.com/article/trump-young-men-voters-election-latinos-democrats-ff30e38698a41132cf90345fffabe579
34. https://www.youtube.com/watch?v=EJ-G_JQz6hU&t=96s
35. https://www.independent.co.uk/news/world/americas/elon-musk-trump-harris-high-status-males-4chan-b2606617.html
36. https://news.sky.com/story/andrew-tate-and-his-brother-tristan-have-left-romania-for-the-us-reports-13317873